TOPOPHRENIA

THE SPATIAL HUMANITIES

David J. Bodenhamer, John Corrigan, and Trevor M. Harris, editors

TOPOPHRENIA

*Place, Narrative, and
the Spatial Imagination*

Robert T. Tally Jr.

Indiana University Press

This book is a publication of

Indiana University Press
Office of Scholarly Publishing
Herman B Wells Library 350
1320 East 10th Street
Bloomington, Indiana 47405 USA

iupress.indiana.edu

Manufactured in the United States of America

Cataloging information is available from the Library of Congress.

ISBN 978-0-253-03770-1 (hardback)
ISBN 978-0-253-03766-4 (pbk.)
ISBN 978-0-253-03769-5 (web PDF)

1 2 3 4 5 23 22 21 20 19 18

For Bertrand Westphal

Contents

Contents

Acknowledgments

It is fitting that, in the acknowledgments section of a book about space, place, and mapping in literature, I should be reminded of the many places that have fired my own imagination and contributed to my thinking, teaching, and writing. As noted throughout this book, with due deference to the brilliant cultural geographer Yi-Fu Tuan, places are endowed with meanings, imbued with subjective experience, and perfectly suited to the sort of interpretative practices typically associated with literature and literary studies.

Perhaps I should begin with my current location at Texas State University in San Marcos, Texas, a place that has enabled me to engage in teaching US and world literature, literary criticism, and theory while maintaining an active program of scholarly activity and professional service. I am very appreciative of the academic and social community here, and I would like to thank many individuals who have contributed to my well-being while living here. First, I want to thank Michael Hennessy, English professor and dean of the College of Liberal Arts, a great champion of literature and of the humanities, who has been an enthusiastic supporter of my work ever since I came to Texas. Next, I am grateful to my students and colleagues at the university, including Devin Baumann, Yasmine Beale-Rivaya, Alejandra Benavides, Bianca Beronio, Flore Chevaillier, Paul Cohen, Taylor Cortesi, Doug Dorst, Geneva Gano, Katrina Goudey, Nancy Grayson, Matt Greengold, Chad Hammett, Craig Hanks, Lucy Harney, Ogaga Ifowodo, Catherine Jaffe, Katie Kapurch, Kitty Ledbetter, Dan Lochman, Whitney May, Kate McClancy, Carolos Abreu Mendoza, Amanda Meyer, Susan Morrison, Marilynn Olson, Cecily Parks, Jessica Pliley, Rebecca Raphael, Benjamin Reed, Shaula Rocha, Deanna Rodriguez, Teya Rosenberg, Aimee Roundtree, Thais Rutledge, Leah Schwebel, Jon Marc Smith, Victoria Smith, Susie Tilka, Nancy Wilson, Sarah Youree, and Taylor Zavala, among others with whom I have discussed these and similar matters over the years. I would like to thank the English Department staff, especially Karen Bryson, and student workers for their help and good cheer. Above all, I thank Reiko Graham for her love and support and the Britches sisters, along with Steve French, for keeping things just unpredictable enough to keep me on my toes.

Although most of the writing of this book was accomplished in San Marcos, my thoughts on these matters have developed and been shaped by my time in many other places I have lived, including Durham, Pittsburgh, and New York. I am extremely grateful to the many friends and advisors in these locales without whom I would not have become the critic or person that I am. These include, without limit, Susan Andrade, Jonathan Arac, John Beverly, Paul A. Bové, Jyotirmoy Banerjee, Jimmy Bridgeforth, Tor Brodtkorb, Susie Bryant, Rodney Draughn, Christopher Edwards, Josefina Melgar, Derek Michalak, Toril Moi, Michael V. Moses, Valentin Mudimbe, Mitch Payton, Charles Rhine, Kirstin Ringelberg, Rick Roderick, James Rolleston, Kenneth Surin, Phillip Wegner, and Holland West. I am especially grateful to my old literature professor, Fredric Jameson, whose example of close reading combined with historical and philosophical contextualization continually inspires me, and whose conception of cognitive mapping, in various forms and incarnations, serves as the basis for my understanding of literary cartography in theory and practice. This volume is dedicated to Bertrand Westphal, my friend and fellow traveler in geocritical exploration.

Many of the ideas or arguments made in this book were first presented at conferences, and I am extremely grateful to the organizers, fellow presenters, and above all the audiences from whom I gained invaluable feedback and encouragement. Among many others, I would like to thank the English Language and Literature Association of Korea, the English Department of the University of Zurich (UZH), the Department of Religious Studies and the Humanities Center at Stanford University, the Italian Graduate Association at Rutgers University, the English Departments at Simon Fraser University and the University of South Florida, the International Studies program at Texas State University, the organizers of the 2015 *Littérature et géographie: l'écriture de l'espace à travers les âges* conference in Lyon, France, and the organizers of the *Congresso Internacional Geopoéticas 2017: Espaços Literários e Territórios Críticos*, held at the University of Porto, Portugal. I am also grateful to the people involved with my panels at conferences of the Society for Novel Studies, the Modern Language Association, the Modernist Studies Association, the American Comparative Literature Association, and the South Central Modern Language Association.

Among the many other individuals who have contributed ideas, support, or encouragement as I worked on this project, I would like to thank David Alworth, Ian Balfour, Herman Beavers, Alexander Beecroft, Ian Buchanan, Eric Bulson, Gerry Canavan, Andrew Cole, Thadious Davis, Colin Dayan, Jeffrey Di Leo, Caroline Edwards, Stuart Elden, Amy J. Elias, Lauren Elkin, Tom Eyers, Molly Gaudry, David Greven, Geosi Gyasi, Dan Hartley, Hsuan Hsu, Hyeryung Hwang, Jeanne-Marie Jackson, Karen Jacobs, Junyoung Verónica Kim, Min-Jung Kim, Youngmin Kim, Adeline Koh, Elizabeth Kollmann, Anna Kornbluh, Cassandra Laity, Catherine Liu, Sophia McClennen, Peta Mitchell, Christian Moraru, Daniel Nutters, Daniel O'Hara, Firat Oruc, David Palumbo-Liu, Joshua Parker, Emmanuelle Peraldo, Ato Quayson, Sangeeta Ray, Johannes Riquet, Jae H. Roe, Robert Rouse, Emilio Sauri, Ben Schreier, Henry Schwarz, David Shumway, William V. Spanos, Hortense Spillers, Mads Rosendahl Thomsen, Amy Wells, Marta

Werner, Bertrand Westphal, Jenny Wills, and Gena Zuroski. While completing this book, I had the good fortune to be part of an international team put together by Professor Ying Liu at Nankai University, and our project, American Literary Geography, has received funding from China's National Social Science Foundation (project number 16ZDA197). I am grateful to Professor Liu and my fellow researchers, and I look forward to continuing my work with them. I have also been lucky to work with Professor Ying Fang of Ningbo University, with whom I am collaborating on a project titled A Study in Spatial Literary Criticism (project number 17BZW057), supported by China's National Social Science Foundation. This book may be considered as work related to both those projects, in which I am honored to take part.

This book contains material that has been previously published; in nearly all cases, however, such material has been revised, expanded, or otherwise modified. As such, this is not exactly the collection of essays I had originally intended, since I found that my earlier versions were, in one way or another, inadequate to the task of the present volume. Although some chapters may stand alone more effectively than others, I propose that the whole may be more useful, if not greater, than the sum of its parts, as the chapters trace a certain, more or less logical trajectory through the literary, critical, and theoretical territories to be explored.

Chapter 1 contains material from "Topophrenia: The Place of the Subject," *Reconstruction* 14.4 (2014) and "Mapping Narratives," in my *Literary Cartographies: Spatiality, Representation, and Narrative* (New York: Palgrave Macmillan, 2014). Chapter 2 includes language from "Situating Geocriticism," *American Book Review* 37.6 (September–October 2016); "The Timely Emergence of Geocriticism," in Bertrand Westphal's *Geocriticism: Real and Fictional Places* (New York: Palgrave Macmillan, 2011); "A Geocriticism of the Worldly World," in Westphal's *The Plausible World: A Geocritical Approach to Space, Place, and Maps* (New York: Palgrave Macmillan, 2013); and "On Geocriticism," in my *Geocritical Explorations: Space, Place, and Mapping in Literary and Cultural Studies* (New York: Palgrave Macmillan, 2011). A version of chapter 3 first appeared as "Geocriticism in the Middle of Things: Place, *Peripeteia*, and the Prospects of Comparative Literature," in *Géocritique: État les lieux / Geocriticism: A Survey*, edited by Clément Lévy and Bertrand Westphal (Limoges: Pulim, 2014); chapter 3 also contains material from "Utopia of the In-Between, or, Limning the Liminal," my foreword to *Landscapes of Liminality: Between Space and Place*, edited by Dara Downey, Ian Kinane, and Elizabeth Parker (London: Rowman & Littlefield International, 2016). A modified version of chapter 4 was published as "Spatiality's Mirrors: Reflections on Literary Cartography," *Journal of English Language and Literature* 61, no. 4 (2015). Chapter 5 appears in a slightly different form as "The Space of the Novel," in *The Cambridge Companion to the Novel*, edited by Eric Bulson (Cambridge: Cambridge University Press, 2018). Chapter 6 contains material first published as "The Novel and the Map: Spatiotemporal Form and Discourse in Literary Cartography," in *Space, Time, and the Limits of Human Understanding*, edited by Shyam Wuppuluri and Giancarlo Ghirardi (London: Springer, 2017) and as "Lukács's Literary Cartography: Spatiality, Cognitive Mapping, and *The Theory of the Novel*," *Mediations* 29, no. 2 (Spring 2016). Chapter 7 appeared in a different form as "Adventures in Literary Cartography: Explorations, Representations, Projections," in *Literature and Geography: The Writing of Space throughout History*, edited by Emmanuelle Peraldo (Newcastle-upon-Tyne: Cambridge Scholars, 2016). A version of chapter 8 was published as "In the Suburbs of Amaurotum: Fantasy, Utopia, and Literary Cartography," *English Language Notes* 52, no. 1: *Imaginary Cartographies*, edited by Karen Jacobs (Spring/Summer 2014). Chapter 9 appeared as "Beyond the Flaming Walls of the World: Fantasy, Alterity, and the Postnational Constellation," in *The Planetary Turn: Relationality and Geoaesthetics in the Twenty-First Century*, edited by Amy J. Elias and Christian Moraru (Evanston, IL: Northwestern University Press, 2015). And some of the language used in the conclusion comes from "Textual Geographies: Real-and-Imagined Spaces in Literature, Criticism, and Theory," *Reconstruction* 14, no. 3 (2014) and "The Map and the Guide," in my *Teaching Space, Place, and Literature* (London: Routledge, 2018). I gratefully acknowledge all of the editors and publishers. In addition, I wish to thank Wendy Chin-Tanner for permission to reprint her poem "On Truth in a Nonmoral Sense," first published in *Vinyl Poetry*, vol. 9 (November 2013).

Finally, I want to thank David J. Bodenhamer, John Corrigan, and Trevor M. Harris, editors of the *Spatial Humanities* series at Indiana University Press for their enthusiasm and support for my project, even as my work represents a bit of a departure from many of the other books in the series. I am also grateful to Jennika Baines and Kate Schramm of Indiana University Press for their patience and generous editorial aid.

Considering the number of people named here, I really ought to be able to find someone to blame, but be assured that any errors or omissions are my responsibility alone.

TOPOPHRENIA

TOPOPHRENIA

Introduction: The Cartographic Imperative

THE MAP IS at once a rather simple tool and a powerful conceptual figure. Everyone already knows what a map is and what it is used for, yet the map is also a much-contested object or metaphor in critical theory and beyond. Mapping has been associated with empire, social repression, and all manner of ideological programs geared toward manipulating the representations of space for this or that group's political benefit, for example. Mapping has also been viewed as crucial to any sort of liberatory political project, as the need for spatial and social representation makes itself all too apparent amid the potential disorientation and alienation of unmapped territories. At a more basic, existentialist level, mapping might be seen as an inevitable (not to say neutral) activity, for the individual subject cannot help but try to orient itself by imagining its position vis-à-vis that of other subjects and in relation to a broader, objective reality. Indeed, notwithstanding the multiple ambiguities attendant to any cartographic enterprise, one might suggest that mapping is almost essential to our being. I map, therefore I am.

The injunction to map makes itself felt most urgently, perhaps, in situations in which one is lost, desperately seeking guideposts or markers that can identify one's place in relation to other places. To call for a map or to demand that someone engage in mapping is to recognize one's own disorientation, one's displacement in space, or one's loss of a sense of place, which is undoubtedly alienating if not also terrifying. The spatial anxiety associated with being lost, somewhat like the angst that accompanies the existential condition à la Martin Heidegger and Jean-Paul Sartre, brings with it a visceral awareness of place and space, which might otherwise be taken for granted or left safely tucked away in the unconscious. The sudden need to map, or at least to have access to a map, propels to the fore the *topophrenia* that remains with humanity at all times: a constant and uneasy "placemindedness" that characterizes a subject's interactions with his or her environment, which is itself so broadly conceived as to include the lived space of any given personal experience (the stroll about the shopping mall, for example) as well as the abstract space whose true representation is beyond any one individual's ken (a larger national, international, or ultimately universal space of a "world system"). Though it may be experienced most keenly in those moments of disorientation, a persistent placemindedness as well as a need to map are constant features of our existence. Topophrenia characterizes nearly all human activity, as a sense of place—not to mention matters of displacement and replacement, of movement between places and over spaces, and of the multifarious relations among place, space, individuals, collectivities, events, and so on—is an essential element of thought, experience, and being. Along those lines, it is worth noting that merely to think of a place is already to be mapping. This cartographic imperative lies at the heart of the spatial imagination. True, as a slogan, "Always map!" does not carry the ironic forcefulness of Fredric's Jameson's "Always historicize!" in the preface to *The Political Unconscious*, and "Always be mapping!" certainly lacks the venomous, predatory alacrity of Alec Baldwin's unforgettable "Always be closing!" in the film version of *Glengarry Glen Ross*. But for all its deficits in pithy memorability, the cartographic imperative makes up for these shortcomings in its apparent universality. We are always mapping, whether we are aware of it or not.

Speaking of cognitive mapping in an era of globalization, an activity understood in part as the self-conscious attempt by individual and collective subjects to represent and to situate themselves in relation to an unrepresentable social totality, Jameson has asserted that it is not merely the case "that we ought to strive for it, but that we do so all the time anyway without being aware of the process."[1] We do so through figures and narratives that carry diverse, even contradictory meanings, but that also operate as the means by which we make sense of the world we occupy and imagine. In this manner, mapping is a persistent, complex, and protean activity. The term must be understood figuratively, of course, but the map is already a figure. It provides a figurative or figural representation of the spaces and places it depicts, and this representation is more or less useful, for a variety of purposes, to those who employ it. And as a number of spatially oriented critics have long asserted, mapping may be seen as an activity not unrelated to literary production. Both practices organize and coordinate the various data of experience and abstract projections or structures in such a way as to constitute a meaningful ensemble, a self-contained whole, if only provisionally and temporarily, which can then be used to make sense of, or give form to, the world as we can then know it. These become ways of orientating ourselves, of establishing a sense of place in relation to other spaces and places, and ultimately of envisioning a somewhat coherent image of the various spatial and social frames of reference, from small-scale interior design to ever larger scales of region, nation, and planet, up to and including the vast world system itself.[2]

As it is used throughout this book, the map needs to be understood as a metaphor, but it is no less powerful for being figurative. Indeed, I would say that it is *only just* metaphorical, since the spatial imagination that is both the motive and the basis for the project of literary cartography is necessarily connected to the "real" spaces, to geography and architecture, for instance, as well as to the imagined spaces that constitute the world, whether conceived of as the social sphere, the planet, or the universe—hence, the value of Edward W. Soja's "trialectical" approach to the conception, perception, and experience of space that posited "real-and-imagined" places as the true object for analysis. Soja conceives of "thirdspace" as a way not only to bridge but also to transform and "Other" the divide between physical and mental spaces, which is to say, the "real" geography out there and the representations of space we carry in our minds (first- and secondspace, respectively). In Soja's view, "*Everything* comes together in Thirdspace: subjectivity and objectivity, the abstract and the concrete, the real and the imagined, the knowable and the unimaginable, the repetitive and the differential, structure and agency, mind and body, consciousness and the unconscious, the disciplined and the transdisciplinary, everyday life and unending history."[3] This holistic view of spatiality informs my sense of *topophrenia*, as well as the projects of literary cartography in narrative and geocriticism in reading, since the spaces and places involved must also be considered in their persistently real, imagined, and "real-and-imagined" states.

If mapping be partly metaphorical, then it still has its literal force in the fact that spatiality is a fundamental aspect of our own being. Moreover, although it cannot be denied that a certain cartographic imperative or mapping project lies at the heart of human experience and aesthetic representation across different historical moments, it does seem that different historical and social formations have produced distinctive spatial organizations, as Henri Lefebvre has maintained,[4] in which case certain times and places have likely called for a greater attention to or awareness of problems of spatial representation or orientation than others. Consequently, levels of cartographic anxiety may vary depending on one's historical, social, and spatial situation, and the need to produce figural maps may be more or less urgent. For a variety of reasons, I follow such thinkers as Michel Foucault, Lefebvre, Soja, and Jameson in recognizing that ours is, and has been for some time now, an epoch of enhanced spatiality. The so-called spatial turn in the humanities and social sciences in recent years is partly the result of this heightened sense of the importance of space, place, and mapping to these fields in the late twentieth and early twenty-first centuries. If Jameson has conceded that his notion of *cognitive mapping* was really a code word for "class consciousness," for instance, it was nevertheless to be understood as a form of consciousness especially suited to "that new spatiality implicit in the postmodern,"[5] and the figure retains "the advantage of involving concrete content (imperialism, the world system, subalternity, dependency and hegemony), while necessarily involving a program of formal analysis of a new kind (since it is centrally defined by the dilemma of representation itself)."[6] Indeed, whether the map be considered as a literal form or as a figure for the sort of narrative representation I have in mind in my use of the term *literary cartography*, the flexibility and effectiveness of mapping make it an exemplary model for literary and cultural studies, if not for the humanities and social sciences tout court.

That our experience of the world and the language we use to describe it can both be considered distinctively spatial (as well as temporal) is not contested. All stories are spatial in one respect or another and more often than not, in many different ways at once. My interest in narrative is no doubt based partly on my own professional formation in the discipline of literary studies, but I also believe that there is a fundamental relationship between narrative and our engagement with the world at an epistemological as well as an aesthetic level; that is, inasmuch as humans are political animals in Aristotle's definition, we are also storytelling animals. I follow Jameson in viewing narrative as "the central function or *instance* of the human mind."[7] This is also related to the cartographic imperative insofar as our comportment toward the world is necessarily topophrenic, so our narratives help to shape the spaces and places we perceive, experience, and inhabit.

The trailblazing linguistic research of Charlotte Linde and William Labov in the 1970s demonstrated the degree to which our perceptions and utterances were guided by distinctive ways of imagining space, place, and our relationships with them. In "Spatial Networks as a Site for the Study of Language and Thought," Linde and Labov famously distinguish between the *tour* and the *map*.[8] The former establishes a sort of spatiotemporal narrative, one which involves a subject who moves through space in a certain sequential order or syntax, whereas the latter postulates a synoptic or synchronic spatial organization in which everything is laid out at once. Looking at the ways that residents of New York describe their apartments, Linde and Labov note the way in which their speech functions to offer a tour of the apartment (e.g., "you enter the kitchen and then you find a dining room to the left"), essentially narrating a spatial story of the environment for the auditor or reader. Only rarely do they find New Yorkers employing the more map-like discourse (e.g., "there is a dining room to the left of the kitchen"). But I would argue that the dynamic movement of the tour and the static description of the map present something of a false dichotomy, since in reality both features are present in any given narrative scenario. The subject's movement through space and among places and his or her perceptions of them presupposes, and is informed by, a more abstract or theoretical vision of a nonsubjective or suprasubjective image: a bird's-eye view that brings order and a sense of objectivity to the limited view of the itinerant subject. What is more, both of these ways of describing space and place are actually cartographic, since the tour also registers locations and their relationships with one another in an imagined space, and the map need not be considered a merely static representation. Each is informed by a spatiotemporality, even if the spatial appears to be more emphatic in the map-like description and the temporal seems highlighted in the movement of the tour. The tour/map distinction is still valuable, as it illuminates two fundamental aspects of the spatial imagination, which in the older discourse of philosophy might simply be transcoded as subjective and objective, and yet as with the long history of this dialectic in philosophy, we find that the two registers cannot long be held separate, as each infuses the other and makes knowledge, and more importantly narrative, possible.

In his analysis of this distinction as part of the discussion of "spatial stories," Michel de Certeau notes the oscillation between alternate terms: "either *seeing* (the knowledge of an order of places) or *going* (spatializing actions)."[9] He then uses this distinction to inform another, in the context of narrative, between the *itinerary* and the *map*. In this vision, the itinerary represents "a discursive series of operations," whereas the map offers "a plane projection totalizing observations," and de Certeau sees these as two distinctive "symbolic and anthropological languages of space."[10] While I agree with the significance of this distinction—which comports with other productive alternatives in literary and social theory, such as narrative versus description (Georg Lukács), class struggle versus mode of production (Karl Marx), or simply, as noted above, subjectivity versus objectivity more generally—I cannot accept de Certeau's conclusion that the one (itinerary, tour) is somehow more liberatory or transgressive, while the other (the map) is repressive, because it is totalizing. In fact, the two registers inform one another, at times mutually reinforcing and at others disjointedly challenging the representations produced in accordance with them. As Jameson observed in his well-known "digression on cartography," itineraries are basically "diagrams organized around the still subject-centered or existential journey of the traveler," whereas mapping proper will require "the coordination of existential data (the empirical position of the subject) with unlived, abstract conceptions of the geographic totality." Moreover, the seemingly subjective, perspectival itinerary and the apparently more objective, speculative, or projective map will necessarily encounter the fundamental problem of representation as such, for "there can be no true maps."[11] With no "true maps," no perfectly mimetic representations of the depicted places and spaces, and no God's-eye view or absolute truth on which to rely, we are left with, but also blessed with, the task of creating, revising, polishing, perhaps discarding, then producing anew our own figural representations. And it is not merely that we ought to make the effort to map these spaces but that we do so all the time. This is the cartographic imperative.

This is also the core concept of literary cartography, for it is through narrative that this figural mapmaking, broadly conceived, takes place. Narrative also *makes* place, establishing relations among places and assigning various levels of significance to different spaces and places.[12] In identifying places, delineating relations among them in space, connecting some while disconnecting others, aggrandizing the importance of some and diminishing that of others, and so on, we are drafting various maps and telling different stories. As Peter Turchi puts it, "To ask for a map is to say, 'Tell me a story,'" to which may be added, and vice versa.[13]

This book is concerned with literary cartography, and my approach to the subject is accordingly that of a literary critic. Some of my readers have asked why I do not include actual maps or other spatial diagrams in any of my writings on the subject, and my answer is in part that *literary* cartography, strictly speaking, is undertaken and accomplished through literature, understood here in its narrower sense as being constituted through the written word.[14] I am not at all suggesting that those spatially oriented critics who do employ maps or other graphics, whether as illustrations, models, or tools, are doing anything wrong, and indeed, my own understanding of these subjects has benefited immensely from their projects. Nevertheless, I do find there to be a certain tension, perhaps a more or less productive rivalry, between text and image, narrative and picture, that can sometimes confuse the issue by causing readers either to conflate one with the other or to feel the need to choose sides. One inevitably compares or contrasts the map created and presented in the language of a text's literary cartography with the visualization of the imaginary space in the map or diagram. In texts that include maps, which are almost always quite helpful to the reader, one cannot help but question the authority of the text relative to its accompanying image. This can lead to productive controversies, but it also takes the reader away from the literary text itself and into entirely different places.

The spatial humanities quite rightly involve interdisciplinary approaches to their areas of inquiry. Whether we name these practices *geocriticism, literary geography, the spatial humanities,* or whatever, researchers engaged in such work cannot help but find themselves working amid the fields of history, literature, philosophy, religion, art and art history, urban studies, architecture, social theory, political economy, sometimes archaeology or geology, even physics and mathematics, and of course geography. Much of the innovation and excitement in the spatial humanities comes from these productive interactions across disciplinary boundaries. Yet I would caution against seeing interdisciplinarity as itself a wholly salubrious phenomenon or an inherently worthy goal. As much as we might value the fruitful collaborations with our peers in other departments, we must also recognize the degree to which disciplinary conventions and practices, while perhaps arbitrary in a purely ontological sense, have developed historically and instantiated themselves within structures of scholarly activity that themselves have value. It is enough to note that philosophers, geographers, and literary critics do not approach their subjects in the same ways, but I would also observe that we do a disservice to ourselves and our colleagues by too eagerly eliding the difference between disciplinary fields. Interdisciplinary scholarship has yielded significant results, but the distinctive power and effectiveness of certain disciplinary practices ought not be disregarded. In this book I maintain an approach that is very much based in literature as a disciplinary field, with literary criticism, literary theory, and literary history understood as key subdivisions of that field. This is not to say that my approach is superior to that of a philosopher, geographer, historian, or other, but only that the perspective of literary studies is distinctive.

In addition to my own comfort level in the field for which my own scholarly training prepared me, I would say that three other considerations have led me to conclude that a literary approach is the right one for this study. First, as noted, Yi-Fu Tuan's definition of *place* with respect to *space* positions the former squarely within the disciplinary bailiwick of literary studies, since place is understood by Tuan to be endowed with meaning and subject to interpretation, and literary criticism (among others fields) takes interpretation, along with analysis and evaluation, to be central to its mission.[15] Second, as Jameson has pointed out, the field of literary studies—in its focus on language and its attention to the need to interpret—prepares us rather effectively to deal with the mystifications or complexities of our current condition:

> Unfortunately, no society has ever been quite so mystified in quite so many ways as our own, saturated as it is with messages and information, the very vehicles of mystification (language, as Talleyrand put it, having been given us in order to conceal our thoughts). If everything were transparent, then no ideology would be possible, and no domination either: evidently that is not our case. But above and beyond the sheer fact of mystification, we must point to the supplementary problem involved in the study of cultural or literary texts, or in other words, essentially, of narratives: for even if discursive language were to be taken literally, there is always, and constitutively, a problem about the "meaning" of narratives as such.[16]

The narrative maps produced through literary cartography are equally subject to hermeneutic investigation, even as they also serve as means by which to interpret the underlying spaces they endeavor to represent. And third, I cite Northrop Frye's impassioned defense and presentation of literary studies as a means of educating the imagination.[17] If the study of literature produces an educated imagination, then the spatially oriented study of literature, focused on literary cartography and geocritical inquiry, can only strengthen the spatial imagination, a faculty all too necessary for making sense of our place and our world today.

For the most part, my examples and my criticism in general focus on the novel, which some readers might consider an odd choice, all the more odd considering the degree to which I rely on fairly traditional or canonical works. After all, many other genres and narrative forms today are arguably more interesting, more relevant to our own time, or more obviously spatial. Cinema, television, video games, comic books, graphic texts, and other media might appear more suited to spatial analysis, and they likely have the additional advantage of being more fashionable. Such forms have perhaps supplanted the novel as the dominant practice of narrative in recent decades. For example, Jonathan Arac has argued that "the age of the novel," the age in which the novel was preeminent in speaking to the broader cultural sphere in modern society, basically ran from the early to mid-nineteenth century to the mid-twentieth in the United States, "from about the time of *Moby-Dick* and *Uncle Tom's Cabin* to that of *Invisible Man* and *Lolita*."[18] This obviously does not mean that novels are not still produced and consumed in great abundance, merely that the cultural significance of the novel or novelist is no longer as notable, particularly in the public sphere. Nevertheless, I would argue that these various newer or more dominant forms are fundamentally novelistic in both their creators' intentions and in their effects. I do not have the space to delve into this here, but one might argue that the emergence, development, proliferation, and (yes) dominance of these new narrative forms has to do with the power of novelistic discourse to transcend its own physical frame, the hardcover's bound volume or paperback, and render other modes more novel-like in the process. That a television series like *The Wire* or a video game franchise like *BioShock* can be compared to the novels of Charles Dickens in its large cast of characters, its narrative complexity, and its realism is merely to say that we are finding different ways to produce novels. In any event, the theory of the novel may be all the more useful and desirable in a moment when novelistic discourse is so pervasive throughout the galaxy of cultural forms available to consumers today. And if the novel is indeed a residual form as Arac suggests, then that residue is nonetheless ample, rich, and rewarding.[19]

The chapters that follow are all devoted to exploring the idea of literary cartography, and in focusing on place, narrative, and the spatial imagination, I attempt to establish the basic terms for such an exploration. A number of these chapters have appeared in earlier versions elsewhere, and as a collection of distinctive essays, each chapter may be viewed as having some degree of semiautonomy. However, I have ordered them in such a way as to suggest a certain logical trajectory that will offer the reader a tour or itinerary through various points on the map of my recent thinking about literary cartography and issues related to it. Given the places and times in which these chapters were first conceived, there is some repetition and overlap among them, which I have tried to alleviate through my revisions to the original versions. Most significant of these repeated points is the fundamental observation, drawn from Tuan, among others, that place is constructed or created as a locus of meaning subject to interpretation and that the representation of place, broadly imagined, necessarily brings with it a literary sensibility. As a unit of literary cartography, place is crucial to the project of narrative mapping and to the more generalized spatial imagination.

In addition to this introduction and a brief conclusion, the contents are arranged in three parts, each comprising three chapters, which correspond more or less directly to the three terms of *Topophrenia*'s subtitle: place, narrative, and the spatial imagination. However, these concepts also appear throughout the book, as they ceaselessly inform my discussion of spatiality, geocriticism, and literary cartography. As with the legends and symbols on a map, the arrangement of the parts and chapters, including their titles, is intended to be helpful and informative, but they are not to be granted a sort of ontological privilege, as they are merely guideposts for explorers of the territories surveyed within and not themselves sights worth seeing. Although I have arranged the chapters with order in mind, readers are certainly free to select their own routes through the book.

Part I focuses on the importance of place for geocritical theory and practice. In chapter 1 I discuss the problem of place while also elaborating on the meaning of the term *topophrenia*, which literally indicates a certain "placemindedness" while also by implication suggesting a condition of disorder or "dis-ease." Drawing on Tuan's earlier concept of topophilia, I look at the ways in which an affective geography of place would necessarily involve the less salutary or utopian visions of place, such as places of fear or loathing that nevertheless condition our approaches to space and place in narrative. Then I discuss how narratives function as mapping machines, dynamic ensembles designed to represent places, spaces, and events in a figural organization that may stand in for the totality of social relations of a given text.

Chapter 2 offers a brief introduction to the theory and practice of geocriticism, an approach to literary and cultural texts that focuses critical attention on place, spatial relations, and the interconnections among literature and geography. Here I discuss the recent work of Bertrand Westphal, the French literary critic who, along with his research team at the Université de Limoges, has done the most to define, elaborate, and promote a geocentric approach to literary and cultural studies. Westphal's *La Géocritique* provided the theoretical and methodological justification of the geocritical endeavor, while his more recent work (most notably in *Le Monde plausible* and *La Cage des méridiens*) has extended and complicated the geocritical project in relation to the exigencies of a truly global approach to world literature. I distinguish my own use of the term *geocriticism* from Westphal's, but I acknowledge the lasting importance of Westphal's work for geocritical explorations in the present. I take geocriticism, conceived somewhat broadly, to be the most effective approach to a critical reading of the narrative maps or literary cartography produced by creative writers. Following the spatial turn in the humanities, the moment is particularly ripe for further geocritical theory and practice.

Chapter 3 takes up this call for theoretical practice in an era that some have suggested is, or ought to be, postcritical or even "posttheory." Looking at the situation of theory in connection to theories of situatedness, I argue for the importance of geocriticism for twenty-first-century literary studies. The logic of the situation, as Jameson has suggested, demands a critical awareness of the relations between things, of spatiotemporal connections to be made, and of the contingencies of the hic et nunc. Drawing on the Aristotelian figure of peripeteia, the reversal of the situation, I discuss the ways in which geocritical theory, and critical theory more generally, remains essential to any literary or cultural studies today. The shifting territories of the present call for new maps, and new maps call for new readings. Geocritical theory and practice are especially well suited to address the challenges of place, narrative, and representation in the uncertain and dynamic world system.

The three chapters in part II deal with the relations among space, place, and mapping and narrative forms, with special attention paid to the theory and history of the novel. In chapter 4, "The Mise en Abyme of Literary Spatiality," I raise a few critical problems associated with literary cartography, which must answer the challenge posed by Jorge Luis Borges's fabulous geographers, whose map was strictly coextensive with the territory it purported to represent. The crisis of representation, as Jameson had suggested, is made manifest in any mapping project. Examining three exemplary moments in classic and modern world literature, I look at the ways in which the narrator or rhapsode constructs the world out of narrative threads and scraps. Then I examine the ways in which an architectonic structure is needed to maintain the seemingly scientific or objective order of this world before looking at the ways in which the subject's own perception of these spaces reflects on him or her, thus rendering the narrative mapping project a reflexive, open-ended meditation. The seemingly infinite reflections of spatiality mirrors serve not only to make clearer but also to complicate the project of literary cartography.

Chapter 5 addresses the space of the novel, and I take the novel form to be perhaps the most important narrative genre for literary cartography. The novel as a historical form emerges, flourishes, and becomes a dominant literary form alongside the rise of cartography, the restructuring of social spaces accompanying developments in capitalist relations of production, the emergence of a colonial and commercial world system, and modernity itself.[20] I look at the ways that space and place are presented in the novel using examples from various texts. The novel is also a distinctively epistemological narrative form, which like the map presents a seemingly realistic but utterly figurative image of the world it depicts. This narrative map can then be used to make sense of, or give form to, the "real" world.

Along those lines, chapter 6 focuses on the different ways in which the novel and the map present, and in some ways produce, knowledge of the world. Delving further into the distinction between itinerary (or tour) and map, I examine the competing registers of experiential or empirical knowledge and a more abstract, theoretical model, showing how both the novel as a literary form and the map as a tool of knowledge exploit the productive tension between these ways of know-ing in order to create a more dynamic *theatrum geographicum* by which to envi-sion the world system. I also look at Lukács's *Theory of the Novel* as a perversely modernist attempt to analyze the novel as a form of literary cartography. Using Miguel de Cervantes's *Don Quixote* and Daniel Kehlmann's *Measuring the World* as exemplary novels, early modern and postmodern visions published four hun-dred years apart, I show how the artificiality of the novel and the map, both pow-erful fictions used to make sense of the world, make possible alternative visions.

The chapters in part III deal in different ways with the fantastic nature of mapping, partly by exploring the discursive mode of fantasy as it is employed by a spatial imagination in literature. Chapter 7 continues the discussion of the ways in which novels produce a literary cartography of their worlds, but here my focus is on the trope of adventure. The adventure story holds a privileged place in the history of narrative, as the hero's departure and homecoming emphasize the spa-tial displacement and return while also mapping out a trajectory of adventures across a variety of distinctive places. Drawing on J. R. R. Tolkien's *The Hobbit*, I argue that the novel of adventure offers an exemplary model for literary cartogra-phy, as the itinerary of the adventurers gives supplementary meaning to the map of the world in which these adventures take place, thus combining the power of each register of literary geography to enhance the experience of spatiality in the text. I examine the way that the tale figures forth spaces and places in the imagi-nary realms of the novel, and I argue that literary cartography has a fundamen-tally fantastic or utopian aspect.

Chapter 8 deals more directly with fantasy and utopia as genres and as modes of thought. I argue not only that these genres are necessarily and inherently spa-tial but also that spatial literary studies must embrace fantastic and utopian criti-cism. I focus especially on Thomas More's *Utopia*, looking at both the text and the accompanying illustration from its 1516 publication, *Utopiae Insulae Figura*, to show the contrast between the highly rationalized order of the Utopian soci-ety and the utterly fanciful or fantastic presentation of it. I argue that, contrary to those critics who would sever utopia from fantasy, favoring the former and disavowing the latter, fantasy is an essential element of the literary cartographic project that, in turn, is indispensable for any utopian thinking in the present.[21] Following China Miéville's critique of cognition as ideology, I embrace a fantas-tic geocritical theory that makes room for dragons even as it explores space.

I elaborate this need for a sort of fantastic thinking in chapter 9, "Beyond the Flaming Walls of the World," which takes its title from an apt phase in Lucre-tius's *De Rerum Natura*. Beginning with the apparently otherworldly perspective of a space alien, which is actually the image of the Earth as photographed by Apollo astronauts, I argue that any literary cartography, even that which strives to appear realistic, must involve the discursive mode of fantasy. The figuration required for literary cartography is related to the fundamentally projective, speculative, or theoretical project associated with fantasy, and I argue that the alterity of fantasy is necessary for resisting the persistent appeals to the status quo or to nostalgic, reactionary formations, particularly nationalism. I move that critics embrace a literary cartography suited to a postnational condition, which would be animated by the critical distance and attention to alterity afforded by the fantastic, whose motive force is theory itself in its vocation as speculative and transformative activity.

Finally, by way of a conclusion, I return to the idea of a cartographic imperative, looking at the ways in which figurative mapping is a necessary and unavoidable aspect of our being-in-the-world. I briefly survey the current landscape of spatial literary studies, which I take to be still in their early stages of development, and I suggest that a geocritical or spatially oriented approach to literature and culture will lead to particularly fecund and fascinating interpretations and analyses. The conclusion is necessarily open-ended, since so much of what is exciting about the spatial humanities likely lies before us in the future. But there is also ample evidence to suggest that the spatial turn in the humanities and social sciences has already produced insightful research on which to produce novel approaches and effects.

If all narratives may be taken as forms of literary cartography, it is in part because of this ineluctable topophrenia at the core of what used to be called the human condition. In telling stories we orient ourselves and others with respect to place and space, not to mention moments in time, and we produce dynamic, multiform, and protean cartographies. A geocritical approach to reading these narrative maps enables us to sense more emphatically the ways that space, place, and mapping condition our lives, attitudes, thoughts, and experiences, as well as our more critically distant claims to knowledge about them. As Frank Kermode once said, it is not for critics to help us make sense of our lives—that is, the burden of the poets and other creative writers—but merely to attempt the lesser task of "making sense of the ways we try to make sense of our lives."[22] In our time, after the "spatial turn," geocritics, spatially oriented critics, and others working in the spatial humanities can offer new interpretations, analyses, and evaluations of these ways of making sense or giving form to our lives. By paying particular attention to the spatial imagination, its motivations, and its results, we may come to see the world, and ourselves, in interesting, new ways.

Notes

1. Fredric Jameson, *The Geopolitical Aesthetic: Cinema and Space in the World System* (Bloomington: Indiana University Press and the British Film Institute, 1992), 2.

2. See, e.g., Amy J. Elias and Christian Moraru, eds., *The Planetary Turn: Relationality and Geoaesthetics in the Twenty-First Century* (Evanston, IL: Northwestern University Press, 2015); see also Christian Moraru, *Reading for the Planet: A Geomethodology* (Ann Arbor: University of Michigan Press, 2015).

3. Edward W. Soja, *Thirdspace: Journeys to Los Angeles and Other Real-and-Imagined Places* (Oxford: Blackwell, 1996), 56–57.

4. See Henri Lefebvre, *The Production of Space*, trans. Donald Nicholson-Smith (Oxford: Blackwell, 1991).

5. Fredric Jameson, *Postmodernism, or, the Cultural Logic of Late Capitalism* (Durham, NC: Duke University Press, 1991), 417–418.

6. Jameson, *The Geopolitical Aesthetic*, 188–189.

7. Fredric Jameson, *The Political Unconscious: Narrative as a Socially Symbolic Act* (Ithaca, NY: Cornell University Press, 1981), 13. See also my *Fredric Jameson: The Project of Dialectical Criticism* (London: Pluto Press, 2014), 58–76.

8. See Charlotte Linde and William Labov, "Spatial Networks as a Site for the Study of Language and Thought," *Language* 51, no. 4 (December 1975), 924–939.

9. Michel de Certeau, *The Practice of Everyday Life*, trans. Steven Rendall (Berkeley: University of California Press, 1984), 119.

10. Ibid.

11. Jameson, *Postmodernism*, 51–52.

12. This is not to say that nonnarrative writing could not also produce literary cartography, and poetry especially, given its "spatial form," has frequently been a subject for spatial literary studies. However, in my view, literary cartography is best executed through narrative for the reasons discussed throughout this book, as the narrative "maps" are more readily visible as dynamic processes or mobile constellations than static images.

13. Peter Turchi, *Maps of the Imagination: The Writer as Cartographer* (San Antonio, TX: Trinity University Press, 2004), 11.

14. From the Latin *littera* or letters. That said, I certain do not mean to rule out narratives from an oral tradition or other unwritten forms.

15. I maintain that interpretation, of one form or another, is a crucial element of literary criticism or even of literary studies in general, even as this view has come under increasing attack in recent years by advocates of a "postcritical" approach to literature. See, e.g., Rita Felski, *The Limits of Critique* (Chicago: University of Chicago Press, 2015).

16. Jameson, *The Political Unconscious*, 60–61. Needless to say, a "literal" interpretation is still a kind of interpretation, as literary texts and the language of which they are made do not simply conform to an objective set of facts but require ways of reading.

17. See Northrop Frye, *The Educated Imagination* (Bloomington: Indiana University Press, 1964).

18. Jonathan Arac, "What Kind of History Does the Theory of the Novel Require?" *NOVEL: A Forum on Fiction* 42, no. 2 (2009), 193; see also Arac's introduction to his *Impure Worlds: The Institution of Literature in the Age of the Novel* (New York: Fordham University Press, 2011).

19. See my "In the File Drawer Labeled 'Science Fiction': Genre after the Age of the Novel," *Journal of English Language and Literature* 63, no. 2 (2017), 201–217.

20. Here I follow a rather traditional and perhaps somewhat outdated vision of the history of the novel, and I am aware that recent theorists and historians of the novel have

demonstrated the wide variety of ancient novels and other forms. See, e.g., the range of work on display in Franco Moretti's massive *Il Romanzo* project, a slightly truncated English version of which appears as *The Novel*, two volumes (Princeton, NJ: Princeton University Press, 2007).

21. See Fredric Jameson, *Archaeologies of the Future: The Desire Called Utopia and Other Science Fictions* (London: Verso, 2005), especially 57–71; see also my *Utopia in the Age of Globalization: Space, Representation, and the World System* (New York: Palgrave Macmillan, 2013).

22. Frank Kermode, *The Sense of an Ending: Studies in the Theory of Fiction* (Oxford: Oxford University Press, 1967), 3.

PART I

PLACE IN GEOCRITICAL THEORY AND PRACTICE

1 Topophrenia

*P*LACE SEEMS so simple—commonplace, in fact—yet the concept lies at the heart not only of some rather complicated geographic theory and practice but also, arguably, of the arts, humanities, and sciences as a whole. The idea of place is crucial to spatial literary studies, unsurprisingly, and as such it deserves further attention. The fact that place can be taken for granted at times is already a sign of its conceptual ubiquity inasmuch as everything is situated in space and in or with respect to a place, but the distinctiveness of this or that place, the relationship of a place to other places and spaces, and the effects of place on persons, events, or narratives occurring or situated in a certain place are certainly worthy of further inquiry. With respect to literature in particular, place is always exerting its influence or making itself known in the text, and narratives frequently display their fundamental spatiotemporality according to the ways in which places, as well as moments in time, are represented. As such, place can be thought of as a sort of unit in literary cartography, which, like actual mapmaking, must register various types of place at the same time as it tries to account for them. Mapping makes visible places, and, in what might seem to be a circular logic, being mapped is what in many respects establishes a place *as* a place. Any study of literary cartography has to take into consideration, or take for granted, the problematics of place.

The Problematics of Place

In his magisterial study *Space and Place: The Perspective of Experience,* Yi-Fu Tuan carefully sets forth the conditions under which what we think of as a place emerges from the almost inchoate or chaotic proliferation of relations associated with space. He identifies a powerfully spatiotemporal dynamic in which a place becomes distinctive and thus knowable, and this dynamic creates meaning for and gives shape to all human experience of the world. For Tuan, a discrete or recognizable portion of otherwise undifferentiated space becomes a place when it occasions a pause, a resting of the eye or the stimulation of some other sense, at which point that now discrete spot becomes imbued with value and meaning. It thus enters the province of literary art, subject to interpretation, as well as to affective appreciation and significance. As Tuan puts it, among the ways that *place* can be defined, place is whatever stable object catches our attention. As we look at a panoramic scene our eyes pause at points of interest. Each pause is time enough to create an image of place that looms momentarily in our view. The pause may be of such short duration and the interest so fleeting that we may not be fully aware of having focused on any particular object; we believe we have simply been looking at the general scene. Nonetheless these pauses have occurred. It is not possible to look at a scene in general; our eyes keep searching for points of rest. We may be deliberately searching for a landmark, or a feature on the horizon may be so prominent that it compels attention. . . .

Many places, profoundly significant to particular individuals and groups, have little visual prominence. They are known viscerally, as it were, and not through the discerning eye or mind. A function of literary art is to give visibility to intimate experiences, including those of place. The Grand Tetons of landscape do not require the services of literature; they advertise themselves by sheer size. Literary art can illuminate the inconspicuous fields of human care such as a Midwestern town, a Mississippi county, a big-city neighborhood, or an Appalachian hollow.[1]

Place, then, by definition is associated with a certain way of seeing that might well be called "critical," even "literary critical," inasmuch as interpretation, evaluation, and analysis of its meaning, functioning, and effects are presupposed the moment a given portion of space becomes recognizable as a place. If in Tuan's view *place* is understood in terms of a pause, a moment of rest, then *space* is associated with movement. Place can then be understood as a relatively fixed, stable, and thus familiar or at least recognizable point, whereas space partakes of the mobile, dynamic, or unfamiliar. Space is likewise associated with the freedom, but also the peril, that comes from being away from home or being on the move. "From the security and stability of place, we are aware of the openness, freedom, and threat of space, and vice-versa."[2] In this somewhat phenomenological conception, the individual subject establishes a place through his or her experience and perception while simultaneously being subject to a place and to the space, abstract or diffuse, against which it is defined. Place is therefore profoundly subjective, but it is also a form of subjection.

A place is not quite the same as a territory, whose tortuous history of shifting relations of power and knowledge is illuminated in Stuart Elden's brilliant genealogy *The Birth of Territory*, but a place must also be understood as an astonishingly dense ensemble of crystallized social relations.[3] These relations might be disclosed in the everyday experiences, attitudes, or memories of those individuals or groups who inhabit, visit, or even just know of such places, which in turn may represent a complicated skein of intersecting historical events, narratives, traumas, and so on. Schematically, we may identify a given place, a "you are here," from which to orient ourselves in relation to other places, but the "here" in question is never merely a location in space, such as would be approximated in the abstract by a set of coordinates on a Cartesian grid or even by a street address. Obviously, there is far more to a place than its mere localizability, but the very idea of localizing, of determining a locus, is essential to producing a place, not to mention experiencing and interpreting it.

In his *Place: A Short Introduction*, Tim Cresswell acknowledges both the simplicity and the complexity of the concept while exploring the many ways in which place or places have been understood by various spatial theorists and critics. One distinction is the difference between an abstract understanding of a given locus and the richer but messier apprehension of the place as experienced or lived. Cresswell illustrates the point by observing that the geographically definitive or specific marker "40.46 degrees North, 73.58 degrees West" does not mean much to most people, but the referent of these coordinates, New York City (or, more precisely, Midtown Manhattan), conjures up a host of images for persons familiar with the area and even for persons who may only know the place from its reputation or from images in books and movies. Pressing further into the analysis of the place, one discovers narratives without limit, social history, cultural traditions, political conflicts, artistic forms, and on and on.[4] Hence, the exact location itself is not necessarily meaningful, at least not to all, but a given place, recognized as such, contains a plenum of meaning so vast as to be nearly overwhelming for an interpreter.

To know a place is really to know only a little about the place, since it would be impossible to achieve anything remotely approaching a complete representation of it. This has been almost comically proven by Georges Perec in his *Attempt at Exhausting a Place in Paris*, in which the writer tries to take note of every person and incident visible to him at a bustling intersection of Place Saint-Sulpice over the course of three days.[5] (Needless to say, perhaps, but even by limiting his inquiry to a single intersection in Paris over a single weekend, Perec can offer little more than an infinitesimal amount of detail, considering the impossibly vast array of potential data to be registered.) This is also why, in Bertrand Westphal's *Geocriticism*, the insoluble problem of the corpus haunts any effort to perform a comprehensive, geocentric interpretation, as I will discuss further in the next chapter.[6] With a nearly infinite number of potential impressions of a particular place at our disposal, at what point does the geocritic feel comfortable that the body of work has achieved some level or threshold of adequate representation? Who is to say where the line would be drawn? Where does one even begin? How does one ever decide where to end?

One approach, certainly, involves a reliance on the subjective experience of space and place that Tuan discusses. In many respects, this remains egocentric, as opposed to Westphal's geocentric methodology, which attempts to avoid bias through a multifocal process in which the place, not the writer or writers representing the place, is central to the investigation at all times. However, the somewhat egocentric approach that focuses on a single observer's subjective experience allows a reader to explore the place *as* perceived or *as* experienced, without necessarily straining to achieve a quasi-scientific categorical knowledge of the place.[7] The admittedly artificial limits on a corpus or on the object under scrutiny need not be debilitating, and these limits can often prove quite constructive. Focusing on a single author or single text, for instance, can enable a range of creative interpretations that may be productive of others. Hence, a geocritical exploration might well take as its starting point a particular text and its relation to a place, whose almost unavoidable polysemy and heteroglossia will ensure that any reading of the text, place, and relations among them will exceed simple personal or autobiographical experience, as if even that were entirely possible to pin down. The problem of place, in this sense, becomes a larger problematic: it is a grand assemblage of problems to be grappled with by the reader and writer. This subjective limit then opens up a *plus ultra* for subsequent, if not endless, exploration.

A key element of such geocritical explorations has been the affective geography made visible through a given subject's own experience with and in places. In an earlier study, Tuan had coined an evocative term, *topophilia*, in order to represent succinctly "all of the human being's affective ties to the material environment." As Tuan explains, these ties "differ greatly in intensity, subtlety, and mode of expression. The response to environment may be primarily aesthetic: it may then vary from the fleeting pleasure one gets from a view to the equally fleeting but far more intense sense of beauty that is suddenly revealed. The response may be tactile, a delight in the feel of air, water, earth. More permanent and less easy to express are feelings that one has toward a place because it is home, a locus of memories, and the means of gaining a livelihood."[8] In Tuan's joyous phenomenology, places are endowed with deeply personal and subjective meanings. They are invested with profoundly affective or emotional content for the subject that perceives, moves about, and in the broadest sense inhabits those spaces that have become demarcated and identified as places. Topophilia, or the love of place, seems an appropriate concept for one who so revels in the sensuous geographies of place, to use Paul Rodaway's suggestive formulation.[9]

Here I might also mention the suggestive notion of *nonplace*, analyzed by Marc Augé in his influential study, *Non-Places: Introduction to an Anthropology of Supermodernity*. Augé focused attention on transitory sites, such as airports, hotels, highways, and supermarkets, which in a sense are not so much *places*— that is, locations imbued with meaning, dense with historical and social reference, the result of creative human endeavor, and so forth—as *nonplaces*, uniform, homogeneous zones of transit in which humans increasingly spend their lives.[10] Siobhan Carroll has referred to these sorts of sites as *atopias*, spaces "antithetical to habitable place," and she adds to the list of man-made atopias such as those mentioned by Augé a number of "natural atopias," such as the North Pole, the middle of the ocean, the desert, or outer space, although she also notes how cyberspace is frequently imagined as a somewhat positive, man-made atopia. Carroll concludes that, whether these atopias are viewed as spaces that either liberate or threaten the individual subject, they have become increasingly useful in "orientating ourselves to the sublime space of the planet and the human networks that span its surface."[11]

Recently, Dylan Trigg has called into question the binary distinction between place and nonplace distinction. Drawing on Maurice Merleau-Ponty's *Phenomenology of Perception*, Trigg argues that "the bodily experience of place operates on several layers" and that this multidimensionality "renders our experience of place ambiguous."[12] Moreover, the phenomenological value of the concept of the nonplace is somewhat compromised by the recognition of the affective complexities and ambiguities associated with the subjective, and especially intersubjective, experience of these apparent nonplaces, as Trigg shows how hospital waiting rooms or beds, as well as airports, can be spaces of friendship as well as of anxiety—that is, "a con-fused space, a layered space where paradoxical aspects are not resolved into a unified whole, but instead becomes emblematic of the ambiguous nature of our spatial experience more broadly."[13] One might also take note of "the betweenness of place," following J. Nicholas Entrikin's analysis of the phenomenon. That is, one can best understand a place, as well as the conception of *place*, from the point of view that is at once situated in the midst of things and attempting to represent the space, much like the way that a narrative operates, combining a subjective, localized perspective with a more speculative or theoretical overview.[14]

Given these complex factors, it may be difficult to maintain a vision of place as essentially homey, familiar, or loved. Tuan's sunny view of topophilia—quite literally sunny, it seems, since he takes as his *Ansatzpunkt* a personal memory of a stunning sunrise he witnessed while camping under the open skies in Death Valley, California—is delightful,[15] yet one cannot help feeling that this perspective on space ignores the more angst-ridden or menacing features of certain places. If "home" is somehow understood to be a topophilic space, then what of the unhomely spaces in which an alienated subject experiences the cartographic anxiety or sense of bewilderment that so typifies many literary representations of space?[16] Like so many Dantes, exiled from our metaphysical or actual homes, we subjected subjects often find ourselves in a *selva oscura*, quite unable to take pleasure in the visceral sensuality of the place or to marvel at its supernal beauty. Martin Heidegger makes note of this eerie sensibility in *Being and Time*, for example, in which he observes that anxiety (*Angst*) is often directly related to one's sense of place: "In anxiety one feels 'uncanny' [*unheimlich*]. Here the peculiar indefiniteness of that which Dasein finds itself alongside in anxiety, comes proximally to expression: the 'nothing and nowhere.' But here 'uncanniness' also means 'not-being-at-home' [*das Nicht-zu-hause-sein*]."[17] This is an apt description of the more quotidian anxiety one associates with being lost, or even just being uncomfortable in a given place, but one can also see how even familiar places might engender in the subject feelings of fear and loathing. It is not uncommon to find oneself in a place that one finds uncomfortable or *unheimlich*, even if it is a fairly well-known area. For example, a workplace that one loathes, a commercial district that one reluctantly visits when required to purchase goods, a locale associated with fear or anxiety (hospitals, funeral homes, cemeteries, etc.), involuntary enclosures (prison, school, factory, church), or other such undesirable places can evoke all manner of bad feelings. *Topophobia* seems the more apt label for the experiences so many people have with so many places.[18] Or, perhaps, a sort of *misotopia* could characterize those places we hate, such as those circles of living hell comprising exurban shopping malls, mass-replicating housing developments, the desert isle or the open field, or other such unloved places. (It is also worth noting that many topophobic sites are thoroughly topophilic for those who gain pleasure from or in them; in my case, the prospect of camping in Death Valley strikes me as rather terrifying, whereas exploring strange, densely populated urban districts sounds like a delightful time.) Affective geography must account for painful or unpleasant emotional responses to places and spaces, presumably, and not limit itself to topophilic relations.[19]

Proliferating neologisms aside, it appears that a crucial consideration of any properly spatial literary study is the pervasive sense, not only of place, but of place-mindedness, which characterizes both the subjective experience and the artistic representation of places, persons, events, and so forth. Fredric Jameson's understanding of narrative as "the central function or *instance* of the human mind," perhaps, is here to be supplemented with the proposition that any such narrative function be understood as itself a form of mapping, which is what I have in mind with the idea of literary cartography.[20] Traditionally, the primacy accorded by narrative criticism and theory to the temporal dimension, with the unfolding of events over time, has sometimes left the more discernibly spatial aspects of narrative to be either ignored entirely, downplayed as a mere backdrop, or reified into a static category, as with certain variations of regionalism or nationalism that condition, if not determine, the text's significance a priori.[21] Yet the dynamic spatiotemporal relations among subject, situation, representation, and interpretation invite critical approaches to literature that are sensitive to the uncertain, often shifting, but always pertinent ways that place haunts the mind.

The Topophrenic Condition

Along these lines, one might propose *topophrenia* as a provisional label for that condition of narrative, one that is necessary to any reading or writing of a text, in which the persistence of place and of the subject's relation to it must be constantly taken into account. Such place-mindedness is not to be understood as a simplistic relation between a given writer and his or her distinctive place (Thoreau at Walden Pond, for example), although any careful analysis of such a relationship would almost certainly disclose that things are not really so simple after all (as when, for instance, the topographic lines of Thoreau's *Walden* narrative extend or reach dead ends, intersect with others, proliferate, combine, and establish new lines entirely). Rather, topophrenia suggests the degree to which all thinking is, in various ways, thinking about place, which also means thinking about the relations among places, as well as those among subjects and places, in the broadest possible sense. In practice, topophrenia represents not so much a *geographical unconscious* as it does an existential comportment toward the world, but it also creates problems as well as opportunities for spatial literary criticism.[22] Topophrenia characterizes the subjective engagement with a given place, with one's sense of place, and with the possible projection of alternative spaces. Moreover, it requires us to consider the apparently objective structures and systems that condition, not to say determine, our perceptions and experiences of space and place.

By *topophrenia*, of course, I mean especially a certain identifiable "place-mindedness" that informs our activities and thinking. The Greek roots of the word justify this definition, but naturally, I am aware of the pertinacious associations of the *phrenia* suffix with disorder, illness, or malfunction. In common parlance as well as in medical discourse, words including *phrenia* almost exclusively designate disease or disorder; indeed, the suffix is likely familiar to most because of the term *schizophrenia*. In some respects, I think that this connotation is also quite suited to the idea of topophrenia as well, for I think that the pervasive place-mindedness infusing our subjective experience in and apprehension of the world is characterized by a profound sense of unease, anxiety, or discontent. Even in the more familiar or homey (*heimlich*) zones of being-in-the-world, we are nevertheless still cognizant of, and affected by, the sense of estrangement that I take to be the persistent condition undergirding the cartographic imperative. To put it differently, even when we are "at home," we maintain our awareness of the unfamiliar, the *unheimlich*, and a subtle, yet visceral feeling of spatial anxiety subtends our thought and actions. In fact, this might be thought of as the fundamental impetus behind the desire for mapping, which is also the desire for narrative.[23]

If topophrenia is not a disease, properly speaking, it is a condition of "dis-ease," something of the sort that Freud indicates in his use of the term *Unbehagen*, which is similar to the French term *malaise* and is translated as "discontent" in *Civilization and Its Discontents*, the English title given to *Das Unbehagen in der Kultur*.[24] Freud had originally considered *Das Unglück in der Kultur* as the title for this book, denoting "unhappiness" in culture or civilization, but he found *Unglück* inapt, replacing it with *Unbehagen*, which captures the more subtle feelings of uneasiness, discomfort, or disquiet. Along the same lines, *topophrenia* would not refer to an unhappiness, and its overall effects could include aspects of both topophilia and topophobia, presumably. Place-mindedness here must be understood to coincide with an entire range of affects, attitudes, conceptions, perceptions, references, and sensibilities that characterize the spatial imagination. In contrast to Tuan's mostly sweet and light *topophilia*, this sensibility or affect is not always pleasant, homely, or secure, but rather takes "place" in a wildly oscillatory but often systemic array of forces that determine the relationship between the subject and the social or even cosmic totality. Yet any topophrenic condition or attitude is also necessarily open to the delights of space and place, to the free play of spatial practices in which we invariably find ourselves both inscribed and inscribing, or to what Louis Marin in his remarkable study of utopia called *jeux d'espaces*.[25]

The experience of a place is therefore no simple matter. Any proper orientation or "sense of place" is definitively connected to and complicated by a seemingly infinite network of spaces and places that not only serve as shifting points of view or frames of reference but also affect the situation of the subject itself. A place is apprehended subjectively, but it is also only understandable as such when located within or in reference to a non- or suprasubjective ensemble of spatial relations, sites, networks, circuits, and so on. In fact, and this brings the matter of *literary cartography* back into the picture for the moment, the apprehension of place is bound up in a discursive or narrative ensemble of relations that—like some metaphor out of modern physics, such as Werner Heisenberg's uncertainty principle or Erwin Schrödinger's wayward cats—determine the outcome by implicating the subjective perception and the objective (or nonsubjective) thing in itself within a tenuous, untrustworthy, and ever-changing system: specifically, that of language. If, as Tuan insists, a place is defined in part as a site imbued with meaning, therefore subject to interpretation and thus an appropriate subject for literary criticism, it also needs to be understood that the language used to describe and to interpret the place itself engenders or conditions the place. The place is a text, but one that is necessarily informed, and indeed formed, by other texts as well.

In *Nausea*, quite possibly the most thoroughgoing analysis of existential anxiety in fiction, Jean-Paul Sartre's protagonist Antoine Roquentin reflects on his time in Morocco two years earlier but concludes that he would be unable to truly apprehend or comprehend the scenes or his experiences because of the intrusive power of words, language, or narrative. "I don't *see* anything anymore: I can search the past in vain, I can only find these scraps of images and I am not sure what they represent, whether they are memories or just fiction."[26] Roquentin realizes not only that the places he has been are utterly imbricated with the various memories he holds of them and the stories he has read or heard about them, such that they cannot be "known" in any reasonably objective way, but also that his own identity as the "experiencer" of these places is unstable. The person who had had experiences in Morocco or Spain or England, wherever, is already a fictional character in a story, now that the story is all there is that remains from which to construct or reconstruct the place and this now-strange person's experience of it. As he continues,

> There are many cases where even the scraps have disappeared: nothing is left but words. I could still tell stories, tell them too well . . ., but these are only the skeletons. There's the story of a person who does this, does that, but it isn't I, I have nothing in common with him. He travels through countries I know no more about than if I had never been there. Sometimes, in my story, it happens that I pronounce these fine names you read in atlases, Aranjuez or Canterbury. New images are born in me, images such as people create in books who have never travelled. My words are dreams, that is all.[27]

Of course, Roquentin's anxiety need not deter anyone from engaging in a project of narrating places and experiences, as if the cartographic imperative could be so easily overruled by the mere sophistry of an angst-ridden intellectual. In fact, the discomfort or uneasiness that Sartre's character experiences is part of the topophrenic condition. One cannot help but think of place and places, visualizing them and putting those images into some sort of narrative framework, at which point the tale and the teller become intertwined with the vast spatial ensemble that makes possible, but also makes difficult, such representations in language. Literary cartography, like "real" cartography, does not deliver the truth of the places it represents, after all. It provides more or less useful figurations by which we come to give shape to or make sense of those places and their significance.

One experiences the visceral force of this topophrenia in Wendy Chin-Tanner's poem, "On Truth in a Nonmoral Sense." Readers will recognize the allusion to Friedrich Nietzsche's brief 1873 essay "On Truth and Lie in an Extra-Moral Sense" (*Über Wahrheit und Lüge im außermoralischen Sinne*), and Chin-Tanner includes as an epigraph Nietzsche's well-known assertion at the end of that essay that the truth is nothing more than "a mobile army of metaphors, metonyms, and anthropomorphisms—in short, a sum of human relations which have been enhanced, transposed, and embellished poetically and rhetorically, and which after long use seem firm, canonical, and obligatory to a people."[28] In Chin-Tanner's stunning meditation on this Nietzschean "truth," the poet bodies forth an entire critique of the human sciences while inviting us to experience the haunting of places—which are themselves *haunts*, of course—by a kind of irrepressible subjectivity.

In sociology, we say *mapping*,
we say *cartography* instead

of *understanding*. To profess
to understand, you see, is hubris.

I am a professional digger. I
should say *excavation* or *archeology*

instead of *digging for the truth*,
which is uncouth. Which is emotional.

And, again, hubris. We should never say
truth. What is the truth, anyway? Instead,

we should say *subjectivity*, as in: *To what
are we subjected*? Or: *What is the subject*

of the story of your life? To name it,
I say *loss*, I say *yearn*, I say *tell me*.

What else can I say? In fall, before
the surgery, we walked, the sky the color

of pigeons. I listened to you breathe, the soft
wheezing. I listened to the sound of your shoes

shuffling, crunching dead leaves into the ground.
I thought I would lose you. How could I betray

you by mapping these cities so far away:
Paris, Prague, Vienna, Kiev? How could

they hurt us? These faint cartographies
drawn in traces of my DNA, and names,

the names escaping me over time and sea
poetically in slant, half, off, and straight

rhymes. I could never escape you. Before
us, our name stands constant, and the City stands

constantly shifting, like truth. Like words and meaning,
making meaningless the crude facts of my making.[29]

Here, one might assert, place becomes less a locale, less a localizable or even recognizable site, and more a subtly reimagined whirlwind of affective, cognitive, and experiential data. The inability to determine the *true* meaning of the place is countered by the literary act of significance, of meaning-making, and the poet's own mapping of the places help to constitute both this sense of place and that of her own subjectivity. As in Nietzsche, the humbling of scientific reason does not augur some ultimately meaningless existence, but rather becomes a step toward unleashing forces of active, creative, speculative thought.[30] The work of art, in this case, forms a map even as it implicitly criticizes the innate epistemic hubris of the cartographic endeavor. One cannot *know* the place, in that older sense, but one can make available a kind of knowledge of both place and self through one's patient, meticulous, creative, and topophrenic activity. A literary cartography emerges as a figuration of subjective experience and objective space, affective geographies combined with abstract principles, forming a sort of constellation by which the poet can navigate her world . . . and, perhaps, even change it.[31]

The fascination with place is a sign of our uneasy, but all-too-necessary relationship with the vicissitudes of space, as we "scan the horizon for a still spot," as Chin-Tanner puts it in another poem.[32] This still spot—also known as Tuan's *pause*, or the site that delights, disturbs, enraptures, and haunts—is the place one might give a name to, investing it with subjective meanings while subjecting it to analytical scrutiny. Caught as we are always in the middest, amid the complex and oscillatory relations of power and knowledge, the geocritic may nevertheless attempt to achieve a sense of place, so long as it is understood to be provisional, contingent, and subject to perpetual modification. Like a map, in fact.

Real-and-Imagined Places

In an early essay titled "Literary Geography" (1905), in which she reviewed two books (one on Charles Dickens, one on William Thackeray) in a Pilgrimage Series intended for enthusiasts who wished to engage in fiction-inspired tourism, Virginia Woolf discusses the relationship between the imaginary spaces or places depicted in a novel and the real-world places to which these appear to refer. Although she admits that certain readers may take pleasure in visiting places that, say, Dickens himself once graced and she concedes that certain biographically oriented critics could make much of how a given environment affected an author's work, Woolf concludes that this attempt to draw meaningful connections between the literary cartography of novel and the physical geography of England is wrongheaded and futile. As she puts it, "A writer's country is a territory within his own brain; and we run the risk of disillusionment if we try to turn such phantom cities into tangible brick and mortar. We know our way there without signposts or policemen, and we can greet the passers by without need of introduction. No city indeed is so real as this that we make for ourselves and people to our liking; and to insist that it has any counterpart in the cities of the earth is to rob it of half its charm."[33] For Woolf, then, the reader's desire to visit the real places that appear in the fiction of a Thackeray or a Dickens ultimately diminishes the affective power of these imaginary places. Woolf's tone is clear: only the naive and foolish should wish to visit in the flesh the places of the imagination.

Umberto Eco, a writer who is certainly neither naive nor foolish, has confessed his own "episode in literary fandom," in which he found himself "looking for the house in Eccles Street in Dublin where Leopold Bloom is supposed to have lived." The pilgrimage to a fictional character's purported haunts undoubtedly satisfies a real desire for many devoted enthusiasts of the fiction, and those places take on additional meanings by virtue of their literary resonances. Nevertheless, like Woolf, Eco recognizes that "to be a good reader of Joyce, it is not necessary to celebrate Bloomsday on the banks of the Liffey."[34] James Joyce's Dublin is not, after all, the "real" Dublin, notwithstanding his own playful assertion that his goal in writing *Ulysses* was "to give a picture of Dublin so complete that if the city one day suddenly disappeared from the earth, it could be reconstructed out of my book."[35] But, then, if *Ulysses* does not provide us with the picture of the "real" Dublin, neither does "the real Dublin" stand ontologically apart from its innumerable narrative representations.

This can even be the case when the geographical reference is a fictional or fantastic one. For example, without having direct access to Lewis Carroll's rabbit hole, C. S. Lewis's wardrobe, or J. K. Rowling's Platform 9¾ and the Hogwarts Express train, how could we visit Wonderland, Narnia, or Hogwarts School of Witchcraft and Wizardry? And at least these places are connected to geospace of our world through such portals.[36] Other realms, such as George R. R. Martin's self-enclosed fantasy world containing the continents of Essos and Westeros are presumably inaccessible except through reading. And yet, not surprisingly, the same bookish wanderlust that motivated late Victorian readers to pore over *The Dickens Country* or *The Thackery Country* in search of meaningful geographical experiences and literary pilgrimages at which a young Woolf gently scoffs has created whole industries for tourism, marketing, and fan culture in the present.

For example, Northern Ireland has been experiencing a significant boost in tourism related not only to its own rich literary and cultural history but also to its connection to "the North" of Westeros in Martin's fantasy world. Various locations represent the setting (more particularly, the film locations) in the HBO series *Game of Thrones*, an adaptation of Martin's possibly interminable saga *A Song of Ice and Fire*. Traveling only a short distance from Belfast, tourists can "Visit Westeros," taking lunch at Winterfell, practicing archery, and meeting direwolves. Likewise, those who wish to go "Beyond the Wall" can do so by signing up for tours in Iceland, where, as one website put it in highlighted bullet points, a person can:

- Visit the areas where Night's Watch men, including Samwell Tarly and Lord Commander Mormont, are attacked by the White Walkers.

- Walk the land that Jon Snow, Ygritte, and the Free Folk cross to reach the Wall.
- Visit the cave where Jon Snow and Ygritte have their first intimate romantic encounter.
- Learn about how the Free Folk, like the ancient Vikings, lived and survived in their harsh environment.[37]

The blending of fact and fiction in this tour is so complete as to almost completely obscure the difference, as if we could visit an actual cave in which two fantastic characters who never existed in the real world, inhabitants of a fantasy realm called Westeros, once canoodled.

Similarly, consider the language used in promoting *Game of Thrones* tourism in Dubrovnik, Croatia, where many of the scenes taking place in the fictional capital King's Landing were filmed: "Climb the old city walls that were attacked by the Baratheons in the first series, and then explore Lovrijenac Fortress—the beautiful 11th-century castle that features heavily in many of the *Game of Thrones* battle scenes. Gaze down at fictional Blackwater Bay from the fort's impressive vantage point, and imagine the bloody Battle of Blackwater taking place outside of its walls."[38] The fact that tourists would flock to these all-too-real places in order to commune with fictional characters, events, and locales is perhaps not very shocking. After all, since at least 2001 we have known that New Zealand is actually Middle-earth, on account of the tremendous success of *The Lord of the Rings* movie trilogy. These and other areas like them are what Rhona Trauvitch has referred to as "transontological spaces," and because they are crucial to our topophrenic experience and worldview, they are necessarily important to any literary cartography of the world.[39]

All of this is to say that Woolf's dichotomy of real versus imaginary places cannot entirely stand, as the imaginary London of *Oliver Twist* is no more a fictional production than the real (but also imagined) space of London, whose contemporary features are in some ways marked by their Dickensian character. Dickens's London was very much a sort of representation of the London in which he lived, but it was also a space of the imagination, in which the most quotidian scenes could be charged with magic and wonder. According to a well-known anecdote related by G. K. Chesterton, a young Charles Dickens was entranced when he discovered the mystical words "MOOR EEFFOC," but the origin of the phrase was rather commonplace; he simply read the sign "Coffee Room" from the other side of a glass door. In Chesterton's view, this is exemplary of "the masterpiece of the good realistic principle—the principle that the most fantastic of all is often the precise fact," and he referred to this as "that elvish kind of realism Dickens adopted everywhere."[40] It seems likely that much of the magic and the reality that both visitors and inhabitants experience in contemporary London owe something to the literary representations of its real-and-imagined spaces by authors like Dickens over the centuries.

Topophrenia, a sort of visceral and persistent place-mindedness, affects us in these places now, and the affective geography of "real-world" topoi is not lessened by the relative fictionality of their representative stories.[41] Thus Langston Hughes's poems may simultaneously map places like Harlem and become themselves maps, no matter how oblique or ironic, engendering the spaces they figure forth and bringing the real-and-imaginary spaces of urban experience to bear on literary representation, and vice versa. Paterson, New Jersey, from the vantage of a William Carlos Williams, is quite different from that viewed on a AAA roadmap, yet the sense of place that emerges from both a literary representation and a geographic information systems (GIS) survey can illuminate the constructedness of a place's *imageability* (to use Kevin Lynch's term), which in turn allows us to imagine otherwise. The streets, parks, and houses of Woolf's own London become examples, in a novel such as *Mrs. Dalloway*, not only of her vibrant spatial imagination but also of the raw materials for other literary cartographers and would-be map readers encountering those spaces afresh. This possible alterity is no more clearly sensed than in the eye (or perhaps the heart, stomach, and loins) of the exile, the expatriate who charts trajectories through a decidedly foreign yet somehow also longed-for place. The Baudelairean *flâneur* in Paris, aching for something always out of reach, traces an entire cartography of a city imbued with proliferating desires, luxuries, and necessities. Critical to all of these formulations is the fact that the spaces represented in the text and in the world partake of the same forms of narrative figuration. The "real" Paris, no less than the "real" Winterfell, is made of stories as much as stones. Geocritical explorations of real-and-imaginary places require readers to pay close attention to those textual spaces that contribute to making a place a place.

Mapping Narratives

Despite the author's stated intention "to give a picture of Dublin so complete that if the city one day suddenly disappeared from the earth, it could be reconstructed out of my book," I would imagine that readers of Joyce's *Ulysses*, even those with a strong background in geography or urban planning, would find it difficult to discern the blueprint of Dublin in the text of the modernist novel. Nonetheless, the cartographic imperative broadly conceived in Joyce's fiction is certainly apparent. From the meticulous descriptions of recognizable locales to the more implicit, affective geography of the intellectual and emotional content of the narrative, a work such as *Ulysses* provides readers a multimodal map of the diverse spaces represented in it. But it certainly is not just the case in Joyce's work. In fact, although certain narratives may be more ostensibly cartographic than others, all may be said to constitute forms of literary cartography. In works of fiction in which the imaginative faculty is perhaps most strongly attached to verbal narrative and description, this mapmaking project becomes central to the aims and the effects of the work. As J. Hillis Miller has put it, "A novel is a figurative mapping."[42]

Speaking figuratively, then, one could agree with Peter Turchi that every writer is also in some ways a cartographer—and vice versa, perhaps. As Turchi puts it in his elegantly written and beautifully illustrated guide to creative writing, *Maps of the Imagination*, "We organize information on maps in order to see our knowledge in a new way. As a result, maps suggest explanations; and while explanations reassure us, they also inspire us to ask more questions, consider other possibilities."[43] In other words, maps presuppose narratives, which in turn may function as maps. The perceived tension between narration and description, like that between text and image or even between time and space, animates the form of narrative discourse, as the struggle between advancing the plot and satisfactorily sketching the scene plays itself out in a given literary work. Turchi refers to this in terms of the overlapping or entangled creative acts of *exploration* and *presentation*. For the writer or literary cartographer, the imperative to arrive at some resolution of the dilemma—or at least to maintain the tension in some sort of productive equipoise—must confront the fact that all spaces and places are necessarily embedded with narratives, just as all narratives must mobilize and organize spaces and places. Thus, for example, it is not enough for Joyce to describe in minute detail the physical features of Dublin, its landscapes, streets, alleys, and houses; to reconstruct Joyce's particular Dublin, we must discern in its unique spaces the narratives that make it a place worth taking note of in the first place, from Buck Mulligan's bowl of lather as described in the opening pages to Molly Bloom's "yes I said yes I will Yes" on the novel's final page. In mapping a place, one also tells a story.

One of my favorite examples of the perhaps unresolvable problem of spatial description and temporal narration comes from Italo Calvino's *Invisible Cities*. In admitting his inability to describe the city of Zaira, the narrator produces an extremely evocative and meaningful picture. As Calvino's narrator, Marco Polo, explains his dilemma,

> In vain, great-hearted Kublai, shall I attempt to describe Zaira, city of high bastions. I could tell you how many steps make up the streets rising like stairways, and the degree of the arcades' curves, and what kind of zinc scales cover the roofs; but I already know this would be the same as telling you nothing. The city does not consist of this, but of relationships between the measurements of its space and the events of its past: the height of a lamppost and the distance from the ground of a hanged usurper's swaying feet; the line strung from the lamppost to the railing opposite and the festoons that decorate the course of the queen's nuptial procession; the height of that railing and the leap of the adulterer who climbed over it at dawn; the tilt of a guttering and

a cat's progress along it as he slips into the same window; the firing range of a gunboat which has suddenly appeared beyond the cape and the bomb that destroys the guttering; the rips in the fish net and the three old men seated on the dock mending nets and telling each other for the hundredth time the story of the gunboat of the usurper, who some say was the queen's illegitimate son, abandoned in his swaddling clothes there on the dock.

As this wave from memories flows in, the city soaks it up like a sponge and expands. A description of Zaira as it is today should contain all Zaira's past. The city, however, does not tell its past, but contains it like the lines of a hand, written in the corners of the streets, the gratings of the windows, the banisters of the steps, the antennae of the lightning rods, the poles of the flags, every segment marked in turn with scratches, indentations, scrolls.[44]

Spatial description and historical storytelling thus merge, and then emerge, as part of a broader literary geography, which in turn becomes the ground for a writer's own literary cartography. A place is suffused with meanings and is thus within the proper provenance of literature and of literary criticism.

Consistent with my view of literary cartography as a fundamental aspect of storytelling, I consider narratives to be, in some ways, devices or methods used to map the real-and-imagined spaces of human experience. Narratives are, in a sense, mapping machines. But narratives—like maps for that matter—never come before us in some pristine, original form. They are always and already formed by their interpretations or by the interpretative frameworks in which they have been situated or in which we, as readers, situate them.[45] Further, we cannot help but fit narratives or spatial representations into some sort of spatiotemporal context in which they make sense to us, thereby also becoming more or less useful to us, in our own attempts to give meaningful shape to the world in which we live. That is, these narratives, which are also maps, must be understood as themselves territories to be mapped. Following the trajectories of the subject and of the object, a narrative is simultaneously something that maps and something to be mapped. This dialectical tendency may not necessarily resolve itself in the unity of opposites à la Georg Wilhelm Friedrich Hegel but may maintain itself in dynamic tension, enabling new creative possibilities for both writing and reading, here understood in terms of literary cartography and geocriticism, respectively.

Ranging widely across centuries, continents, genres, and perspectives, world literature reveals the various means by which writers form literary cartographies of the worlds represented in their narratives. In reading the narrative maps produced by such a diverse array of writers, critics shine a light on the manner in which the spaces represented in those original texts become parts of the real-and-imagined places in our world, contributing to our own topophrenic activities in the here and now. Mapping narratives—that is, narratives that map, as well as our readerly activity in mapping the narratives we encounter—make possible novel spaces. To be sure, Joyce's Dublin is not the same as the "real" Irish capital, and it may be rather unlikely that that city's geospace could be reconstructed from scratch through the careful study of Joyce's fiction. And yet, *Ulysses* is indeed a map, a spatial and narrative representation of Dublin and of the modern world. The figural mapping project of the novel may disclose different ways of seeing and of experiencing the territories surveyed in the text. Through our own geocritical explorations of such literary cartographies, we come to make better sense of their distinctive spaces and places, as well as our own.

Notes

1. Yi-Fu Tuan, *Space and Place: The Perspective of Experience* (Minneapolis: University of Minnesota Press, 1977), 161–162.
2. Ibid., 6.
3. See Stuart Elden, *The Birth of Territory* (Chicago: University of Chicago Press, 2014).
4. Tim Cresswell, *Place: A Short Introduction* (Oxford: Blackwell, 2004), 2–3.
5. See Georges Perec, *Attempt at Exhausting a Place in Paris*, trans. Marc Lowenthal (Cambridge, MA: Wakefield Press, 2010).
6. Bertrand Westphal, *Geocriticism: Real and Fictional Spaces*, trans. Robert T. Tally Jr. (New York: Palgrave Macmillan, 2011), 117; see also my *Spatiality* (London: Routledge, 2013), 143–145.
7. Westphal's geocentric approach makes no claims to objectivity, but by insisting on multiple perspectives, it tries to register the ways in which a place has been experienced, represented, and "read" by a number of different people with different backgrounds and distinctive perspectives. A chief benefit of using multiple points of view is that this approach would minimize personal biases, offering a more well-rounded if not complete image of the place in question.
8. Yi-Fu Tuan, *Topophilia: A Study of Environmental Perception, Attitudes, and Values* (New York: Columbia University Press, 1990 [orig. 1974]), 93.
9. See Paul Rodaway, *Sensuous Geographies: Body, Sense, and Place* (London: Routledge, 1994).
10. See Marc Augé, *Non-Places: Introduction to an Anthropology of Supermodernity*, trans. John Howe (London: Verso, 1995).
11. Siobhan Carroll, "Atopia / Non-Place," in *The Routledge Handbook of Literature and Space*, ed. Robert T. Tally Jr. (London: Routledge, 2017), 159, 164–165.
12. Dylan Trigg, "Place and Non-Place: A Phenomenological Perspective," in *Place, Space, and Hermeneutics*, ed. Bruce B. Janz (New York: Springer, 2017), 130.
13. Ibid., 138–139.
14. J. Nicholas Entrikin, *The Betweenness of Place: Towards a Geography of Modernity* (Baltimore, MD: Johns Hopkins University Press, 1991), especially 1–26.
15. See Yi-Fu Tuan's "Preface to the Morningside Edition," *Topophilia: A Study of Environmental Perception, Attitudes, and Values* (New York: Columbia University Press, 1990), xi–xiv.

16. On "cartographic anxiety," see Derek Gregory, *Geographical Imaginations* (Oxford: Blackwell, 1994), 70–73.

17. Martin Heidegger, *Being and Time*, trans. John Macquarrie and Edward Robinson (New York: Harper and Row, 1962), 233, bracketed terms in original.

18. See Dylan Trigg, *Topophobia: A Phenomenology of Anxiety* (London: Bloomsbury, 2016).

19. Of course, Yi-Fu Tuan is also well aware of this. Indeed, his *Landscapes of Fear* (New York: Pantheon, 1979) offers a detailed study of the ways that fearful spaces and places affect individuals and communities.

20. Fredric Jameson, *The Political Unconscious: Narrative as a Social Symbolic Act* (Ithaca, NY: Cornell University Press, 1981), 13, 123.

21. See Westphal, *Geocriticism*, especially 9–36.

22. See Argyro Loukaki, *The Geographical Unconscious* (London: Ashgate, 2014).

23. See Entrikin, *The Betweenness of Place*, 133–134.

24. See Sigmund Freud, *Civilization and Its Discontents*, trans. James Strachey (New York: W. W. Norton, 2010 [orig. 1930]).

25. Louis Marin, *Utopics: The Semiological Play of Textual Spaces*, trans. Robert A. Vollrath (Atlantic Highlands, NJ: Humanities Press International, 1984), xiv.

26. Jean-Paul Sartre, *Nausea*, trans. Lloyd Alexander (New York: New Directions, 1964), 47–48.

27. Ibid., 48.

28. Friedrich Nietzsche, "On Truth and Lie in an Extra-Moral Sense," in *The Portable Nietzsche*, ed. and trans. Walter Kaufmann (New York: Viking, 1977), 46–47.

29. Wendy Chin-Tanner, "On Truth in a Nonmoral Sense," available online at http://vinylpoetry.com/volume-9/page-30/.

30. See Gilles Deleuze, *Nietzsche and Philosophy*, trans. Hugh Tomlinson (New York: Columbia University Press, 1982); see also Daniel T. O'Hara, *The Art of Reading as a Way of Life: On Nietzsche's Truth* (Evanston, IL: Northwestern University Press, 2009).

31. On affective geography and poetry, see Heather H. Yeung's *Spatial Engagement with Poetry* (New York: Palgrave Macmillan, 2015).

32. See Wendy Chin-Tanner, "No Moon," in *Turn* (Alexander, AR: Sibling Rivalry Press, 2014), 38.

33. Virginia Woolf, "Literary Geography," in *Books and Portraits: Some Further Selections from the Literary and Biographical Writings of Virginia Woolf*, ed. Mary Lyon (New York: Harcourt, Brace, Jovanovich, 1977), 158–161.

34. Umberto Eco, *Six Walks in the Fictional Woods* (Cambridge, MA: Harvard University Press, 1994), 84.

35. See Frank Budgen, *James Joyce and the Making of Ulysses, and Other Writings*, ed. Clive Hart (Oxford: Oxford University Press, 1989), 69.

36. In fact, the actual King's Cross station in London now has a Platform 9¾ (Hogwarts Express), complete with Harry Potter–themed gift shop, as a tourist attraction.

37. "Myvatn, Mystery, and Magic: *Game of Thrones*-Themed Tour," Iceland Travel, accessed August 16, 2017, https://www.icelandtravel.is/tour/item700728/myvatn-mystery-magic-game-of-thrones-themed-tour-2/.

38. "Viator Exclusive: Game of Thrones' Tour," Lonely Planet, accessed August 16, 2017, https://www.lonelyplanet.com/croatia/southern-dalmatia/activities/viator-exclusive-game-of-thrones-tour/a/pa-act/v-5360GAMETHRONES/1319358.

39. See Rhona Trauvitch, "Charting the Extraordinary: Sentient and Transontological Spaces," in *Literary Cartographies: Spatiality, Representation, and Narrative*, ed. Robert T. Tally Jr. (New York: Palgrave Macmillan, 2014), 199–213.

40. G. K. Chesterton, *Charles Dickens: A Critical Study* (New York: Dodd Mead and Co., 1906), 47–48.

41. This is related in part to what Edward W. Soja called "real-and-imagined places," as he attempted to break down the dichotomy between the perceived or real spaces and the conceived or imagined spaces in his innovative conception of "thirdspace." See his *Thirdspace: Journeys to Los Angeles and Other Real-and-Imagined Places* (Oxford: Blackwell, 1996).

42. J. Hillis Miller, *Topographies* (Stanford, CA: Stanford University Press, 1995), 19.

43. Peter Turchi, *Maps of the Imagination: The Writer as Cartographer* (San Antonio, TX: Trinity University Press, 2004), 11.

44. Italo Calvino, *Invisible Cities*, trans. William Weaver (New York: Harcourt, 1974), 10–11.

45. See Jameson, *The Political Unconscious*, 9–10.

2 Introducing Geocriticism

GEOCRITICISM HAS BECOME an increasingly significant practice within literary studies over the past few years, even if the exact meaning of the term itself, along with its characteristics and methods, has not been definitively settled. The emergence of geocriticism is connected to a broader spatial turn in the humanities and social sciences. This turn is frequently associated with developments in critical theory, as exhibited in Michel Foucault's now-famous declaration (initially spoken in 1967 but published only in 1984) that ours is an "epoch of space."[1] This sense has been amplified by the discourse on postmodernity, of which a peculiar "new spatiality" is a key feature, as registered in the work of Fredric Jameson, Edward W. Soja, David Harvey, and Nigel Thrift, to name but a few of the more influential figures.[2] These theorists and others have called attention to material developments of the post–World War II era, especially the acceleration of the processes of globalization and financialization as factors in both the experiential and the structural "time-space compression" in postmodern societies, which has in turn brought matters of space, place, and mapping to the fore in contemporary debates in social theory as well as cultural and literary studies. To be sure, there are numerous predecessors, and one could well argue that the pronounced spatiality of the postmodern condition is merely the continuation of the sort of modern transformations that social critics such as Walter Benjamin, Georg Simmel, Georg Lukács, or even Karl Marx and Friedrich Engels long before them were already addressing. Moreover, one can certainly find in earlier epochs and disparate places social and cultural formations in which space or spatiality featured prominently.[3] Nevertheless, the rapid expansion in the number and quality of works focusing on spatial or geographical concerns in the last forty years, particularly in the humanities and social sciences, have registered the degree to which a "spatial turn" has occurred.[4]

Concomitantly, it seems, with the rise of geocriticism, literary geography, and the spatial humanities more broadly, the significance of spatiality has only grown. The explosion in the number of books and articles on these subjects has been supplemented and supported by major international conferences in Europe, Asia, and the Americas by innovative scholarly journals, such as *Literary Geographies* and *GeoHumanities*, and new book series such as Indiana University Press's Spatial Humanities or Palgrave Macmillan's Geocriticism and Spatial Literary Studies (which I edit). Geocriticism, which has burgeoned in these last ten or fifteen years especially, partakes of this overall interest in space, place, and mapping, while also establishing its own place within literary and cultural studies. In this chapter I would like to offer a brief introduction to geocriticism as I understand it, and I will situate it among other literary critical and scholarly practices in order to get a sense of the state of various fields of spatially oriented literary and cultural studies as they currently stand. The attempt will not, and likely cannot, be exhaustive, but I hope that this discussion demonstrates different ways in which geocriticism may be brought to bear on contemporary critical theory and practice.

Defining Geocriticism

Like most labels, the term *geocriticism* has an interesting, potentially contested, and not entirely clear history. In the early 1990s while in graduate school, I started to use the term *geocriticism* to refer to an aspect of my research project through which I hoped to bring a greater emphasis to space, place, and mapping in literary studies, which ultimately resulted in a much narrower dissertation topic. At the time I imagined geocriticism as the critic's counterpart to what I viewed as the writer's literary cartographic project. Engaging in a practice of literary cartography, a writer maps the social spaces of his or her world, be that understood as the referential "real world," the "storyworld" of the text, or something more like the "real-and-imagined" spaces that Soja analyzes in his *Thirdspace*; indeed, most literary cartographies involve all three.[5] A geocritic, in my view, would read these "maps," drawing particular attention to the spatial practices involved in literature. That is, geocriticism was to have served as the name of a spatially oriented approach to literature in which the inherently cartographic aspects of narratives were brought to the fore in their analysis and interpretation.

Although I thought I may have coined the term, I was certainly not so bold as to think I had come up with the idea all on my own. In my view, a large number of scholars, critics, and theorists had been producing works that might be labeled *geocritical*, even if they themselves would not necessarily embrace the name. Among those I had in mind, Kristen Ross's fascinating work on Rimbaud in *The Emergence of Social Space*, Edward Said's "geographical inquiry into historical experience" in *Culture and Imperialism*, and Fredric Jameson's expanded notion of cognitive mapping in *The Geopolitical Aesthetic* provided several then-current examples. But I also considered earlier works, such as Raymond Williams's *The Country and the City*, Walter Benjamin's writings on Paris and especially his unfinished *Arcades Project*, Mikhail Bakhtin's study of "chronotopes," and Joseph Frank's idea of "spatial form" to be fundamental to any geocritical project. And this list could be expanded in many different directions at once, especially when one allows for figurative uses of space and mapping. In using the word *geocriticism*, I also wanted to indicate a counterpart in literature to what Gilles Deleuze and Félix Guattari in *What Is Philosophy?* had termed *geophilosophy*; along those lines, I also wished to register something of the *geohistory* suggestively evoked in the work of Fernand Braudel, not to mention the phenomenological investigations of spatial experience in Gaston Bachelard's *The Poetics of Space*, the "spatial history" one encountered especially in many of Foucault's writings, and the powerful sense of the historicity of spaces made manifest in Henri Lefebvre's *The Production of Space*. Even as I wished to give *geocriticism* definition, I wanted to make sure it remained broad enough to encompass a number of different spatial and critical practices. Geocriticism, at least as much as ecocriticism and other emerging approaches, needed to be flexible.

After experiencing a few spatiotemporal displacements of my own, I returned to these preliminary inquiries around 2005. In completing my study of Herman Melville's literary cartography, *Melville, Mapping and Globalization*,[6] which was loosely based on my dissertation research, I was pleased to rediscover a number of critics engaged in geocriticism, including one who used the term itself, albeit in French (*géocritique*): Bertrand Westphal, director of the research group devoted to Espaces Humains et Interactions Culturelles at the Université de Limoges. Reading his foundational essay on the subject, "Pour une approche géocritique des textes: esquisse" (in *La Géocritique mode d'emploi*),[7] I realized that Westphal's view of geocriticism was not the same as mine, but that he was clearly a kindred spirit. I made contact with Westphal just after his book-length theoretical explication of geocriticism, *La Géocritique: Réel, fiction, espace*, was published, and we began our efforts to bring it out in an English translation.[8] Westphal is quite rightly the theorist and critic most closely associated with geocriticism, and I discuss Westphal's geocritical theory and practice in greater detail in the subsequent sections of this chapter.

The term *geocriticism* gained currency with the publication of Westphal's book, but Westphal and I—along with many other critics, undoubtedly—had been separately thinking through the concepts associated with geocriticism years earlier. I was particularly interested in the ways that a spatial critical theory, which I labeled "cartographics," could be brought to bear on an analytical or interpretive practice (geocriticism) that would be geared toward understanding the ways in which narratives represented, shaped, and influenced social spaces (i.e., literary cartography).[9] Whether focused on a particular location or examining works in a different geographical register entirely, geocriticism provided a way of reading literature with a heightened sensitivity to spatial relations, as well as to place and to mapping, in and around the texts under consideration.

In any event, what I took to be my idea of geocriticism was related to but rather different from the work Westphal and his team were doing. Whereas I focused on how various writers, such as Melville, mapped the real and imagined places of their world, Westphal turned from the author-centered or ego-centered interpretations to emphasize the place itself, making the project a geocentric one. That is, geocritics following Westphal's approach would begin by locating a place, then attempt to form a corpus or archive of literary and cultural representations of that place. In this way, the location's multifaceted image comes into focus through a variety of lenses and perspectives. A salutary effect of this method is that any reading will be far less likely to be subject to ethnocentric or narrow interpretations, as individual biases or prejudices become leavened with multiple and diverse points or view. Westphal's geocentric reading of a place allows its various textual, artistic, or even commercial incarnations in various media— novels, poems, films, travelogues, tourist brochures, ethnographic studies, and so forth—to flesh out the meanings of the place, both in the world of letters or images and in the real world. After all, the place is not merely coordinates on a map but the living embodiment of the polysensory experiences of those many people who attempt to represent both it and the experiences associated with it. The meanings of a given place, according to Westphal's theory, emerge from the multiple perspectives of those representing the place.[10]

My own view of geocriticism, as a set of practices according to which the reader focuses attention on the ways that literature represents, shapes, or is formed by the real and imagined spaces with which it engages, is a bit more expansive than Westphal's geocentric approach, but I think it is perfectly consistent with it as well. The crucial point is to understand space as more than an empty container, a mere background in which characters are situated and events take place; in that view, the characters and events are necessarily deemed far more significant than the spaces and places in which they appear. Rather, space and spatial relations are active and present, continuously informing if not actually determining all the elements of a story, thus also positively affecting the formation of characters, events, and so on. Geocritical approaches require us to take space and place seriously as dynamic features of a text, which constantly interact with and affect other features. Geocriticism also means recognizing the degree to which the writer, the reader, and the text are part of a larger spatiotemporal ensembles that gives form to the literary experience as a whole. Geocriticism often involves interdisciplinary or transdisciplinary work, such as that which brings literary critics and geographers together,[11] but it also specifies a distinctive critical approach to literature, which has its own internal logic, one might say. The spaces of literature call for a geocritical theory and practice suited to their dynamic complexity and imaginative power.

Westphal's *Geocriticism*

In *Geocriticism: Real and Fictional Spaces*, Westphal elaborates and advocates a geocentric approach to literature and cultural studies that would allow a particular place to serve as the focal point for a variety of critical practices. Thus, for example, in Westphal's edited collection on the Mediterranean, the contributors looked at the various depictions of that multifaceted zone—whether using classical myth, modern fiction, historical works, cinematic visions, tourist brochures, and so on—to form a pluralistic image of the place.[12] In some respects, a more informal version of a project of this sort could be said to bring the place in question into being, transforming the otherwise unrepresented space all around it into a recognizable border, thus making it a meaningful locus. After all, a place is only a place because of the ways in which we, individually and collectively, organize space in such a way as to mark the *topos* as special, to set it apart from the spaces surrounding and infusing it. Our understanding of a particular place is determined by our personal experiences with it, but also by our reading about others' experiences, by our point of view, including our biases and our wishful thinking. Drawing on interdisciplinary methods and a diverse range of sources, geocriticism attempts to understand the real and fictional spaces that we inhabit, cross through, imagine, survey, modify, celebrate, disparage, and on and on in an infinite variety.

Geocriticism allows us not only to emphasize the ways that literature interacts with the world but also to explore how all ways of dealing with the world are somewhat literary. The geographer is a kind of writer (e.g., *earth-writing* being the essential meaning of "geo-graphy"), and the representational techniques used in such sciences are often analogous, if not identical, to those used in so-called imaginary writing. In a brief review of Westphal's *La Géocritique*, I noted that "all writing partakes in a form of cartography, since even the most realistic map does not truly depict the space, but, like literature, figures it forth in a complex skein of imaginary relations."[13] Indeed, the realistic London of Charles Dickens or Paris of Honoré de Balzac are part of what I call the *literary cartography* of the world, but so is Amaurotum, capital city of Thomas More's Utopia, or Minas Tirith, capital of Gondor in J. R. R. Tolkien's Middle-earth. So is William Faulkner's Yoknapatawpha County, which would seem to combine the referential space of Faulkner's own Lafayette County, Mississippi, with the imaginary spaces traversed by fictional Compsons, Bundrens, and Snopeses. But really all places are like Yoknapatawpha County, combining the real and the imaginary, for the perception, conception, knowledge, and experience of a given place cannot be definitively disentangled. As Westphal points out, the referentiality of fiction (and of other mimetic arts, for that matter) allows it to point to a recognizable place—real, imaginary, or a bit of both at once—while also transforming that place, making it part of a fictional world. In this sense geocriticism allows us to understand "real" places by understanding their fundamental fictionality, and vice versa, of course. We understand "fictional" spaces by grasping their own levels of reality as they become part of our world.

Westphal draws heavily on the insights of poststructuralism and postmodernism, among other nonscholastic schools of thought, but Westphal insists on a kind of referentiality that such theoretical practices as Derridean deconstruction or the Baudrillardian analysis of hyperreality were to have called into question, if not permanently banished from critical discourse. But Westphal takes such arguments seriously, and he certainly does not attempt to return to an unsophisticated notion of fiction's being able to offer a mirror reflection of the "real" referent out there. Rather, Westphal understands that the referentiality operating between fiction and the real world is characterized by constant movement, or *oscillation* as he puts it, whereby one can never really fix or pin down the referent—only the text of God could purport to do such a thing, after all—but neither does one simply abandon the effort. Indeed, the inability to fix a referent in a literary text makes the project of geocriticism all the more worthwhile, as the critic may look at the multiple, almost infinite, variety of texts that refer to a place in order to shape the vision, an ever-shifting, ever-developing image of the "real-and-imagined" place, thus examining that "thirdspace" (as Soja has dubbed it) that troubles or "others" the reductive binary of subjective perception and objective reality.[14]

This also encourages further explorations. As Westphal explains, geocriticism will involve what he calls *multifocalization* and *polysensoriality*, among other things, insofar as the approach moves beyond merely a single author's perspective (e.g., James Joyce's Dublin or Fyodor Dostoevsky's St. Petersburg) and engages all five senses, not limiting itself to that by far most dominant visual register. By bringing together a wide variety of authors, including multiple genres and disciplines—for example, reading tourist brochures or listening to songs alongside studying Homer makes for a productive examination of Mediterranean spaces and place—the geocritic orchestrates a number of different points of view, allowing diverse perspectives to flesh out, to round out, and perhaps to overcome the stereotyping or otherwise limiting images of a given place. By taking time to focus on senses other than merely the visual, the geocritic can register the sensuous plenum of a place, where the fragrance of jasmine commingles with the flavor of some Proustian tea-soaked cookie, or the texture of the cobblestones echoes the bone-rattling clamor of horse-drawn hearses, to cite a nursery rhyme exhumed and reiterated for the epigraph of Neil Gaiman's *The Graveyard Book*. These senses do not overthrow but rather supplement the kingdom of the visual, of *le regard* ("the gaze" in the tradition of Jean-Paul Sartre and Foucault, among many others), rendering the polysensorial place more completely realized in our interactions with fictional and nonfictional texts. Naturally, the idea of *completing* the geocritical analysis of a place is as false as the idea of fixing it in a permanent, unchanging, and static image. A total representation of the place is impossible, as is the critical attempt to interpret all attempts at representing the place. But if failure is inevitable, then the goal must be to fail in interesting ways. And geocriticism offers interesting ways to engage with the spaces of fiction and reality.

The title of Westphal's *Geocriticism* is deceptively categorical. The book does not once and forever provide a definitive answer to the question, "What is geocriticism?" That too is probably impossible. *Geocriticism* surveys a territory, speculates about others, suggests possible paths to take, argues in favor of certain practices and against others, all while peregrinating around multiple discourses of space, place, and literature. In a world in which fiction may be as reliable as any form of understanding the world, what grounds do we have for analysis? What methods can we use to make sense of things? Indeed, in his introduction Westphal indicates his paradoxically tentative and yet bold project: this book is "an attempt—one trial, among many other possible ones—to answer these questions, to capture if only fleetingly the mobile environment in a cautious, humble way."[15]

Geocriticism is an *essay*, in the strongest and broadest sense of the word, an attempt to make sense of things, to make sense of the ways we make sense of things, which is after all the role of the critic. As Frank Kermode has said in a book dedicated to the study of temporality rather than to spatiality but no less apt: "It is not expected of critics as it is of poets that they should help us to make sense of our lives; they are bound only to attempt the lesser feat of making sense of the ways we try to make sense of our lives."[16] So too with geocritics. *Geocriticism* offers Westphal's attempt, one among many he has made and likely will continue to make and one among the very many being made by other critics (whether they would embrace the term *geocriticism* or not) working with real and fictional spaces to make sense of the ways we make sense of our world, of our places in the world, and of our various and complex mappings of those worldly and otherworldly spaces. The final word in *Geocriticism* is quite fittingly the verb *explore*, for, notwithstanding the seemingly categorical title, Westphal intends for geocriticism to be an exploratory critical practice whereby readers, scholars, and critics engage with the spaces that make life, through lived experience and through imaginary projections, meaningful. As is apparent by the rapidly growing library of books and articles devoted to such projects, this is a timely moment for the emergence and proliferation of geocriticism.

Geocriticism and the Worldly World

As we have seen, a literary or cultural critic using Westphal's approach thus would begin by focusing attention on a singular geographical place, such as a city or a body of water, as opposed to a particular author, literary genre, or historical period. The geocritic would then examine the ways in which that place has been represented in a variety of texts, which could include not only works of literature proper but also films, travel narratives, governmental surveys, and so forth.[17] The geocritical method advocated by Westphal would allow readers to see the ways in which various texts represent the spaces of the locale selected, and by examining a variety of perspectives, geocritical scholars could develop a relatively nonbiased, though inevitably incomplete, image of the place.

However, this method presents one problem, one readily acknowledged by Westphal, which could confound any serious geocritical inquiry: the question of the corpus. How does one determine exactly which texts could, in the aggregate, reasonably constitute a meaningful body of material with which to analyze the literary representations of a given geographical site? If the Dublin as represented in the work of James Joyce is far too limited since it relies on the perspective of a only single author or a few of his own writings, then how many authors and texts representing Dublin would constitute a feasible and credible starting point for a geocritical study of the Irish capital? How many poems, novels, short stories, and plays about or set in Dublin would a geocritic need in order to feel comfortable in pronouncing the resulting picture somewhat complete? How many geographical surveys, travel narratives, tourism-related documents, historical writings, letters, or postcards would be used to supplement, flesh out, or color in the picture? Who determines whether enough material has been taken into account? How would one know? Even a relatively remote place would prove the subject of multiple representations by a number of different writers across an array of genres, such that it would present difficulties for any geocritic attempting to explore the meaning or meanings of the place. With certain places, such as Paris, London, Rome, or New York, their almost mythic status and the seemingly innumerable textual references to them render any geocritical analysis, at least those laying claim to a kind of scientific value, impossible. As Westphal admits, "To attempt to undertake a full-scale geocritical analysis of those hotspots would be madness."[18] Principles of selectivity must be established, as even a rather large corpus will inevitably leave whole swaths of material aside. And with selection comes exclusion and ultimately something like censorship, no matter how much the critic hopes to avoid it. Hence, the geocentered approach, if it aims truly to avoid the perception of bias, seems somewhat doomed from the start.

Another potential problem with Westphal's geocentric method, one which Eric Prieto has addressed, is that it does not adequately take into account the conflicting forces and views that condition the ways in which various spaces come to be recognizable as places. Prieto notes that Westphal's focus, perhaps understandably, has been on the "*hauts lieux* of the literary tradition: places that have a distinct cultural and topographical profile and that have given rise to a whole body of literature."[19] In his revision of the geocritical project, Prieto considers the textual emergence of various types of place, including what appear to be nonplaces, such as improvised shantytowns or the French *banlieues*, along with already identified, recognizable topoi.[20] By examining the ways that certain kinds of social spaces come into being as places for interpretation, this sort of geocriticism offers intriguing opportunities for understanding how literary representation and spatiality interconnect. To state it somewhat differently, geo-criticism would need to examine not only the real-and-imagined places of litera-ture but the conditions for their possibility as well.

In *The Plausible World: A Geocritical Approach to Space, Place, and Maps*, which in some ways can be imagined as a sequel to *Geocriticism*, Westphal dem-onstrates the degree to which he too was puzzling through such problems as the geocritical corpus and the sites made available for critical inquiry. As a follow-up to his more programmatic and introductory study, *The Plausible World* explores a rich variety of texts from antiquity to the present and draws on numerous cultural and linguistic traditions from all over the planet. In this extravagant, sometimes sprawling but also intensely curious performance, Westphal explores a wealth of material in an attempt to characterize the many ways in which indi-viduals and cultures enact a sort of literary cartography of their worlds. Westphal argues that a certain kind of cartographic practice associated with a rational or scientific discourse developed in the West. It is embodied perhaps most vividly by the networks of imaginary lines—latitudinal and longitudinal—that imprison the spaces of the world in a Cartesian grid.[21] However, at the same time alterna-tive mapping practices arose and flourished in other, non-Western civilizations, and Westphal envisions these countermaps as implicit, and occasionally explicit, challenges to the hegemony of the more limited Western spatial imagination.

I believe that Westphal's use of the unproblematized geopolitical metaphors of the West and non-West is itself rather problematic and sometimes smacks of a discourse of Orientalist oversimplification, as when Michel Foucault notoriously contrasted a "Western" *scientia sexualis* with the "Eastern" *ars erotica*.[22] In an age of globalization, if not much earlier, the skein of power/knowledge relations that makes possible the imaginative cartography of our world is far more com-plicated, even if it is undoubtedly influenced by the legacies of imperialism and a worldview shaped by them. As the historical record bears out, even the most hegemonic mapping practices—like most practices, in fact—entail apparently counterhegemonic ones and vice versa. For instance, the imposition of a grid-like plan for an urban space has never really stopped the wayward *flâneur* from taking a shortcut, perhaps even a non-Euclidean shortcut, but it is equally clear that errant wanderers who make their own paths are frequently discovered to be pathfinders for an even more rigid stratification, as today's shortcut becomes tomorrow's one-way street.

Along these lines, the geocritic does well to remember Gilles Deleuze and Félix Guattari's discussion of smooth and striated space, a distinction that partly underlies Westphal's own theories. Even prior to his collaboration with Guattari in *Difference and Repetition*, Deleuze had begun to distinguish between Cartesian and what he called "nomad" space, which he later took up in a famous distinction between State philosophy and nomad thought. In *A Thousand Plateaus* Deleuze and Guattari explicitly argue that such nomads have a qualitatively different kind of space from that of the state: "It is the difference between a *smooth* (vectoral, projective, topological) space and a *striated* (metric) space: in the first case 'space is occupied without being counted,' and in the second case 'space is counted in order to be occupied.'"[23] But notwithstanding the clear sense that Deleuze and Guattari seem to favor nomadic smooth space to the state's striated space, the authors insist that the opposition cannot be maintained as such. "What interests us in operations of striation and smoothing are precisely the passages or combinations: how the forces at work within space continually striate it, and how in the course of its striation it develops other forces and emits new smooth spaces." As Deleuze and Guattari note, "Even the most striated city gives rise to smooth spaces," but they hasten to add, "smooth spaces are not in themselves liberatory. . . . Never believe that a smooth space will suffice to save us."[24]

Likewise, one cannot really feel confident in proposing nonhegemonic maps or representations of place that escape the relations of power (of power/ knowledge, in Foucault's sense of the terms) that contribute to its character and understanding. In terms of the legacies of imperialism, for example, it seems that Edward W. Said's contrapuntal approach is most productive insofar as it recognizes the degree to which the formation of the modern world system and its representations are part of a dynamic, ever-shifting process rather than a unilinear movement from one agent to a subjected, largely passive, or reactionary other.[25] Generalizations such as "East" and "West" may retain value as cultural or political heuristics, but they are not always helpful in describing existing social formations, particularly in an era of globalization. Nevertheless, despite this objection to what I consider an oversimplified and perhaps overly moralizing conception of the West and its "others," the overall project of *The Plausible World* is entirely worthwhile, as it provides a much more substantial experience of space, place, and mapping than the more introductory writings on geocriticism could hope to deliver. Westphal's comparative literary treatment of spatial representation is both fascinating and stimulating, with interpretations that will encourage readers to read more and to read otherwise. By moving away from the strictly geocentric approach outlined in the methodological sections of *Geocriticism*, Westphal connects his critical practice to a broader field of spatiality studies that does not resist the allure of an individual author's perspective, while also paying closer attention than in the former study to the problem of the *emergence* of places. Hence, *The Plausible World* nicely extends the project of *Geocriticism* and at the same time strikes out in interesting new directions in search of unexplored territories.

In *The Plausible World*, Westphal challenges the view that perceptions and representations of space are largely stable and straightforward. For example, although maps often give the impression that the geographical knowledge of the

world at any given moment is complete, that the planet has lost any sense of wonder now that all has been not only found but also mapped, Westphal believes this
is a misleading characteristic of a peculiarly Western conception of modernity.[26]
Throughout its history, in Westphal's view, the West—through direct imperialism and through scientific practices—has repeatedly confronted open spaces of
the world and transformed them into closed places. But enclosures of such places
have never been definitive or unchanging. Westphal finds in the non-Western
arts a countergeography to the cartographic pressures of the Western modernity.
The visual art of the Aztecs, the cartographies of the Far East, and the chanted
lines of Australian Aborigines confirm that the West never held a clear monopoly
on geographic images of the world. These twists and turns through spaces and
places of the past and present postulate the existence of not just the one "real"
world or infinite possible worlds, but a *plausible world*, a new conception of *the
world as plausible*. Acknowledgment of the merely plausible world, as Westphal
sees it, would spell the end of the hegemonic claims of the West. The geocritical exploration of these alternative ways in which spaces and places have been
imagined not only leads to new insights into our world but also discloses hitherto
invisible or unknown elements that a purely Eurocentric model has left hidden or
ignored. In a sense, Westphal's book aims to make visible a new world.

Drawing on his background in classical literature, Westphal begins *The
Plausible World* with an examination of ancient Greek mythology, looking particularly at the conception of an omphalos, "navel," or center of the world. From
this point of departure, Westphal gradually proceeds through various traditions
of spatial representation through modernity and across multiple cultural formations. In Westphal's view, the modern West attempted to master space, and the
exploration and colonization of new spaces by Columbus and those who followed
formed part of this cartographic program. However, as Westphal also insists,
beginning with Alvar Nuñez Cabeza de Vaca and continuing through twentieth-
century Third World writers and artists, alternative perceptions and depictions
of space emerged.

Westphal attempts to elude and to augment a strictly Eurocentric perspective by looking at various non-Western traditions, such as those to be found in
Africa, Australia, and China. He argues that the ethnographic (and ethnocentric) character of Western spatial sciences must be replaced by a multicultural
and multifocal perspective. Westphal draws heavily on postcolonial theory in
his geocritical reading of the texts under consideration, and he introduces such
lesser-known practices as Aztec mapmaking, transoceanic voyages by explorers
from China and Mali, or Aboriginal representations of space. These alternative
spatialities allow geographically oriented critics to rethink the ways they imagine
the world. The alternatives do not, and ought not to, simply replace the Western
models, nor do they somehow reveal a "true" world that the ideologically suspect

West presented falsely. Rather, the critic's engagement with multiple spatialities makes possible a *plausible* world that does not claim for itself immutable, apodictic reality. Westphal's commitment to the plausible world, as opposed to the more definitive singular (*the* world) or to loose pluralities (of possible or multiple worlds), indicates the flexible and still-tentative view of such a far-reaching and theoretically ambitious geocritical project. Along the way, *The Plausible World* does an excellent job of surveying a broad territory while also performing readings of specific literary and historical texts.

Westphal's conception of a plausible world, while implicit throughout the book, is not discussed at any length in it. As noted above, plausibility offers Westphal a helpful middle ground between the dubious idea of one true "real world" and the potential mise en abyme that the theory of possible worlds seems to invite. Plausibility makes possible the practical overcoming of the problem of referentiality, something Westphal found difficult but necessary in formulating his view of geocriticism in his earlier book; geocriticism after all relies on a great deal of poststructuralist theory, including notions—such as Jacques Derrida's notorious assertion that there is no *hors du texte*—that call literary referentiality into question. Certainly the Paris of Victor Hugo's *Notre-Dame de Paris* is not the same as the "real" Paris, since the former is obviously a literary setting in which fictional characters lead their fictional lives. But neither is Hugo's Paris *not* Paris, which must be equally obvious.[27] In *The Plausible World*, Westphal is able to consider simultaneously the places as they appear in literature and in "the world," while avoiding a position of either arrogance or ignorance. It is a bit like Gianni Vattimo's notion of *il pensiero debole* (or "weak thought"), insofar as the *plausible* recognizes the humility with which the geocritic must approach the subject of geocritical inquiry.[28]

This subject, I maintain, is the worldly world itself. Any geocriticism that is worth the effort must engage actively and considerately with the *worldly*, by which I do not simply mean the secular or mundane, although these are necessarily a part of it. I mean that geocriticism maintains a comportment toward the world that embraces the entirety of spatial and social relations, which in turn constitutes the literary cartography produced in those multifarious ways of making sense of, or giving shape to, that world. Stated less circuitously, geocriticism approaches texts as literary maps that, regardless of the ostensible real or imagined spaces depicted, help us to understand our world. Of course, by *worldly world* I do not mean to fall back onto some naive vision of the "real" world as opposed to figural spaces of fiction or of fantastic otherworlds. Indeed, I refer especially to that surprising and revelatory sense of Erich Auerbach's *irdische Welt*, which he discovered in the seemingly paradigmatic Otherworld of Dante's *Commedia*. As Auerbach writes, "The *Comedy* is a picture of earthly life. The human world in all its breadth and depth is gathered into the structure of the hereafter and there it stands: complete, unfalsified, yet encompassed in an eternal order; the confusion of earthly affairs is not concealed or attenuated or immaterialized, but preserved in full evidence and grounded in a plan which embraces it and raises it above all contingency."[29] Such a description would not be out of place in a discussion of the ways that literature serves to map the world, combining those material elements of earthly experience with the intelligible forms of the imagination. Not every mapmaker is the literary cartographer that Dante is, of course, but Auerbach's assessment of the Florentine "*als Dichter der irdischen Welt*" (i.e., as the poet of the worldly world) figures forth a critical approach to comparative literature and the worldly world.

Ralph Manheim's translation of *irdisch* as "secular" highlights the irony of Auerbach's title, but it is not a literal translation; as in the quoted lines above, *irdisch* means "earthly," whereas *weltlich* is closer in German to "secular" or "mundane." However, in this case, the earthly or worldly aptly registers the ways in which Dante's "divine" *Commedia*, even in its otherworldliness, truly represents the world as we experience it in life and literature in all its literal and metaphorical worldliness. In this respect the worldly world is also emphatically a plausible world. Geocriticism is necessarily *of* this world, and a geocritical approach to world literature may disclose novel representations and interpretations of its diverse, protean spaces.[30]

Geocriticism without Boundaries

Although Westphal clearly aims to distinguish geocriticism from other critical practices or schools—such as structuralism, iconology, or reception theory to name but a few—he does not want to define it so narrowly that it would overlook useful materials or approaches that could benefit our greater understanding of literature, space, and place. Hence, one encounters his frequent recourse to a tentative or provisional language, where one can see Westphal's desire to encompass a variety of methods and texts without losing sight of the expressly *geocritical* project he has in mind. This balancing act deserves a bit of sympathy or generosity, a recognition of the degree to which complex ideas and practices are poorly served by explanations that confuse simplification for clarity. Westphal and I had originally thought of giving the English version of *La Géocritique* a more ambiguous title, such as "A Theory of Geocriticism" or "Towards a Theory of Geocriticism," as a way of indicating our own view that there might be other, perhaps even opposed, versions of "geocriticism" out there. Yet in the end we decided that the simplicity of the title was preferable, inasmuch as it might better provoke discussion about the nature of geocriticism or related critical practices. By suggesting that *this* is what geocriticism is, the book invites others to engage in the discussion, to argue and to disagree, as well as to listen and to concur. By throwing down the gauntlet in this way, a more productive discussion might possibly ensue. In any case, the *Geocriticism* of Westphal, together with his other recent work along these lines, provides an excellent point of departure for the multiple geocritical explorations to come.

Indeed, in the final line of *Geocriticism*, Westphal writes that geocriticism "operates somewhere between the geography of the 'real' and the geography of the 'imaginary' . . . two quite similar geographies that may lead to others, which critics should try to develop and explore."[31] It is fitting that Westphal closes with the word *explore*, because the active *exploration*—in every sense of the word, for better or for worse—of the real and imaginary spaces of literature is the goal of geocriticism. Geocriticism certainly does not provide all the answers, and it is more likely to generate further questions. Geocriticism explores, it seeks, it surveys, it digs into, it reads, and it writes a place; it looks at, listens to, touches, smells, and tastes places. In doing so, geocriticism does not provide a complete representation of a place, which is as we have seen not only impossible but possibly even undesirable; that is, who (other than Georges Perec, perhaps) really wants to "exhaust" a place like that?[32] But the geocritical project does allow us to engage with place, to consider the degree to which our own perceptions of space and place come to determine our attitudes toward the world and all within it, while also recognizing the ways that place, space, and spatial relations actively shape us, forming us as individual or collective subjects and affecting the way we encounter and experience the world. These mutually reinforcing processes highlight the topophrenia underlying our general being-in-the-world, revealing the cartographic imperative while also underscoring the importance of geocritical reading as a key to understanding the figurative maps by which we make sense of the spaces we inhabit and imagine.

Many of the scholars and critics currently engaged in the spatial humanities, including some who have adopted the term *geocritical* in describing their own work, challenge Westphal's or my views, and many offer positions quite different from what either Westphal or I intend by the term. This is all to the good as far as I am concerned, since a great deal of this work maintains that spirit of geocritical exploration that we hope to foster and promote, and the diversity of approaches befits the overall enterprise of geocriticism. Undoubtedly, as more scholars and critics explore the spaces, places, and mappings of literature, geocritical practices and readings will further multiply. Such, in any case, is my hope, and I rather think that even if it appears in hitherto unseen and unforeseeable forms, geocriticism will be a vital part of literary and cultural studies in the years to come.

Geocriticism, whatever else it may be, is a way of looking at the spaces of literature, broadly conceived to include not only those places that readers and writers experience by means of texts but also the experience of space and place within ourselves, our *situatedness* in space as a condition of our own existence.

With geocriticism one emphasizes this inherent spatiality while also focusing one's critical gaze on those aspects of literature, along with other texts not always deemed literary, that give meaning to our spatialized sense of being. In the diversity and scope of the work undertaken in its name, geocriticism may be used to ask new questions, to read differently, to engage with other disciplinary methods, and to interpret the ways that we make sense of our own spaces, of our own mappings. Recent work suggests some of the directions that geocriticism and geocritics may take in the future, as readers and writers—some lost in space, some at home in the world—continue to explore in ongoing adventures.

Notes

1. See Michel Foucault, "Of Other Spaces," trans. Jay Miskowiec, *Diacritics* 16 (Spring 1986), 22–27.

2. Among the many influential texts by these theorists, see Fredric Jameson, *Postmodernism, or, The Cultural Logic of Late Capitalism* (Durham, NC: Duke University Press, 1991); Edward W. Soja, *Postmodern Geographies: The Reassertion of Space in Critical Social Theory* (London: Verso, 1989); David Harvey, *The Condition of Postmodernity* (Oxford: Blackwell, 1990); and Nigel Thrift, *Spatial Formations* (London: SAGE, 1996).

3. See, e.g., Tom Conley, *The Self-Made Map: Cartographic Writing in Early Modern France* (Minneapolis: University of Minnesota Press, 1996); Paul Carter, *The Road to Botany Bay: An Essay in Spatial History* (London: Faber and Faber, 1987); Ricardo Padrón, *The Spacious Word: Cartography, Literature, and Empire in Early Modern Spain* (Chicago: University of Chicago Press, 2004); and Leonard Goldstein, *The Social and Cultural Roots of Linear Perspective* (Minneapolis: MEP, 1988).

4. See, e.g., Barney Warf and Santa Arias, eds., *The Spatial Turn: Interdisciplinary Perspectives* (London: Routledge, 2008).

5. See Edward W. Soja, *Thirdspace: Journeys to Los Angeles and Other Real-and-Imagined Places* (Oxford: Blackwell, 1996).

6. See my *Melville, Mapping and Globalization: Literary Cartography in the American Baroque Writer* (London: Continuum, 2009).

7. See Bertrand Westphal, "Pour une approche géocritique des textes: esquisse," in *La Géocritique mode d'emploi*, ed. Bertrand Westphal (Limoges: Pulim, 2000), 9–39.

8. See Bertrand Westphal, *La Géocritique: Réel, fiction, espace* (Paris: Minuit, 2007); see also Bertrand Westphal, *Geocriticism: Real and Fictional Spaces*, trans. Robert T. Tally Jr. (New York: Palgrave, 2011).

9. Readers of my *Spatiality* (London: Routledge, 2013) will recognize the use of these terms in that work. See also my "Jameson's Project of Cognitive Mapping: A Critical Engagement," in *Social Cartography: Mapping Ways of Seeing Social and Educational Change*, ed. Rolland G. Paulston (New York: Garland, 1996), 399–416.

10. See Westphal, *Geocriticism*, especially 111–147.

11. See, e.g., Marie-Laure Ryan, Kenneth Foote, and Maoz Azaryahu's *Narrating Space / Spatializing Narrative: Where Narrative Theory and Geography Meet* (Columbus, OH: Ohio State University Press, 2016); see also the wide variety of essays in Emmanuelle Peraldo's

edited collection, *Literature and Geography: The Writing of Space throughout History* (Newcastle-upon-Tyne: Cambridge Scholars, 2016).

12. See Bertrand Westphal, *Le Rivage des mythes: Une géocritique méditerranéene* (Limoges: Pulim, 2001).

13. See my review in *L'Esprit Créateur: The International Quarterly of French and Francophone Studies* 49, no. 3 (Fall 2009): 134. On "literary cartography," see my *Melville, Mapping and Globalization: Literary Cartography in the American Baroque Writer* (London: Continuum, 2009).

14. See Soja, *Thirdspace*.

15. Westphal, *Geocriticism*, 4.

16. Frank Kermode, *The Sense of an Ending: Studies in the Theory of Fiction* (Oxford: Oxford University Press, 1967), 3.

17. For example, Westphal has made a geocritical study of the Dalmatian islands, examining the literary representation of that geographical domain; see Bertrand Westphal, "Îles dalmates: L'odysée des îles," in *L'Oeil de la Méditerranée* (La Tour d'Aigues: Éditions de l'Aube, 2005), 177–198.

18. Westphal, *Geocriticism*, 126–127.

19. Eric Prieto, "Geocriticism, Geopoetics, Geophilosophy, and Beyond," in *Geocritical Explorations: Space, Place, and Mapping in Literary and Cultural Studies*, ed. Robert T. Tally Jr. (New York: Palgrave Macmillan, 2011), 22.

20. See Eric Prieto, *Literature, Geography, and the Postmodern Poetics of Place* (New York: Palgrave Macmillan, 2012).

21. Bertrand Westphal's most recent book, in fact, is *La Cage des méridiens: La littérature et l'art contemporain face à la globalization* (Paris: Minuit, 2016); it is arguably the third volume in a trilogy also comprising *Geocriticism* and *The Plausible World*.

22. See Michel Foucault, *The History of Sexuality, Volume I: An Introduction*, trans. Robert Hurley (New York: Random House, 1978), 57–73.

23. Gilles Deleuze and Félix Guattari, *A Thousand Plateaus*, trans. Brian Massumi (Minneapolis: University of Minnesota Press, 1987), 361–362.

24. Ibid., 500.

25. See Edward W. Said, *Culture and Imperialism* (New York: Knopf, 1993), 62.

26. Here one might think of Marlowe's "blank space[s] of delightful mystery" in Joseph Conrad's *Heart of Darkness*. In "Geography and Some Explorers," Conrad praised the "honest" maps that left unknown or unexplored territories blank rather than filling them with fanciful creatures or allegorical illustrations. Of course, what is left unsaid is the degree to which even scientific maps are projecting figural representations that stand in for "real" places, and these are no more or less real in an objective sense than the dragons or sea serpents of antique charts.

27. See, e.g., my *Spatiality* (London and New York: Routledge, 2013), 79–86.

28. See Gianni Vattimo, "Dialectics, Difference, Weak Thought," in *Weak Thought*, ed. Gianni Vattimo and Pier Aldo Rovatti, trans. Peter Carravetta (Albany, NY: SUNY Press, 2012), 39–52.

29. Erich Auerbach, *Dante: Poet of the Secular World*, trans. Ralph Manheim (New York: New York Review Books, 2007), 133.

30. Westphal's most recent book, *La Cage des méridiens*, addresses this worldliness head on. Indeed, I view this as the culmination of the geocritical trilogy (with *Geocriticism* and

The Plausible World as the first two parts), as Westphal's complicated critical and theoretical trajectory has taken him from discrete places to multiple worlds and on to the planet itself, while also recursively finding his way back to a grounded, earthly (*geocritical*) practice. See Amy Wells, "Bending the Bars of the Meridian Cage," *American Book Review* 37, no. 6 (September/October 2016): 7–8.

31. Westphal, *Geocriticism*, 170, ellipsis in original.

32. See Georges Perec, *An Attempt at Exhausting a Place in Paris*, trans. Marc Lowenthal (Cambridge, MA: Wakefield, 2010).

3   Geocritical Situations

W~AS IT BERTOLT~ Brecht who pointed out that the soldier enlisted to fight in the Thirty Years' War almost certainly did not know that it would one day be called "the Thirty Years' War"? The observation serves as an apt reminder of the limited perspective afforded by our inevitably historical situation *in mediis rebus*, in which the sense of our own place cannot be fully apprehended so long as we are restricted to its vantage point. It is the experience of being in the midst of actions and events of which one has little control or even understanding: in other words, it is to experience history and geography themselves. Like Gilles Deleuze's nomads, whose lives are ever the intermezzo,[1] those of us located in the middle of things (i.e., all of us) attempt to make sense of the present as best we can. It is in this situation that theory, which was always defined by its speculative aspect (*theoria*), is most needed in order to envision and to project new ways of making sense of the world in which we are inescapably a part. Geocritical theory seems well suited to addressing the cartographical anxiety of life "in the middest." Finding ourselves always in the middle of things is no less spatial than temporal, as we need to find ways both of representing our own position in the dynamic world system (an intensively *local* theoretical practice) and of imagining the world system in which we are positioned (a seemingly impossible *global* vision), and apparently we need to do both at once and at all times in a continuous project of mapping and remapping.

A Utopia of the In-Between

In *The Sense of an Ending: Studies in the Theory of Fiction*, Frank Kermode observes that "Men, like poets, rush 'into the middest,' *in medias res*, when they are born; they also die *in mediis rebus*, and to make sense of their span they need fictive concords with origins and ends, such as give meaning to lives and poems."[2] Kermode is, of course, speaking of a temporal register, but his point applies equally to the experience of space, place, and spatial relations more generally. As individual or collective subjects, we find ourselves always and already in the midst, located in a perpetual-though-mobile state of the *in-between* or *entre-deux*.[3] Ever bound to a particular situation—that is, at a site within a cognizable spatial assemblage or formation—we define our position in relation to others, establishing limits, boundaries, borders, or other such markers to help determine our sense of place amid the expansive, perhaps unrepresentable extension of space. As with time and space, so too with history and geography, the phenomenological subject is situated in the middle, which is itself determined by imaginary limits that can be taken for spatiotemporal boundaries. One cannot imagine the middle ages without some sense of an anterior classical period and a posterior modern one; likewise, one cannot imagine a middle ground without reference to cognizable areas to the left or right, above or below. Yet in some very real sense, we are always in the middle, as times and zones are envisioned as boundaries surrounding this essentially intermediary position. Making sense of this condition is, as Kermode notes, a principal vocation of literature, whereas the critic is bound only to the lesser task of "making sense of the ways we try to make sense of our lives."[4] From the inescapably middling situation in which we find ourselves, the creative writer creates a map, giving form to the spaces and places of our experience, while the critic, also ensconced in the middle of things, endeavors to make sense of this literary cartography.

Recognition of this fundamentally intermediary experience perhaps accounts for the increasing interest in liminality.[5] The discourse of liminality itself is perhaps a symptom of the cartographic anxiety or spatial confusion characteristic of the present moment, whether it be associated with poststructuralism, postmodernity, globalization, or some other conditioning condition.[6] Undoubtedly, certain aspects of this anxiety could be related to what we used to call the human condition, as when Martin Heidegger associates anxiety (*Angst*) with the uncanny (*unheimlich*), which in turn is revealed to be a sense of homelessness (*das Nicht-zu-Hause-sein*).[7] The celebrated cultural geographer Yi-Fu Tuan famously distinguished place and space by positing the former as a site of security and the latter as a zone of freedom; however, as in the existentialist tradition, with freedom comes anxiety, the dis-ease that Jean-Paul Sartre evocatively referred to as nausea, and with security comes all the potential for bad faith.[8] Yet if this be part of the human condition, it is difficult to deny that the pervasiveness of spatial anxiety has seemed to increase in the twentieth and twentieth-first centuries. In our time, the "epoch of space" as Michel Foucault dubbed it,[9] spatial relations appear to be at least as significant as temporal ones, and artists, critics, social theorists, and others have found it necessary to develop novel approaches to their subjects, in part to account for this new or enhanced spatiality. The "spatial turn" in the humanities and social sciences in recent years is one name for this polyvalent critical phenomenon. Not surprisingly then, the rise in a discourse surrounding the liminal, that auspicious space or place of in-betweenness, appears to be thoroughly concomitant with the burgeoning of spatiality studies more generally.

As may be readily surmised, the concept of liminality lies somewhere between space and place. The two terms are distinct, but they are also inextricably interrelated, such that it is difficult, even undesirable, to speak of one without reference to the other. As Tuan explains, "The ideas 'space' and 'place' require each other for definition. From the security and stability of place we are aware of the openness, freedom, and threat of space, and vice-versa. Furthermore, if we think of space as that which allows movement, then place is pause; each pause in movement makes it possible for location to be transformed into place."[10] Elsewhere, Tuan asserts that a place comes into being through this *pause*: "As we look at a panoramic scene, our eyes pause at points of interest," thereby transforming these previously undifferentiated expanses of space into places, which, in being identified as such, take on meanings.[11] Thus, they become subject to interpretation, the traditional jurisdiction of literary art and criticism. In establishing the place-ness of a place in this manner, one creates a text to be read, as well as a topography to be mapped, and the contours of its form are largely arbitrary. Place relative to space thus requires the insistence and the persistence of the limit, points and lines demarcating the space in such a way as to form the boundaries of place.

Hence, the situation in-between or *entredeux* requires some sense of boundaries, borders, or limits. In Latin this was indicated by the term *limes* (plural *limites*), which could be used to designate any number of limits but which also stood for the frontier or boundary of the Roman Empire itself. The *limes* represents an end, the outer boundary, or the mark of enclosure. However, what we think of as liminality is far from the closed space of a delimited territory but instead an in-between space of potentiality. In a ruse of etymology, one of those philological phantasms that trick the mind with false similitude or homophony, the *limes* does not necessarily share a root with the *limen*, the latter designating a threshold. To be sure, a boundary or border might become a threshold, but only when it is transgressed. The *limen* suggests a space more explicitly understood as a site of transgressivity, a point of entry into another zone.[12] Unlike the closed space or place given form by its perceived limits (*limites*), the liminal space or site of the *limen* is one of opening, unfolding, or becoming. Indeed, the liminal is figured in the form of the Deleuzian nomad, living in the intermezzo, ever deterritorializing without reterritorialization, occupying smooth spaces subject to intense striation over and over again.[13] One could say that a political program of liminality, if there were any, would have to involve the transformation of the *limes* into a *limen*.

Here we might invoke Siegfried Kracauer's idea of "anteroom thinking," which he employs as a way of representing the historian's fundamentally *situated*, intermediary position with respect to history. From the perspective of one located in the anteroom, the historian can avoid the errors of a thoroughly abstract, bird's-eye view theorizing based on received ideas or set laws. Exploring "an area which borders on the world of daily life," the historian embraces the basic ambiguities of the *Lebenswelt*. In this, there is not so much attention to the beginnings and ends as there is the recognition of powers of the middle. In this "intermediary" situation, Kracauer observes, "we usually concentrate not so much on the last things, as the last before the last."[14] The *teloi* are not the true goals in this sort of critical thinking. "Indeed," writes Kracauer, referring to a historian criticized for not following a problem through to its logical end, "a stopping mid-way may be ultimate wisdom in the anteroom."[15] "What does this imply for historians and other inveterate anteroom dwellers?" asks Kracauer, before concluding:

> Ambiguity is of the essence in this intermediary idea. A constant effort is needed on the part of those inhabiting it to meet the conflicting necessities with which they are faced at every turn of the road. They find themselves in a precarious situation which even invites them to gamble with absolutes, all kinds of quixotic ideas about universal truth. These peculiar preoccupations call forth specific attitudes, one of which appears to be particularly fitting because it breathes a true anteroom spirit. . . . It points to a Utopia of the in-between—a terra incognita in the hollows between the lands we know.[16]

Only from this "utopian" perspective, perhaps, can one adequately limn the liminal, which must remain something of a terra incognita even as it is occupied and transgressed.

Liminality signifies a threshold between two zones, an anteroom distinct from that which could be said to be definitely inside or outside, here and there. The term *ambiguity* literally refers to "both ways," and one who is located in the space of the liminal must be ever attuned to the presence of adverse or conflicting possibilities. Liminality also suggests a sort of neutrality, an aspect that confirms its connection with utopia, as Louis Marin made clear in *Utopics: Spatial Play.*[17] Utopia is both a "good place" (*eu-topos*) and a "no place" (*ou-topos*) in Thomas More's homophonic pun, and the island itself is simultaneously profoundly real, insofar as it serves as a satirical critique of English and other European governments and social orders, and utterly imaginary, inasmuch as it exists only in the fancy of the author and reader. Along similar lines, the *neutral*—deriving from the Latin *ne* and *uter*—literally expresses "neither one nor the other," which for Marin opens up a utopian space distinct from the official zones designated real or imaginary. Neutrality should not be confused with disinterestedness, even less with objectivity. Here the neutral becomes another figure for the anteroom, the threshold, utopia, or the space that is neither the one nor the other, a site of perpetual ambiguity. Is it surprising that Dante punishes the neutral (that is, those who refused to take sides in the wars between good and evil) *not* in Hell itself, but in a vestibule just outside the gates of Hell, the ante-Inferno? Although it is hardly a utopian vision, Dante's creation of an ante-Inferno populated by the souls of the neutral, quite literally on the threshold of Hell, is indicative of the degree to which liminality itself can appear diabolical. However, from a perspective that is beyond good and evil, the liminal is suggestive of infinite possibilities.

Finally, as "a Utopia of the in-between," the liminal cannot be adequately represented, but it might be limned in our always tentative, provisional, and exploratory efforts to make visible the potential so often obscured by a tyrannical status quo, to transform the limit into a threshold, and to cross over into alternative domains, perhaps also creating in them new spaces of liberty. What I have been referring to as *topophrenia*, an intensive and extravagant place-mindedness, connects the characterizing consciousness to the spaces and places that, in their interrelations, give form to the world, defining its contours and disclosing its potential alternatives. The project of limning the liminal is perhaps especially well suited to literature, which is the art form most closely associated with the faculty of the imagination. In fact, borrowing the phrase from Northrop Frye, one might say that the "educated imagination,"[18] which is the aim and result of literary study, is precisely what is most needed to assess the character and potential of liminality in all its utopian otherness and ambiguity. At the threshold one may be able to see both sides at once, finding a boundary to be transgressed, thus rendering the *limes* a *limen*. It is a situation in-between space and place, but one that joins the two in productive ambiguities. Geocriticism, in insisting on a critical perspective situated in the midst, is at its most effective in imagining, analyzing, and extrapolating from these liminal zones, sites of alterity and becoming, in which meanings proliferate, connect to one another, and extend into other, possibly unforeseen territories.

Dialectical Reversals

The intellectual work taking place in this situation, the form-giving or sense-making activity of theory itself, might be aptly labeled a *postcontemporary intervention*,[19] as the trace of some tenebrous future might be glimpsed, if only tentatively and provisionally, in a present moment which has already passed in the instant that it is recognized. Heraclitus notoriously observed that one cannot step into the same river twice, but we know that in its onrushing and turbulent flow, history cannot truly be experienced even once. The vantage of the vicissitudinous present, the middle in which we muddle, sharply limits the vistas of the past and future. And what has seemed a certainty may quickly be revealed to be quite otherwise, while other uncertainties crystallize into recognizable forms. Ideally, as Aristotle explains in *The Poetics*, such a reversal (*peripeteia*) is accompanied by a new recognition and understanding of things (*anagnorisis*), and the ensuing images are clearer, if only temporarily.

In Aristotle's explanation of *peripeteia* in *The Poetics*, he refers specifically to that moment in *Oedipus the King* when the messenger, who had ostensibly brought welcome tidings to cheer the perplexed Oedipus, delivered the revelations that had the opposite effect.[20] This moment of peripety is accompanied by a form of recognition, or the "movement from ignorance to knowledge," where Oedipus now understands, precisely through the reversal, what is really going on. Significantly then, the reversal is a necessary component of the new knowledge, or as Aristotle puts it, "The best form of recognition is coincident with the reversal of the situation."[21] The dialectical reversal, a ruse of history, the unforeseen consequences of this or that action or reaction, these are the events that ultimately press a stamp of significance on the given moment or situation. Peripety, then, is an essential element of theoretical practice or of theory itself, whose speculative vocation in the end can only be successful once the various reversals of fortune are disclosed. This applies equally to geocritical theory and practice, since the place one attempts to map is itself only comprehensible through a speculative activity that can account for its own uncertainty amid the shifting, protean spaces of which it is necessarily a part.

Although Aristotle's theory concerns the ways and means of producing effective drama, the concept of peripety appears to be a crucial part of historical and geographical understanding more generally. Almost like a kind of spatiotemporal *Nachträglichkeit* (to evoke a Freudian term), one does not really "know" the event or its meaning until after it has happened, and more often than not the import of the event is disclosed only in connection with a later reversal. For example, as Fredric Jameson has argued, peripety is the fundamental element, as well as the most significant revelation, of dialectical thought:

> The basic story which the dialectic has to tell is no doubt that of the dialectical *reversal*, that paradoxical turning around of a phenomenon into its opposite . . . . It can be described as a kind of leap-frogging affair in time, in which the drawbacks of a given historical situation turn out in reality to be its secret advantages, in which what looked like built-in superiorities suddenly prove to set the most ironclad limits on its future development. It is a matter, indeed, of the reversal of limits, of the transformation from negative to positive and from positive to negative.[22]

In 1971's *Marxism and Form*, Jameson's timely example of such a dialectical reversal in contemporary history involves the Cold War arms race. He notes that the technological superiority of the United States in producing atomic weapons led the Soviet Union to experiment with missiles that could carry their much more cumbersome nuclear bombs, which resulted in a benefit to their space program; but the consequent Soviet superiority in rocket technology led the Americans to develop smaller, more efficient transistorized instruments, and so on. An apparent disadvantage turns out to have been a clear advantage when judged from a certain point of view, but this situation is itself reversed at a different spatiotemporal vantage. As Jameson concludes, this example neglects the various events and reversals that came before but constituted the conditions for the possibility of the technological arms race or space race: "A complete picture of this particular set of dialectical reversals would ultimately have involved a reimmersion in the very element of concrete history itself."[23]

Such too, I think, is the situation of theory in what is today called—sometimes gleefully, sometimes elegiacally—a "posttheory" epoch, particularly in literary studies but extending into other fields in the humanities and social sciences in the United States and elsewhere. Recently, various postmortems have attempted to assess the gains or losses of the era of high theory, with such leading figures as Terry Eagleton in *After Theory* lamenting the pervasiveness of anti-theoretical scholarship, especially in the United States, centered on trendy popular culture or consumerist models of intellectual sexiness, or Ian Hunter's rather negative intellectual history of a decidedly *past* "moment of theory," or François Cusset's thoughtful assessment of the life and afterlives of "French theory" in the United States and in Europe.[24] Jameson, though not alone, is one of the few figures from the heyday of high theory in the United States to continue to produce high-level theoretical and critical writings, not only in his recent studies of Georg Hegel and Karl Marx, but through his ambitious and far-reaching *Poetics of Social Forms* multivolume project, two volumes of which are still forthcoming.[25] Perhaps owing to his conviction that the dialectical reversal is the fundamental element of the narrative of history, Jameson recognizes the degree to which the enthusiasm for critical practices and literary scholarship *after theory* may more clearly set the stage for theory's inevitable return. Or just as likely, this may set the stage for the revelation that theory was with us all along. Amid the crowing or lamenting variations of the "end of theory" arguments in recent years, one finds a sense of desperation, a pervasive but indefinite feeling of need, which ironically might only be met by some form of theorizing. Hence the dilemma faced by those who toil in the fields of literature or, more broadly, cultural or critical studies: at a profoundly anti-theoretical moment, we find ourselves more in need of the ability to theorize.

In another kind of dialectical reversal, the rise and fall of "high" theory—the monumental figures of Ferdinand de Saussure, Claude Levi-Strauss, Jacques Lacan, Louis Althusser, Roland Barthes, Michel Foucault, Gilles Deleuze, Jacques Derrida, Julia Kristeva, Luce Irigaray, Pierre Bourdieu, and perhaps, at twilight, Alain Badiou (to name but a few of the well-known Francophone theorists)—is a narrative of victory as well as defeat. While these figures no longer carry the cultural cachet they had maintained in the United States in the 1970s or 1980s, the residual effects of their writings and the various critical works performed under the sign of their writings continue to inform literary and cultural studies in innumerable ways. If "theory" has gone away, it is at least partly because theory has been absorbed into so much of what is understood as literary and cultural studies that it need no longer be granted its separate and distinct place in the curriculum. Arguably, the dissemination of theoretical practices throughout literary and cultural studies obviates the need for a study of theory *qua* theory, and the famous Deleuzian metaphor of the toolbox becomes the dominant figure for how theory will operate within and alongside literary criticism.[26] The end of theory in that case is merely the next stage of theory, moving us from the moment of speculative formulation and abstract analysis to practical deployment and ultimately to unconscious influence. Citing John Maynard Keynes, Eagleton has noted that those "who disliked theory, or claimed to be able to get along better without it, were simply in the grip of an older theory."[27] But in this case, the older theory is theory itself, diluted and rinsed out, perhaps now blending in with other critical discourses in more or less interesting ways, but keeping itself politely in the background of the discussion. Or worse, as Eagleton feared, theory becomes so commoditized and fetishized that it loses any of its critical edge, sinking into a jargon-filled, professionalized, and anti-intellectual form of anodyne cultural studies. Any theoretically coherent geocriticism must countenance these threats and be on guard against them.

Yet the present historical conjuncture in the age of globalization is marked by such dynamism and turbulence that the calls for pragmatic or common-sense philosophies, as opposed to the so-called abstractions of theory, seem almost quaint. The cultural consequences of the continuing global economic crisis of 2008, for example, which was both caused and exacerbated by financial instruments specifically engineered as means for lowering economic risk, will not be adequately apprehended without a speculative and subtle mode of thought, one that is well attuned to such peripety and to the dramatic ironies that the Hegelians associate with the ruse of history. The posttheory critical approaches that seek to identify particular or partial points of reference—such as identity politics, environmental concerns, national frameworks, and so on—can only appear parochial and incomplete when confronted with the dynamic world system. In this era of postmodernity, or maybe now post-postmodernity, theory itself stages its dramatic comeback, not as an answer to our hitherto unanswered questions, but as an attempt to ask new questions and tell new stories. These novel queries and narratives may account for elements previously omitted or unseen or re-tell stories in a new, different way. The peripeties of globalization, including the rise and fall of national interests in an increasingly postnational system and the pervasive sense of placelessness associated with an enhanced spatiality, call for rigorous theoretical practice, and geocriticism offers a powerful framework in which to pursue this practice. Thus, to borrow Jameson's language for use in a slightly different context, I might say that theory "characterizes the way our spectatorship and our praxis alike construct portions of the world with a view towards changing them."[28] The situations of theory in this world system may enable new, possibly better, and certainly different vantages and vistas for twenty-first-century criticism.

Geocritics maintain that a properly critical approach to the spatiotemporal subjects, texts, and events under consideration must be informed by a theoretical practice equipped to deal with the shifting and protean conditions for the possibility of criticism itself. That is, geocritical theory offers a sort of Archimedean point, though now necessarily tentative and provisional, from which to comprehend the situation *in mediis rebus*, and theory provides a critical impetus for reimagining the given situation in the context of the world system with a view toward both its past and future. The peripety or "ruse of history" disclosed by theoretical practice enables that recognition or understanding of the world, and only through such a process does one begin to imagine radical alternatives. Hence, a utopian or fantastic project also subtends the vocation of theory, which allows critics to project an imaginary map in order to navigate the real spaces more effectively and perhaps gain a vista into other potential spaces beyond.[29]

The turbulent and shifting constellations of power in the era of globalization undoubtedly make it difficult to ascertain the cultural tendencies of the present, much less to predict the future. Geocriticism aligns itself with the speculative vocation of fantasy or utopia, each of which being a form of "radical alterity" in China Miéville's phrase, inasmuch as theory will maintain its fundamentally critical function in mapping the present world system, but it will do so while in the service of imagining other worlds. In this sense, the situations of theory in a dynamic world system may be revealed to be the point of view for global peripeties, just as the reversals that make possible the recognitions of the true state of affairs are themselves indications that this state is also provisional, tentative, and subject to radical transformation. Situated always in the middle of things as it were, geocritical theory maps the territories while projecting alternative visions where new spaces are possible, even necessary.

A Discourse of Alterity

The recent spatial turn in literary and cultural studies has generated a great deal of interest in the relations among space, place, mapping, and literature.[30] This has resulted in a growing body of critical scholarship in the interdisciplinary field of spatiality studies, broadly defined so as to encompass geocriticism, geopoetics, and the spatial humanities, among other emerging critical and theoretical practices. In my *Spatiality* I attempt to provide a general introduction to spatial literary studies, which undoubtedly offer innovative insights into various disciplines, but which I believe will be especially valuable to comparative literature.[31] Even more than those disciplinary fields whose focus is limited to a particular national body of writings or a single linguistic literary tradition, comparative literature has always paid close attention to those elements that spatially oriented critics highlight in their research. Notably, the comparative study of literature requires some focus on different places, on places understood *as* being *different* from others as well as on different perspectives of the various sites under consideration. The intensive awareness of alterity is part of the substance of comparative literature. Unlike those fields or scholars that favor identity over alterity, as Gayatri Chakravorty Spivak has put it, "Comparative Literature . . . goes rather toward the other."[32] With its own conceptual grounding in a discourse of alterity, geocriticism is particularly well suited to the timely exploration of space and comparative literature today.

For those familiar with the term, it may seem a bit ironic to specify *geocriticism* as committed to alterity or otherness in the way Spivak suggests. As discussed in chapter 2, the geocritical approach outlined by Bertrand Westphal, for example, seems to take as its point of departure an identifiable *place*, which can then be the subject of geocritical analysis. In *Geocriticism: Real and Fictional Spaces*, Westphal argues for a geocentric, as especially opposed to an egocentric, approach. By this Westphal means that the geocritic would study a singular geographical place, such as a city or a region, and then examine the ways in which that place has been represented in a variety of texts, which could include not only traditional works of literature, poetry, or fiction but also films, travel narratives, governmental surveys, tourist brochures, and so forth. A major benefit that Westphal sees in the geocentric approach is that, because it avoids the limited perspective of a single author or group, its multifocal perspective can yield a relatively nonbiased, though inevitably incomplete image of the place.

However, this vision of geocriticism presents a couple of rather serious problems for comparative literature, one practical and the other more theoretical. First, there is the inevitable question of the corpus. How does one determine exactly which texts could, in the aggregate, reasonably constitute a meaningful body of material with which to analyze the literary representations of a given geographical site? That is, if the Paris of Honoré de Balzac is far too limited since it relies on the perspective of only a single author or a few of his own writings, then how many authors and texts representing Paris would constitute a feasible and credible starting point for a geocritical study of the French capital? Also, the seemingly innumerable textual references to well-known places such as Paris would seem to render any geocritical analysis impossible. Westphal argues that the corpus would have to reach "the threshold of representativeness" but concedes that this would be difficult to ascertain.[33] The second problem with Westphal's geocentric method is that it assumes the unproblematized identity of a "place," without adequately take into account the conflicting forces and views that condition the ways in which various spaces come to be recognizable as places. In his revision of the geocritical project in *Literature, Geography, and the Postmodern Poetics of Place*, Eric Prieto examines the textual emergence of various types of place, including what appear to be nonplaces, such as improvised shantytowns or the French *banlieues*, along with already-identified, readily recognizable *topoi*.[34] By examining the ways that certain kinds of social space come into being as places for interpretation, this sort of geocriticism offers intriguing opportunities for understanding how literary representation and spatiality interconnect.

In my own view geocriticism would have to move beyond a geocentric method, returning to philological and historical approaches that might also include examinations of single authors or texts, genres, or periods in order to address the protean spaces of literature. But it should also be clear that the aims of geocriticism are best served by a decidedly comparative scope of literary studies, since the spaces and their representation to be geocritically analyzed are also established in their tentative but recognizable shapes through the related effects of multiple authors, languages, and historical forms. Westphal has in practice always embraced a thoroughly comparative approach. In his follow-up to *Geocriticism*, titled *The Plausible World: A Geocritical Approach to Space, Place, and Maps*, Westphal explores a rich variety of texts from antiquity to the present, drawing on numerous cultural and linguistic traditions from all over the planet, and he ably characterizes the many ways in which individuals and cultures enact a sort of literary cartography of their worlds.[35] By moving away from the strictly geocentric approach outlined in the methodological sections of *Geocriticism*, Westphal connects his critical practice to a broader scope of spatiality studies that does not resist the allure of an individual author's perspective, while also paying closer attention than in the former study to the problem of the *emergence* of places. Hence, *The Plausible World* nicely extends the project of *Geocriticism* while at the same time striking out in interesting, new directions in search of unexplored territories.

The relations between space and literature, mapping and writing, and description and narration are as complex and numerous as they are interesting. To attempt to know a place, one maps it, but one also reads it and narrates it. In *Space and Place: The Perspective of Experience*, Yi-Fu Tuan has noted that a given portion of space becomes a place once it occasions a pause, a resting of the eyes, which—however brief—transforms it into a subject for storytelling. As one's eyes rest on something long enough to distinguish it from within an undifferentiated sweep of scenery, the space-turned-place takes on *meanings*, the traditional bailiwick of "literary art."[36] And one might add vice versa—that is, a literary work becomes infused with the places that it explores, places that make it what it is. In narrative fiction, particularly visible in works employing a first-person narrator or a focalized point of view, the narrator maps the spaces of the narrative while also exploring them, often forcing the reader to project his or her own "map" of the text while attempting to follow the itinerary of the narrator through this space. One thinks of Joseph Frank's discussion of spatial form in James Joyce's *Ulysses*[37] but also of the spatiotemporal ramblings of Benjy or Quentin Compson in William Faulkner's *The Sound and the Fury*. As narratives move across borders, which by their very nature they inevitably do, those spaces and places become all the more significant. Geocriticism provides a flexible critical approach to the literary cartography produced in such writings, revealing how the transnational border crossings of comparative literature actively determine the real-and-imaginary spaces, to use Edward W. Soja's expression from his *Thirdspace*,[38] that readers encounter and explore.

Comparative literature discloses the degree to which even familiar places are made strange in the process of reading or mapping them, and the multiple and diverse points of view taken into account by any comparative study will highlight the alterity inherent in literary representation as well as in our comportment to the world itself. As Spivak writes, "To be human is to be intended toward the other. We provide for ourselves transcendental figurations of what we think is the original of this animating gift: mother, nation, god, nature. These are names of alterity, some more radical than others."[39] Through literature we encounter this alterity, incorporating its very strangeness into who we are but also recognizing the simultaneously alluring and unsettling otherness of the places and experiences depicted. Of course, all fiction, no matter how realistic, maintains the power of estrangement that can make possible alternative prospects. But comparative literature in an age of globalization has as its *raison d'être* a commitment to difference. As a method of examining the shifting but distinctive spaces of literature, geocriticism also takes alterity as its *Ansatzpunkt*. Although geocriticism may certainly focus attention on this or that particular place or on a recognizable type of place, geocriticism does not rely on (or admit as possible) any sense of stable, unchanging geographic identity. On the contrary, a geocritical approach understands and demonstrates the degree to which a given "place" is formed through the interrelations of multiple forces and representations. The mythic stability or static identity of a particular city, region, nation, or continent is belied by the diverse literary representations of such apparently identifiable geographical ensembles. Spatially oriented approaches to comparative literature can open up new vistas, establish different vantages, and disclose alternative prospects for mapping the real-and-imagined spaces of the world in which we live. The prospects of comparative literature are, in an almost literal sense, fantastic, opening up before our eyes a realm in which monsters may appear. As in the early world maps that the popular imagination, if not actual history of cartography, discerns the words *hic sunt dracones*, we readers of comparative literature may find ourselves in the presence of dragons.

In the final words of his famous essay on *Beowulf*, J. R. R. Tolkien eloquently argues for the cultural significance of this medieval epic and urges readers, whom he clearly imagines as strictly English, to see themselves in it. Unlike Greek epics or mostly French romantic lays, he argues *Beowulf* belongs to "our" northern heritage. Speaking to Englishmen alone, of course, Tolkien insists that the epic is part of "us":

> There is not much poetry in the world like this; and though *Beowulf* may not be among the very greatest poems of our western world and its tradition, it has its own individual character, and peculiar solemnity; it would still have power had it been written in some time or place unknown and without posterity, if it contained no name that could now be recognized or identified by research. Yet it is in fact written in a language that after many centuries has still essential kinship with our own, it was made in this land, and moves in our northern world beneath our northern sky, and for those who are native to that tongue and land, it must ever call with a profound appeal—until the dragon comes.[40]

Tolkien was adamantly opposed to nearly all forms of cosmopolitanism, but here he unintentionally reveals the power of literature's radical alterity to disrupt the somewhat nationalist, rather culturally isolated, and identitarian perspective the philologist tended to embrace. Not that this is Tolkien's point, but the moment of estrangement—when the dragon comes—is what makes the literary text so valuable, and not the many moments of seeming familiarity or purported kinship. The power of literature resides in its defamiliarizing effects, in that productive alienation that makes us begin to question our own former certainties, or in the exploration of spaces hitherto unknown, spaces we had thought homely but which turn out to be profoundly foreign and suddenly novel.

The dragon is perhaps the very avatar of radical alterity, the creature that Tolkien saw as paradigmatically otherworldly and that Jameson identified as itself almost a *differentia specifica* between fantasy and science fiction.[41] Where the dragon appears is irremediably in another world. Yet in the apprehension or even just the glimpse of the fantastic otherworld, the reader encounters the spaces of the so-called real world afresh, seeing them quite differently. Leaving the genre or mode of fantasy, one recognizes that the places of one's own homey and familiar world are transformed through the literary cartographies intended to make sense of them. The productive alterity of comparative literature makes possible hitherto undisclosed prospects, and with a geocriticism attuned to the places unexpectedly rendered visible by this experience, literary critics can begin to sketch new maps.

Empowering the Imagination

The situations in which the study of literary and cultural criticism finds itself in at present, in the age of globalization, the post–American Century, or whatever it might be labeled, are necessarily uncertain, shifting, oscillatory, and subject to sudden turnabouts. For example, there must be an almost-cosmic irony, if we want to think about it that way, in the fact that the end of the American

Century coincided with, and in no small part was caused by, the supreme victory of the United States and of the capitalist mode of production more generally, over the Soviet-styled communist systems at the end of the Cold War, with the fall of the Berlin Wall, the establishment of apparently more democratic political institutions in Eastern Europe, and the extension of free market economies to nearly all corners of the globe.[42] The present, equally global financial crises in the twenty-first century, as well as the social and economic insecurities not too distantly related to such crises, are unthinkable without this well-nigh total victory of the West, and yet the tragic consequences of that triumph create other sources of hope, as is audible in the rhetoric of anti-globalization movements. Of course, the exuberance of new social movements must be leavened with the memories of Tiananmen Square, the Prague Spring, the anti-war movements, and so on. The "reversal of the situation" or *peripeteia*, which Aristotle had identified as a crucial element of tragedy, is also and always a key feature of both history itself and our historical situatedness in the dynamic world system. As noted above, Jameson once suggested that a basic purpose and consequence of dialectical thought is to detect and disclose the dialectic reversal. More recently Jameson has pointed out that the dialectic is committed to the "logic of the situation," as opposed to logics of individual consciousness or abstract notions such as "society." As he puts it, "The emphasis on the logic of the situation, the constant changeability of the situation, its primacy and the way in which it allows certain things to be possible and others not: that would lead to a kind of thinking that I would call dialectical."[43] I would argue that the role of critical theory at the present world-historical conjuncture is also to focus its critical lens on the situation in which we find ourselves, within the broader spatiotemporal configuration of the world system itself. Geocritical theory, which is already attuned to the site-specific character of our perceptions, experiences, and thought, as well as to the spatial relations that determine these, is especially well suited for this project.

The situation of theory in this system, then, is problematic. Theory is needed as a means for giving form to and making sense of texts and events, but theory is also limited by its own situatedness in the protean and turbulent system it is supposed to make visible or clear. How can we gain the recognition or understanding, Aristotle's *anagnorisis*, that was to have accompanied the *peripeteia*?[44] The perspective of the foot soldier on the battlefield is rather different from that of the general on the hilltop, and both viewpoints are immeasurably limited when contrasted with the eye of history. The concept of peripety, its fundamental or even its paradoxically essential presence in all historical experience, requires one to approach the present with a sense of irony. Perhaps this is an instance of the time-tested historiographical practice of wait and see, in which one needs to witness the reversal in order to gain that recognition, to experience viscerally the passage from ignorance to knowledge as Aristotle would have it. Through the perspective afforded by theory, we may discern more clearly the characterizing aspects of one's actual situation, only afterward, once these things have resolved into some newly recognized pattern. Or to use Hegel's phrase, which hits the ears as a cloak-and-dagger passcode whispered among coconspirators, the Owl of Minerva flies at dusk.[45] But of course we know that the ultimate end of history, the supreme vantage from which to view all things, is itself a chimera, and we must remain "in the middest," *in mediis rebus*, where the best we can hope for is a sort of tentative or provisional project, developed in connection with a postcontemporary, geocritical theoretical practice: that is, this project involves a recognition of the present *hic et nunc* in its bewildering dynamism, where the peripeties or reversals are taking place. Here one's perspective is grounded in the historical while simultaneously being directed toward a speculative activity that finds each limit as nothing more than a defining boundary of another space beyond. In other words, our experience is entirely bound up with the vocation of theory itself.

Geocritical theory today, whatever else it does, must therefore involve some theory of the imagination, or perhaps a theory of our own lack of imagination. The question will not be, how can we know with absolute certainty the world and our place in it? The project is not epistemic in that sense. Rather the questions will be, how can we tell new and different stories, how can we think the limits of the status quo while projecting alternatives to it? I am thinking partly of the utopian impulse, as in the theories of Ernst Bloch, Herbert Marcuse, or Jameson, and in fact Jameson has suggested at several points in his career that dialectical thought (which is a code word for "theory" itself, properly understood in this way) is really a mode of thinking for the future—that is, the dialectic a specific kind of thought suited to utopia itself.[46] But this intensive meditation on the limits of thought in the present situation is made possible in part by the patient, meticulous study of the texts and theories of the past, seen from the vantage of an imaginative and projective geocriticism. It is something like Deleuze's assessment of Jean-Paul Sartre in 1964, at a moment when the founder of existentialism was starting to be considered rather passé by the younger generation: "Sartre allows us to await some vague future moment, a return, when thought will form again and make its totalities anew, like a power that is at once collective and private. That is why Sartre remains my teacher."[47]

The speculative project, to use a Sartrean term, of postcontemporary critical theory involves the exercise of the imagination, the utopian "scandal of qualitative difference" (as Marcuse called it),[48] and the radical alterity that is made conceptualizable by fantasy or by a fantastic mode, in which the dragons of our imagination mingle with the all-too-real exigencies of our existential experience of the world. Fantasy in this sense is not a means of escape from the world but an engaged mode in which we may critically apprehend the so-called real world. For example, China Miéville points out that under a fairly orthodox understanding of

Marxist theory, the so-called real world represented by a wholly mimetic realism is actually delivering a false picture; Marx's own critique of the political economy revealed how the capitalist mode of production tends to mask the real social relations, as with the commodity, with its "metaphysical subtleties and theological niceties."[49] As Miéville explains, "In a fantastic cultural work, the artist pretends that things known to be impossible are not only possible but real, which creates mental space redefining—or pretending to redefine—the impossible. This is sleight of mind, altering the categories of the not-real. Bearing in mind Marx's point that the real and the not-real are constantly cross-referenced in the productive activity by which humans interact with the world, changing the not-real allows one to think differently about the real, its possibilities and its actualities."[50] Such "sleight of mind" may also be accomplished through critical theory, which examines the all-too-real situation of the present moment and spatial configuration while attempting to detect the traces of some radical alternatives in the transient, shimmering, or oscillatory vistas made possible, as it turns out, by theory. Such fantastic theory is well suited to the uncertainties of the age of globalization, since it is attuned in advance to the peripety inherent in the world system. Like theory itself, as Miéville concludes, "the fantastic . . . is good to think with."[51]

In the present, still-postmodern condition in which the simulacrum all too often turns out to be the real and where authentic fakery trumps the anti-gravitational force field of a carefully commoditized "reality," this fantastic critical theory may serve literary and cultural criticism far better than some of the more properly philosophical or scientific theories, whose aims are ultimately epistemological rather than speculative or projective. An educated and empowered imagination, fundamental to any geocritical practice, is needed to make sense of this dynamic world system and our mobile, protean situations within it. In bracing for the inevitable peripety, geocritical theory today makes possible any recognition of place and its role in a global totality, and an imagination informed by and productive of theory is equally necessary if we are to glimpse possible alternatives.

Notes

1. See Gilles Deleuze and Félix Guattari, *A Thousand Plateaus: Capitalism and Schizophrenia*, trans. Brian Massumi (Minneapolis: University of Minnesota Press, 1987), 381.
2. Frank Kermode, *The Sense of an Ending: Studies in the Theory of Fiction* (Oxford: Oxford University Press, 1967), 7.
3. See Eric Prieto, *Literature, Geography, and the Postmodern Poetics of Place* (New York: Palgrave Macmillan, 2013), 1–2.
4. Kermode, *The Sense of an Ending*, 3.
5. See, e.g., Dara Downey, Ian Kinane, and Elizabeth Parker, eds., *Landscapes of Liminality: Between Space and Place* (Lanham, MD: Rowman & Littlefield International, 2016).

6. On "cartographic anxiety," see Derek Gregory, *Geographical Imaginations* (Oxford: Blackwell, 1994), 72–73; see also Edward W. Soja, *Postmodern Geographies: The Reassertion of Space in Critical Social Theory* (London: Verso, 1989).

7. Martin Heidegger, *Being and Time*, trans. John Macquarrie and Edward Robinson (New York: Harper & Row, 1962), 233.

8. Yi-Fu Tuan, *Space and Place: The Perspective of Experience* (Minneapolis: University of Minnesota Press, 1977), 3.

9. Michel Foucault, "Of Other Spaces," trans. Jay Miskowiec, *Diacritics* 16 (Spring 1986): 22.

10. Tuan, *Space and Place*, 6.

11. Ibid., 161–162.

12. See Bertrand Westphal, *Geocriticism: Real and Fictional Spaces*, trans. Robert T. Tally Jr. (New York: Palgrave Macmillan, 2011), 41–43.

13. Deleuze and Guattari, *A Thousand Plateaus*, 380–381.

14. Siegfried Kracauer, *History: The Last Things before the Last*, ed. Paul Oskar Kristeller (Oxford: Oxford University Press, 1969), 211.

15. Ibid., 213.

16. Ibid., 216–217.

17. See Louis Marin, *Utopics: Spatial Play*, trans. Robert A. Vollrath (Atlantic Highlands, NJ: Humanities Press, 1984), 12.

18. See Northrop Frye, *The Educated Imagination* (Bloomington: Indiana University Press, 1964).

19. Such is the title of the famous, influential, and recently terminated Duke University Press book series edited by Stanley Fish and Fredric Jameson.

20. Aristotle may be conflating two messengers from Sophocles's play: one from Corinth who announces the "good news" that Oedipus's parents (i.e., his adopted parents) had died a natural death and that therefore Oedipus could not kill his own father, and the other who confirms the old shepherd's narrative, which explains how, as a newborn baby, Oedipus was saved from death and spirited far away from his biological parents.

21. Aristotle, *The Poetics*, trans. Malcolm Heath (New York: Penguin, 1996), section XI.3.

22. Fredric Jameson, *Marxism and Form: Twentieth-Century Dialectical Theories of Literature* (Princeton, NJ: Princeton University Press, 1971), 309.

23. Ibid., 310. More recently in *Valences of the Dialectic*, Jameson uses an example better suited to an age of economic globalization by looking at the "reversals" evident in India's role in the modern world system in the late twentieth century—that is, as Jameson explains, the seemingly negative (from the point of view of Western capitalism), Soviet-style policies of Jawaharlal Nehru in the 1960s led to the formation of technical institutes, thus creating a generation of well-educated workers perfectly suited to the (positive) outsourcing booms of the 1990s. But the dot-com bust (negative) facilitated the cheaper employment of outsourced Indian labor (positive). Such dialectical reversals remain part of the geopolitical and economic history of the present. See Fredric Jameson, *Valences of the Dialectic* (London: Verso, 2009), 40–41. More bizarre still, at least for some readers, is Jameson's argument about how Walmart's production and distribution networks form a model for utopian practice— peripety indeed! (see *Valences*, 411–433).

24. See Terry Eagleton, *After Theory* (New York: Basic Books, 2003); Ian Hunter, "The History of Theory," *Critical Inquiry* 33, no. 1 (Autumn 2006): 78–112; and François Cusset, *French Theory: How Foucault, Derrida, Deleuze, & Co. Transformed the Intellectual Life of the*

United States, trans. Jeff Fort (Minneapolis: University of Minnesota Press, 2008). For a pro-theory and Marxist response to Hunter's essay, see Fredric Jameson, "How Not to Historicize Theory," *Critical Inquiry* 34, no. 3 (Spring 2008): 563–582.

25. See Fredric Jameson, *The Hegel Variations: On the Phenomenology of Spirit* (London: Verso, 2010) and *Representing Capital: A Reading of Volume One* (London: Verso, 2011). For his comments on the forthcoming volumes in the six-volume Poetics of Social Forms study, see Maria Cevasco, "Imagining a Space That Is Outside: An Interview with Fredric Jameson," *minnesota review* 78 (2012): 89. The third volume in the project but the fourth published is *The Antinomies of Realism* (London: Verso, 2013); the remaining two will address allegory and myth, respectively.

26. See Deleuze's comment in Michel Foucault, "Intellectuals and Power: A Conversation between Michel Foucault and Gilles Deleuze," in *Language, Counter-Memory, Practice*, ed. Donald Bouchard (Ithaca, NY: Cornell University Press), 208.

27. Terry Eagleton, *Literary Theory: An Introduction*, 2nd ed. (Minneapolis: University of Minnesota Press, 1996), ix.

28. Jameson, *Valences of the Dialectic*, 290.

29. On this matter, please see my *Utopia in the Age of Globalization: Space, Representation, and the World System* (New York: Palgrave Macmillan, 2013).

30. A different, earlier version of this section appears as "Until the Dragon Comes: Geocriticism and the Prospects of Comparative Literature," *Inquire: Journal of Comparative Literature* 3, no. 2 (Fall 2013), http://inquire.streetmag.org/articles/125.

31. See my *Spatiality* (London: Routledge, 2013).

32. Gayatri Chakravorty Spivak, *Death of a Discipline* (New York: Columbia University Press, 2003), 92.

33. Bertrand Westphal, *Geocriticism: Real and Fictional Spaces*, trans. Robert T. Tally Jr. (New York: Palgrave Macmillan, 2011), 127.

34. See Eric Prieto, *Literature, Geography, and the Postmodern Poetics of Place* (New York: Palgrave Macmillan, 2013).

35. See Bertrand Westphal, *The Plausible World: A Geocritical Approach to Space, Place, and Maps*, trans. Amy Wells (New York: Palgrave Macmillan, 2013).

36. Yi-Fu Tuan, *Space and Place: The Perspective of Experience* (Minneapolis: University of Minnesota Press, 1997), 161–162.

37. See Joseph Frank, *The Idea of Spatial Form* (New Brunswick, NJ: Rutgers University Press, 1991).

38. See Edward W. Soja, *Thirdspace: Journeys to Los Angeles and Other Real-and-Imagined Places* (Oxford: Blackwell, 1996).

39. Spivak, *Death of a Discipline*, 73.

40. J. R. R. Tolkien, "Beowulf: The Monsters and the Critics," in *The Monsters and the Critics and Other Essays*, ed. Christopher Tolkien (New York: HarperCollins, 2006), 47–48.

41. See Tolkien, "On Fairy-Stories," in *The Monsters and the Critics and Other Essays*, ed. Christopher Tolkien (New York: HarperCollins, 2006), 135; see also Fredric Jameson, *Archaeologies of the Future: The Desire Called Utopia and Other Science Fictions* (London: Verso, 2005), 63–64.

42. For a perspicacious analysis of this post–Cold War moment, see Phillip E. Wegner's excellent *Life between Two Deaths, 1989–2001: U.S. Culture in the Long Nineties*.

43. Fredric Jameson, "Interview with Xudong Zhang," in *Jameson on Jameson: Conversations on Cultural Marxism*, ed. Ian Buchanan (Durham, NC: Duke University Press, 2007), 194.

44. For Jameson's own extended analysis of the Aristotelian poetics in connection to the valences of history, see *Valences of the Dialectic*, 551–612.

45. See G. W. F. Hegel, *Hegel's Philosophy of Right*, trans. T. M. Knox (Oxford: Oxford University Press, 1967), 13.

46. See, e.g., Jameson, "Interview with Xudong Zhang," 194.

47. Gilles Deleuze, *Desert Islands and Other Texts, 1953–1974*, ed. David Lapoujade, trans. Michael Taormina (New York: Semiotext[e], 2004), 79.

48. See Herbert Marcuse, "The End of Utopia," trans. J. Shapiro and S. Weber, in *Five Lectures: Psychoanalysis, Politics, and Utopia* (Boston, MA: Beacon Press, 1970).

49. Karl Marx, *Capital, Capital: A Critique of Political Economy*, vol. 1, trans. Samuel Moore and Edward Aveling (New York: Random House, 1906), 81.

50. China Miéville, "Editorial Introduction," *Symposium: Marxism and Fantasy*, in *Historical Materialism* 10, no. 4 (2002): 45–46.

51. Ibid., 46.

Part II
Spatial Representation in Narrative

4   The Mise en Abyme of Literary Cartography

JORGE LUIS BORGES's "Of Exactitude in Science" is among the most recognizable, even canonical, texts in spatiality studies. At once elegiac and absurd, the fragment—or more specifically, a complete text conceived of and presented as a fragment from a larger narrative—makes reference to an imaginary empire in which the passion for mimetic accuracy in mapmaking had reached its zenith with the creation of the ultimate chart of the imperial territory, drawn up according to a one-to-one scale. Citing a fictional source (Suárez Miranda, *Viajes de varones prudentes*, Libro IV, Cap. XLV, Lérida, 1658), Borges writes:

> In that Empire, the Art of Cartography attained such Perfection that the map of a single Province occupied the entirety of a City, and the map of the Empire, the entirety of a Province. In time, those Unconscionable Maps no longer satisfied, and the Cartographers Guilds struck a Map of the Empire whose size was that of the Empire, and which coincided point for point with it. The following Generations, who were not so fond of the Study of Cartography as their Forebears had been, saw that that vast Map was Useless, and not without some Pitilessness was it, that they delivered it up to the Inclemencies of Sun and Winters. In the Deserts of the West, still today, there are Tattered Ruins of that Map, inhabited by Animals and Beggars; in all the Land there is no other Relic of the Disciplines of Geography.[1]

Borges's story of a map coextensive with its territory has become a haunting reminder of the absurdity of the quest for "exactitude" in cartography. Much earlier, in his *Sylvie and Bruno Concluded*, Lewis Carroll produced a more humorous version of the story while making a similar point about the exactitude of this science. After boasting of his countrymen's skill in making a map "on the scale of *a mile to the mile*," Mein Herr concedes that it has never actually been spread out and used. "The farmers objected: they said it would cover the whole country, and shut out the sunlight. So now we use the country itself, as its own map, and I assure you it does nearly as well."[2] The cheerful absurdity of this vision, along with the more melancholy tone of Borges's fable, has been famously reproduced in Jean Baudrillard's conception of late-twentieth-century hyperreality, in which the simulacrum precedes the reality it was supposed to mimic and the map precedes and engenders the territory it is supposed to depict.[3] In his own variation on the theme of the map coextensive with the territory it purports to represent, the contemporary fantasist Neil Gaiman has extracted a more distinctively literary lesson from these parables, asserting that "One describes a tale best by telling the tale. You see? . . . The tale is the map which is the territory."[4]

From the perspective of the geographical sciences, these speculations over the perfectly mimetic representation of territorial space in a map are, quite rightly, amusing absurdities, thought experiments that remind us that all representation is figurative, metaphorical, or allegorical. With respect to literary cartography, such reminders are surely unnecessary, for the act of writing presupposes multiple acts of figuration. The writer is intensely aware that, as Friedrich Nietzsche has observed, "truth" is but "a mobile army of metaphors, metonyms, and anthropomorphisms."[5] It is not just that a perfectly accurate map would also be perfectly useless; it is clear that such a map is neither possible nor desirable. Like the cartographer, the storyteller creates a representation of the world presented in the work, but this representation cannot be a simple reflection of the "real" world in a more figurative form. One does not, as the saying goes, merely hold up a mirror to reality. As with the mise en abyme, any reflection will presuppose further reflections, and the effort to describe the persons, places, events, and so on will inevitably shape them. For instance, one lesson of Borges's parable is that the narrative seems to trump the image; just as scraps of maps litter the territory they had once been intended to represent, so the stories about them proliferate and find new meanings long after the "exact" map's static image was set down. They are now part of its history and part of the landscape, which are now altered, as the entire domain is marked as one in which maps and their remnants are themselves mobile but persistent geographical features. The territory is not necessarily the map or vice versa, but the maps and the territories disclose themselves to be constitutive of one another.

In *Maps of the Imagination*, which is a guide for creative writers as well as a beautiful meditation on the theory and practice of literary cartography, Peter Turchi identifies two distinct but overlapping activities that together make possible an effective "map" for the reader. These are *exploration*, understood as "some combination of premeditated searching and undisciplined, perhaps only partly conscious rambling," and *presentation*, the deliberate creation of "a document meant to communicate with, and have an effect on, others."[6] Although they do not necessarily align perfectly, I believe that this distinction maps well onto that made between *narrative* and *description* in Georg Lukács's well-known essay "Narrate or Describe," even if Lukács's point was primarily to identify the *differentia specifica* between what he took to be a socially useful form of realism and a politically crippling naturalism.[7] The productive tension between these two modes characterizes any literary cartography, which must negotiate, or rather navigate, between the need to advance a plot (thus acceding to a relentlessly temporal register) and the equally pressing imperative to pause, which not only allows the literary cartographer to depict the spaces under consideration but also, in the view of geographer Yi-Fu Tuan, summons into existence the "place" itself, making it subject to apprehension and interpretation.[8] That is, a place does not become a "place" at all until it has distinguished itself from the undifferentiated spaces of which it is a part, and places are invested with significance only by being noticed "in the first place." In telling a story, one necessarily projects an itinerary and paints a picture, and both of these aspects of storytelling in turn shape the world that unfolds. The rivalry between text and image, narrative and description, is thus shown to be both false and inevitable, as the literary cartographers simultaneously create and represent the territories as they map them.

In these reflections and projections on literary cartography in this chapter, I will examine the concomitant activities of exploration and presentation in three exemplary scenes from world literature. Obviously, the list could be extended almost infinitely, even within the highly canonical "great books" tradition from which I have drawn here. It cannot be entirely accidental that the narratives I have in mind happen to coincide with the three great odysseys identified by the poet and postmodernist Charles Olson, who saw in Homer's *Odyssey*, Dante's *Commedia*, and Herman Melville's *Moby-Dick* the three discontinuous stages of the development of "Western man," the "central quality" of which is "*search*."[9] In my estimation, these scenes are somehow representative of three distinctive aspects of the literary cartographic project: namely, the world-making effects of a narrator's presentation, as the itinerary of the individual explorer becomes a map of the world; the abstract or architectonic system that undergirds such a created world, as the geography is shown to conform to a logic in order to demonstrate its "truth"; and finally the intensely reflexive character of the project, as the mapmaker cannot help but be marked by the cartographic endeavor.

These three features do not in any way constitute an exhaustive inventory, as if such a thing were possible. Turchi's guidebook devotes seven chapters to what he takes to be the distinctive elements of a creative writer's literary cartography, and each of them may be subdivided into various categories. But these scenes are evocative of that mise en abyme into which spatial representations in literature inevitably place us, where the contours of the map melt into the distinctive features of the landscape, which in turn shape our own perceptions and narratives, and so on. Along with Odysseus, Dante, and Ahab, we find ourselves on the brink of a great abyss, whose recursively reflecting reflections generate new visions, projecting potentially alternative arrangements by simultaneously mapping the territory and territorializing the maps.

Odysseus the Bard

Toward the middle of the *Odyssey*, there is a striking scene in which the narrative shifts dramatically from an almost literally Olympian point of view to a first-person account.[10] Although his true identity remains unknown to his gracious hosts, Odysseus enjoys a banquet in the court of the Phaeacians, where he applauds the skills of Demodocus, a blind bard, and begs him to tell the tale of the Trojan Horse. In praising the singer, Odysseus specifically highlights his gift for verisimilitude: "I respect you, Demodocus, more than any man alive— / surely the Muse has taught you, Zeus' daughter, / or god Apollo himself. How true to life, / all too true . . . you sing the Achaeans' fate" (8.546–549, ellipsis in original). So sad, beautiful, and above all realistic is the bard's skillfully told story that Odysseus breaks down in tears. Noticing his guest's distress, King Alcinous then calls for Demodocus to rest, before inviting the stranger to recount his own history: "But come, my friend, / tell us your own story now, and tell it truly. / Where have your rovings forced you? / What lands have you seen, what sturdy towns, / what men themselves?" (8.642–646). Book 9 of the *Odyssey* thus begins, "Odysseus, the great teller of tales, launched out on his story," and for the most part Books 9 through 12 will be the first-person narrative of Odysseus. The epic hero has been transformed for these sections into a bard.

Odysseus takes this role as seriously as any duty to which a warrior or king would be bound. Like any storyteller, he first attempts to organize his plot: "Well then, what shall I go through first, / what shall I save for last?" (9.15–16). Straightforwardly enough, it seems, he opts to begin by naming himself[11] before recounting the events that befell him in chronological order, from the fall of Troy up to his time with Calypso in Ogygia. In presenting a narrative of his adventures, Odysseus establishes a literary cartography of the Mediterranean world, identifying places and regions but also enlarging the known world through narrative. Is it merely coincidental that the tales Odysseus himself tells in these books include many of the most famous scenes in the epic? The Lotus-eaters, the Cyclops, Aeolus, the Laestrygonians, Circe, the visit to the underworld (along with its memorable conversations with Tiresias, Anticleia, Agamemnon, and Achilles), the Sirens, Scylla and Charybdis, the cattle of the sun—these are unquestionably some of the most memorable scenes in the *Odyssey*, if not all of world literature. Odysseus's tale, "told once, and told so clearly" (12.491), not only sketches the simultaneously mythic and real geography of his world but also fills it in with populations, places, and events. Homer's *Odyssey* already does this, of course, but the scene of the telling, in which the adventurer himself becomes the bard whose song concerns the exploits of the adventurer, underscores the productive tension between exploration and presentation, opening a vista into the mise en abyme of its literary cartography.

Myth, which is to say also plot or narrative (in Greek, *mythos*), is a means by which human beings make sense of and give form to the world. In representing the spaces of the world, narratives help to shape those spaces into meaningful places and forms. The bard, a surveyor of space and a rhapsode whose rhapsody brings disparate places into cognizable relations to one another, thus actively creates the world in which his stories unfold, and these places become "real" to the extent that the stories draw them into the intelligible universe of the narrative. Etymologically, the rhapsode is one who weaves or sews, stitching together various songs or stories. In a like manner, the rhapsode connects places; the rhapsody produces a map through the carefully arranged weaving together of discrete spatial representations, which in turn forms a new, enlarged, and more diverse image. By becoming a bard in these sections of the *Odyssey*, Odysseus shapes both the narrative and the world in which it unfolds.

In his study of Herodotus's *Histories*, François Hartog notes that any such narrative is the result of both the geographical project of the *surveyor* and the meticulously synthetic processes of a *rhapsode*, a seamster or seamstress who stitches together disparate parts into a whole.[12] For Hartog, the narrator of these texts becomes, seemingly by turns but also coexisting in mutually reinforcing roles, a surveyor of spaces, a rhapsode who sews these spaces into a new unity, and a bard who ultimately "invents" the world so surveyed and assembled. Hartog writes that "the narrator is thus a surveyor and, in a number of senses, a rhapsode, but he is also a bard, in that the inventory of the *oikoumene* cannot fail to be an invention of the world, if only by reason of the use of the space of language, for correlations exist between 'the order of the discourse' and the order of the world." As Herodotus produced "his inventory of distant peoples and border territories," asks Hartog, "did he not invent the *oikoumene* and set the human world in order? The space of the narrative purports to be a representation of the world and he, the rhapsode, is the one who *eidea semainei*, who indicates the forms, who makes things seen, who reveals; he is the one who knows."[13] Clearly, such knowledge derives from the survey of the spaces and the rhapsodic stitching together of these places, but it is also made possible by the bard's singing. That is, the literary cartography that renders the world a knowable place emerges from the formation and presentation of the narrative itself.

According to this view, narrative is not just a form of representation but a form of world making, which in the end may turn out to be the same thing. As the storytellers survey the territory they wish to describe, they weave together disparate elements in order to produce the narrative, and these elements may include scraps of other narratives, descriptions of people or places, images derived from firsthand observation as well as from secondary reports, legends, myths, and inventions of the imagination. In producing this *bricolage* or patchwork representation of a world, the bard also invents or discovers the world presented in the narrative. For readers, this narrative conjures into being a more or less useful image of the spaces depicted, much like that of a map, and the literary cartography presented in one narrative can become a part of future surveys, rhapsodies, and narratives—that is, the scraps of images and stories arranged by the skillful bard form the substance of future narrative maps. Thus have Odysseus's wanderings become so integral to the discourses of Western civilization (among others) that the very word *odyssey* can transcend its original Mediterranean space and apply with equal force to any peripatetic adventure whatsoever and wheresoever. But again, many of the most memorable adventures from Homer's *Odyssey* are those surveyed, stitched together, and brought into a sort of spatiotemporal whole by the rhapsode Odysseus in his elaborate presentation before the Phaeacian assembly.

The *oikoumene* made visible, made real even, by Homer's or Odysseus's narrative is, in a sense, part of a historical plenum, a literary world filled with stories to be stitched together in various ways and with various effect, but which all appear to fit within a cognizable totality. This is what Lukács referred to when he characterized the age of the epic in terms of "closed" (*geschlossene*) civilizations in *The Theory of the Novel*.[14] In theory this also explains why various stories may be pieced together in such different ways, with some seemingly significant stories left out entirely and others placed in the foreground. The notorious absence of the Trojan horse from Homer's *Iliad* is a shock to many modern readers, but just because the world of the ancient Greek epic contained that tale in no way required this particular epic to include the episode. Aristotle, in *The Poetics*, rightly praises Homer for recognizing that the unity of a plot does not involve the exhaustive account of a single character's career: "In composing the *Odyssey* he did not include all the adventures of Odysseus—such as his wound on Parnassus, or his feigned madness at the mustering of the host—incidents between which there was no necessary or probable connection; but he made the *Odyssey*, and likewise the *Iliad*, to center round an action that in our sense of the word is one."[15]

Similarly, what Lukács considers the *Lebenstotalität* of the classical epic makes available to the rhapsode the spatial form that, among other things, allows for virtually any entry point in a given narrative to be as valid as any other. The classic epic begins in medias res, but as Edward W. Said astutely observed some time ago, this is merely "a convention that burdens the beginning with the pretense that it is not one."[16] Obviously, chronology alone—in some unilinear, rigid, and untheorized version of this or that "In the beginning" genesis leading to an absolute, unchanging, and ineluctable telos—has never dictated the form of narrative, and even if the storyteller wishes, naturally enough, to employ chronology as a structuring device, the vicissitudes of time tend to thwart the effort again and again. Odysseus, for example, wonders where to begin, and in stating his name ("I am Odysseus, son of Laertes, known to the world / for every kind of craft"), he immediately shifts to his homeland and its distinctive geography (9.21–32), before mentioning that Calypso had delayed his return to Ithaca. Only then does he launch out on his apparent chronicle of events leading from the beaches of Troy to Calypso's arms, but this chronological account makes little sense without the knowledge of the before and after. As Lukács puts it, "The way Homer's epics begin in the middle and do not finish at the end is a reflexion of the truly epic mentality's total indifference to any form of architectural construction."[17] Moreover, the persistence of fate and the unaccountable whims of the gods ensure that, whatever twists and turns the adventurer might take, a larger, supra-individual structure or system determines the shape of the adventure. The rhapsode or bard, god-like, also gives shape to these seemingly disparate, autonomous, or unrelated elements, sewing them together into a form that, much like a map, can then be used to make sense of the world. In other words, Odysseus-the-hero's Mediterranean itinerary becomes a somewhat more totalizing map in the transformative rhapsody of Odysseus-the-bard.[18]

This in turn makes possible new visions as well. Referring to James Joyce's *Ulysses*, perhaps the most elaborate reinvention of Homer's epic in modern literature, Fredric Jameson has observed that "it is not the meaning of the *Odyssey* which is exploited here, but rather its spatial properties. The *Odyssey* serves as a *map*: it is indeed, on Joyce's reading of it, the one classical narrative whose closure is that of the map of a whole complete and equally closed region of the globe, as though somehow the very episodes themselves merged back into space, and the reading of them came to be indistinguishable from map-reading."[19] In apprehending the world of the *Odyssey* in its totality as a spatial form, the modernist artifice becomes a representational mode suited to the far more complex geopolitical system in the twentieth century.[20] The map, like the narrative, is ultimately a means of making sense of the world it depicts, which is why both have such persistent value as tools of knowledge.

At the core of his being as an epic hero, Odysseus thirsts for knowledge and experience, which he can then incorporate into his stories or maps. Mark how it is in the famous episode with the Sirens. Following Circe's counsel, Odysseus has each member of his crew plug their ears with beeswax so that they will not succumb to the Siren song. However, Odysseus cannot allow himself to miss the experience; he orders that he be lashed to the mast, with his ears left unblocked, and he therefore goes through the excruciating torment of the Sirens' deadly, alluring call. Yet because he has done this, Odysseus alone among his crew can describe the song and its effects. His knowledge makes possible a story, and this story in turn is incorporated into the mythical substance of classical literary geography.[21]

The rhapsode creates the world as he or she explores it, but that does not necessarily make the world "true." Odysseus is best known for his trickster cunning, his ingenuity, and his inventiveness, and not infrequently these traits are displayed in his deliberate falsehoods. Although Athena clearly approves of Odysseus's deceits, which are after all signs of intelligence and thus serve to honor the goddess of wisdom, the morality of a subsequent epoch would condemn him. Knowing the facts but delivering the lie may have baleful consequences. We recall that when Dante encounters him in Hell, Odysseus (or Ulysses) is consigned to the infernal *malebolgia* reserved for fraudulent counselors.[22] Encased in flame, the epic hero there takes over the bard's role once again, telling of another journey beyond Ithaca and past the Pillars of Hercules. Eventually, as Ulysses recounts in this narrative, he comes within view of Mount Purgatory—a place where sins may presumably be cleansed—but before Ulysses can reach it, he, his ship, and all its crew are swallowed into a great whirlpool, a modern Charybdis from which he cannot escape (*Inferno* XXVI.112–142). The story told by Dante's Ulysses involves a greatly expanded geographical range, not only enlarging the Mediterranean *oikoumene* by venturing out across the River Ocean, but enlarging the scope of literary cartography to include a highly structured moral geography.

Dante's Geography Lesson

The *Odyssey* presents a map of the classical Mediterranean world, establishing for the Homeric epic the entire *oikoumene* to be represented. Dante's *Commedia* expands the purview of its literary mapmaking to the decidedly otherworldly spaces of the Hereafter, but it does so according to a rigorously logical, as well as an elaborately poetic, plan. If Odysseus's considered narrative of his own wanderings can be viewed as emblematic of the productive tension between exploration and presentation in any attempt at literary cartography, then the grand architectonic structure developed by Dante, who is also both the adventurer in and the singer of the canticles, enlarges and refines the cartographic project. Where Odysseus combined personal experience, cunning, and a gift for storytelling (or lying) to weave together the spaces of his world into a recognizable unity that can then become a source of knowledge of that world, Dante draws on an impersonal, transcendent, and well-nigh scientific ordering of imaginary geographies to establish a "truer" map.

The distinction between Dante-the-poet and Dante-the-pilgrim is more clearly defined than that between Odysseus-the-hero and Odysseus "the great teller of tales," who is, after all, still experiencing his adventures among the Phaeacians even as he plays the role of bard. In his poetic exploration of the otherworldly realms, Dante registers his knowledge as the expert architect of these places while simultaneously exploring them in the guise of the relatively naive traveler. Thus the wary pilgrim, like the reader, is exposed to the most wondrous and bizarre experiences as he moves through the various levels of the afterlife, while the poet reflects on the adventures, given his privileged spatiotemporal position in a here and now as opposed to the there and then. But the poet also maintains the godlike role of the creator of these domains, one who fabricates, orders, and arranges the spaces and events encountered by the wandering hero. The very arrangement of the *Commedia* into three canticles, comprising one hundred cantos, with a *terza rima* scheme mirrors the moral and geographical formations of the realms themselves. At one point in the *Inferno*, the travelers pause to discuss this moral geography, allowing the pilgrim, as well as the reader, to see what the poet is doing.

Beginning with canto 3, with its famously ominous inscription (*Lasciate ogne speranza, voi ch'intrate*) on the gates, Dante and Virgil move rapidly through the circles of Hell. Nearly each canto of the *Inferno* covers an entire circle of the upper level, respectively, such that by the end of the tenth canto, out of thirty-four total, the adventurers have already explored six of the nine circles of Hell. Canto 11 thus stands out in dramatic contrast, for all forward momentum of the journey draws to a halt as Virgil and Dante are forced to pause, overwhelmed by the infernal atmosphere.[23] In this canto, the characters' itinerary through the underworld pauses, but the narrative itself does not. While the pilgrim Dante does not explore the Sixth Circle further or interview any new souls in this section, he does profit by gaining a valuable lesson in the spatial and moral geography of the place. Perched almost literally on the edge of the abyss—that is, peering down from the Sixth Circle of Hell into the Seventh, Eighth, and Ninth Circles below—Virgil explains how the entire geography of Hell is organized according to a strictly logical, divine plan.

Although geographical features play important roles throughout the *Inferno*, including rivers, lakes, forests, valleys, cliffs, and the like, the geography lesson here relies on a broader theory of ethics. Virgil begins by sketching the geographical or geometric diagram for Dante but quickly shifts to a moral register as he describes the territories through which they must travel: "My son, / within these boulders' bounds are three more circles, / concentrically arranged like those above, / all tightly packed with souls; and so that, later, / the sight of them alone will be enough, / I'll tell you how and why they are imprisoned" (XI.16–21). Virgil explains that sins of violence and of fraud are far more hateful in the eyes of Heaven than the sins of incontinence or the underregulation of the appetites, which are themselves natural and therefore not evil. Thus, while the lustful, gluttonous, slothful, wrathful, and the avaricious Dante and Virgil had previously encountered are justly punished, often in horrifying ways, their sins are not as grievous as those below (see XI.67–90). The Seventh Circle, which is itself subdivided into three rings, contains those whose violence against themselves, against others, or against God condemns them to their memorable punishments. The poet's principle of *contrapasso*, in this circle as elsewhere, sees to it that the punishments fit the crimes in a more or less reasonable manner. Virgil explains that "since fraud belongs exclusively to man, / God hates it more" (XI.25–26), so the Eighth and Ninth Circles contains the souls of various types of the fraudulent, with a major division between so-called lesser and great fraud, defined primarily by a fiduciary duty owed to the victim of the fraudulent activity (XI.52–54), marked topographically by another steep drop into the well of the Ninth Circle. The greater complexity of these levels—the ten discrete *bolgias* of Circle 8 and the four distinctive zones of Circle 9—reflect the nuance and subtlety of such sins. Thus without direct reference to the various topographical features to be encountered along the way, Virgil lays out a kind of moral geography of lower Hell.

For all the philosophical abstraction that comes with using the *Nicomachean Ethics*, leavened with Thomist theology, to organize the infernal domains, the intensely physical or corporeal aspects of this scene are all the more noteworthy. The whole reason that Virgil and Dante have paused at the edge of the Seventh Circle, and thus the reason they have time to engage in this lesson in moral geography, is that the foul smells emanating from that region prevented them from going further. Canto 10 had ended with the travelers walking "a path / that strikes into a vale, whose stench arose, / disgusting us as high up as we were" (X.134–136). At the brink of the next circle, "the disgusting overflow of stench / the deep abyss was vomiting forced us / back from the edge," and Virgil states that "Our descent will have to be delayed somewhat / so that our sense of smell may grow accustomed / to these vile fumes" (XI.4–6, 10–12). This noisome zone carries allegorical import, no doubt indicating the degree to which the sins of violence and fraud are far more obnoxious than the previously encountered sins of the appetites or even heresy (not that the sinners in those regions were enjoying a walk in the park, of course). But the physicality of the moral geography is itself a sign of the merger of theory and practice in Dante's literary cartography. Hell, like the *Inferno*, is laid out according to a strictly logical plan, but it is experienced viscerally. The grander abstractions that make possible the architectonic of Dante's carefully ordered afterlife territories are accompanied by the all-too-concrete, corporeal, and sensual experiences of the itinerant subject moving through these realms. While they may at times be viewed as competing modes, the presentation and the exploration of these narratives spaces combine to render the literary cartography meaningful.

The abstract yet corporeal experience of canto 11 indicates a sort of dialectical advance in the literary cartography of the epic. Whereas Odysseus's wanderings furnished the raw materials for the rhapsode to stitch together into a new whole, Dante's itinerary is largely restricted by the predetermined, logical structure of the territories through which he travels. As with the *Odyssey*, there is still danger and uncertainty, but the literary mapmaking now relies on an impersonal, supra-individual, or even objective body of knowledge to determine its "truth." In Lukács's history of epic forms, this represents a powerful break from the earlier epic tradition and a distinctive move in the direction of modern novel:

> Dante is the only great example in which we see the architectural clearly conquering the organic, and therefore he represents a historico-philosophical transition from the pure epic to the novel. In Dante there is still the perfect immanent distancelessness and completeness of the true epic, but his figures are already individuals, consciously and energetically placing themselves in opposition to a reality that is becoming closed to them, individuals who, through this opposition become real personalities. The constituent principle of Dante's totality is a highly systematic one, abolishing the epic independence of the organic part-unities and transforming them into hierarchically ordered, autonomous parts.[24]

In Lukács's view, the epic *Commedia* is already verging on the epistemological and social form of the novel insofar as it registers the fissure between soul and world, or to put it in other words, between the perceiving or experiencing subject and the global totality or world system. Ironically, perhaps, for such an important religious poem, this is not unlike the technological or scientific developments in the history of cartography.

Another modern (or postmodern) example might be useful in this context. In his elaboration of cognitive mapping, which he took to be an existential and political strategy for coming to grips with the alienating spatial anxiety of the postmodern condition, Jameson illustrates his point by examining similarly cartographic practices from earlier historical epochs.[25] This "digression on cartography" starts by looking at the ancient itineraries or portolan charts, which in effect were "diagrams organized around the still-subject-centered or existential journey of the traveler, along which various significant key features are marked." With the advent of a more abstract philosophical mindset, as well as a certain scientific method aided by such technical developments as the use of a compass or sextant, mapping introduces a new element, "the relationship to the totality," which will "require the coordination of existential data (the empirical position of the subject) with unlived, abstract conceptions of the geographic totality."[26] Although the Aristotelian ethical order and late-medieval Catholic moral theory are not what we would normally associate with technological or scientific advances in geography and astronomy, Dante's literary cartography in the *Inferno* does just this, as it coordinates the pilgrim's supernatural itinerary with an abstract totality that ultimately shapes the entire terrestrial (and celestial) space and furnishes its significance through the interactions of the individual traveler's experience and the objective reality, whose contours are essentially guaranteed by "Divine Omnipotence . . . and Highest Wisdom joined with Primal Love" (III.5–6). For Dante this vision can therefore be "true."

Jameson continues to a third stage, just after Dante's era but still well before the postmodern epoch in which mapmaking abandons all hope of achieving the sort of true maps that Borges's imperial cartographers dreamed of. With the advent of the first terrestrial globe in 1490 and the subsequent Mercator projection, "a third dimension of cartography emerges," which occasions a practical crisis of representation with respect to what Jameson calls "the unresolvable (well-nigh Heisenbergian) dilemma of the transfer of curved space to flat charts." It is at this point when the "naively" mimetic maps—that is, those in which cartographers have honestly attempted to depict the figured space as realistically as possible—are proven to be entirely impossible; indeed, they are no longer particularly desirable as even their ultimate use value comes increasingly into question. Maps based on the Mercator projection, for instance, dramatically distort the spaces presented, grotesquely aggrandizing spaces further from the equator such that—to use the familiar image—a place like Greenland can appear to be about the same size as South America, when in fact it occupies less than one-sixth of the area. However, during the Age of Discovery and subsequently, such maps became much more useful for navigators plotting courses over long distances, since it allowed them to make use of straight lines on a two-dimensional chart that figuratively represented the curvilinear space of a three-dimensional planet. Following this development and others like it, it rapidly becomes apparent that there can be no "true maps," but it also becomes clear that "there can be scientific progress, or better still, a dialectical advance, in the various moments of mapmaking."[27] Jameson asserts that this moment represents a watershed in the history of mapmaking, as the impossibility and undesirability of perfectly mimetic maps opens up the possibility of better and more useful maps, maps which are, it may be added, by design expressly figurative or metaphorical.

The rise of cartography in the fifteenth and sixteenth centuries coincides with these practical and philosophical developments, but the medieval world of Dante's *Commedia* formed an important and indispensable precursor. As Ricardo Padrón has observed, the fascination of Renaissance artists with drawing maps of Dante's Hell owes much to the apparently cartographic nature of the *Inferno* itself. In Padron's view, "The *Inferno* clearly suggests that Hell is an orderly, well-bounded space, however vague and contradictory it may be about the details or size, proportion, distance, and location. Spaces of this sort seem like they should be visible, and therefore suggest that they might be mappable."[28] However, literary cartography as literature undoubtedly troubles the sense of certainty or of abstract reasoning implied by geographical science or cartographic exactitude, and Dante's multivalence vision with its four distinctive registers of meaning (literal, moral, allegorical, and anagogical) makes trouble for any too facile representation of the otherworldly spaces. Whereas mapping may require "visibility, stasis, hierarchy, and control," writes Padrón, "Literature often works to subvert these things. It has us experience space and place in myriad ways that have little to do with mapping it, just as it has us experience time in many ways that cannot be measured by a clock."[29]

The logical, hierarchical, and almost scientific vision of Dante's literary cartography must succumb to the spatiotemporal vicissitudes of a "world abandoned by God," as Lukács memorably called it, in an age "in which the extensive totality of life is no longer directly given, in which the immanence of meaning in life has become a problem."[30] In such an epoch, the age of the novel,[31] the literary cartography of the world system cannot help but reflect the interiority of the mapmaker. The mise n abyme of the map takes on new meanings as the cartographer him- or herself becomes subject to deterritorializations and reterritorializations. In that situation, world making of the ancient rhapsode and the structured totality of the architectonic are destabilized as the oscillating subjectivity of the mapmaker and the subject of the map call into question the accuracy of the literary representation. But then this uncertain situation also makes possible infinitely new and different maps.

Ahab and His Chart

It seems fitting that so major a work of literary cartography as *Moby-Dick* would include a chapter entitled "The Chart."[32] The narrator himself, a chapter later, insists on its significance to the novel as a whole: "So far as what there may be of a narrative in this book, . . . the foregoing chapter, in its earlier part, is as important a one as will be found."[33] It depicts a scene that takes place shortly after Ahab's dramatic revelation to the crew of his true purpose—that is, to hunt and kill the white whale, and it follows a series of chapters in which various crew members, including Ishmael, reflect on this matter. In its opening paragraphs, "The Chart" illuminates the reflexive nature of Ahab's maniacal mapping project, which is suggestive of other projects as well:

> Had you followed Captain Ahab down into his cabin after the squall that took place on the night succeeding that wild ratification of his purpose with his crew, you would have seen him go to a locker in the transom, and bringing out a large wrinkled roll of yellowish sea charts, spread them before him on his screwed down table. Then seating himself before it, you would have seen him intently study the various lines and shadings which there met his eye; and with slow but steady pencil trace additional lines over spaces that before were blank. At intervals, he would refer to piles of old log-books beside him, wherein were set down the seasons and places in which, on various former voyages of various ships, sperm whales had been captured or seen.
>   While thus employed, the heavy pewter lamp suspended in chains over his head, continually rocked with the motion of the ship, and for ever threw shifting gleams and shadows of lines upon his wrinkled brow, till it almost

seemed that while he himself was marking out lines and courses on the wrinkled charts, some invisible pencil was also tracing lines and courses upon the deeply marked chart of his forehead. (215)

The image of Ahab as he pores over his maps and logbooks, themselves repositories of spatiotemporal bodies of knowledge (geography and history), is emblematic of a modern literary cartography. While fervently reading old notations and jotting down new information, examining remembered itineraries and tracing out novel trajectories, reflecting on past seascapes and projecting future directions for scientific inquiry, Ahab charts the world that *Moby-Dick* produces and represents. In the context of Ahab's hunt for the white whale, the scene serves an important narrative function: It convinces the perhaps skeptical reader that it is truly possible for an experienced fisherman using detailed geographical and historical wisdom to locate a single, uniquely marked, and quite memorable whale in so vast a space as the world's oceans. (The subsequent chapter, titled "The Affidavit," piles on the evidence, in case the reader remains dubious.) But just as Ahab uses his pencil to fill in "spaces that before were blank," the "shifting gleams and shadows of lines" mark the blank spaces of Ahab himself, who in a much more figurative sense represents a territory to be explored, to be mapped, and to be known. *Moby-Dick* is as much a novel about this "undiscovered country" as it is a study of the whale. At this moment in the novel, the immense magnitude of the world system and the enigma of the tragic hero coincide in an explicitly cartographic image. In order to make sense of this world at both the macroscopic level of the terraqueous globe and the microscopic level of the individual subject, Melville's strictly literary cartography—note the absence of any diagrams or maps in his text—manages to disclose the real-and-imagined spaces of the world, as Edward W. Soja has called them,[34] as they emerge from the encounter with the subject who attempts to map them.

Moby-Dick is one of the most ambitious, unwieldy, and extravagant attempts to produce a literary cartography on a global scale, and the narrator's effort "to manhandle this Leviathan" requires that he be "omnisciently exhaustive in the enterprise" (496). Said has noted that "in its vast spaces and in Melville's blazingly original style, *Moby-Dick* is about (it seems silly to say it this way) the whole world; it willingly incorporates everything, leaving such small matters as resolution, inconsistency, and indeed evaluating the *consequences* of so tremendous as shattering an experience to lesser natures."[35] In another famous passage from *Moby-Dick*, the narrator concedes that his book is concerned less with the voyage of one Ishmael, mad Ahab's monomaniacal quest, or the white whale of the title, and rather more with "the whole circles of the sciences, and all the generations of whales, and men, and mastodons, past, present, and to come, with all the revolving panoramas of empire on earth, and throughout the whole universe, not excluding its suburbs" (497). The entire "terraqueous globe" is the setting for such an outrageously extravagant novel, and the dramatic action is traced, with Moby Dick himself, along "the devious zig-zag world-circle of the Pequod's circumnavigating wake" (218). In mapping such a space, Melville cannot help but enfold the individual subject within the comprehensive cartography.

The opening scene of "The Chart" is not just a metaphorical case of the mapper being mapped. In this chapter Melville evokes what Jonathan Arac has called "a new mode of trans-subjective agency,"[36] in which the narrator directly compromises the distinction between subject and object, leading ultimately to an interpretive perplexity over which character is the hunter and which the hunted. For example, without setting off Ahab's speech or thoughts in quotation marks, the following lines blend the presences of Ahab, the narrator, and the whale, subjects and objects complicated in an intertwining skein: "And have I not tallied the whale, Ahab would mutter to himself, as after poring over his charts till long after midnight he would throw himself back in reveries—tallied him, and shall he escape? His broad fins are bored, and scalloped out like a lost sheep's ear! And here, his mad mind would run on in a breathless race; till a weariness and faintness of pondering came over him" (218–219). The grammatical subject, direct and indirect objects, and narrative voice itself swirl about as the tallying Ahab "tallies *him*" and identifies "*His* broad fins" (the white whale), while the narrator sees "*his* mad mind" (i.e., Ahab's). Arac highlights a similar "pronominal transfer" of the word *his* later in the novel,[37] specifically that memorable scene during which for the first time the reader encounters Moby Dick in the flesh: "At length, the breathless hunter [Ahab] came so nigh his seemingly unsuspecting prey, that his entire dazzling hump was distinctly visible, sliding along the sea as if an isolated thing" (596). A few pages later, after the whale attacks Ahab's boat, the phrase "his prey" is used again, although the meaning has been reversed, as Ahab is now the object of Moby Dick's hunt (599). As becomes clear—or rather as remains somewhat unclear in the mise en abyme of *Moby-Dick*'s exploration and presentation—Ahab's vaunted individualism and iron will are troubled by the vicissitudinous forces that overwhelm him, which are ultimately figured in the persona of the white whale himself.[38]

Such doublings of Ahab and the whale are frequent throughout *Moby-Dick*, as each becomes a kind of map on which Ishmael or the reader projects possible meanings. A "marked" man, Ahab is introduced by reference to his scars, particularly a "rod-like mark, lividly whitish," which runs from the tops of his head to (rumor has it) the soles of his feet (134–135). And like the lines drawn on Ahab's face by the lamplight in "The Chart," the whale is marked by "numberless straight marks in thick array," "obliquely crossed and re-crossed" with "hieroglyphical" lines that "remain undecipherable" (333), although that does not stop them from being interpreted. For Ishmael, who is perhaps the misreader par excellence,[39] the lines and shadings of the map are shown to be sources of infinitely inscrutable significance, while the quest for knowledge, the dream of a "true map," founders.

"The Chart" concludes with a fearsome depiction of Ahab, who is so marked by his intense mapping project, split between his subjective and objective conditions, a subject without agency, that his very soul seems at odds with his mind. "But as the mind does not exist unless leagued with the soul, therefore it must have been that, in Ahab's case, yielding up all his thoughts and fancies to his one supreme purpose; that purpose, by its own sheer inveteracy of will, forced itself against gods and devils into a kind of self-assumed, independent being of its own. Nay, could grimly live and burn, while the common vitality to which it was conjoined, fled horror-stricken from the unbidden and unfathered birth" (219). The narrator goes on to conclude that the person who *seemed* to be Ahab in these moments was in fact "but a vacated thing, a formless somnambulistic being, a ray of living light, to be sure, but without an object to color, and therefore a blankness in itself" (220). Thus are the opening and closing images of "The Chart" tied together in "scorching contiguity," as the cartographer who fills in "spaces that before were blank" and who is himself marked by "some invisible pencil" is revealed to be a paradoxically striated and erased blankness.

This is another view from the mise en abyme of literary spatiality. The hero's journey creates itineraries—lines—that crisscross the spaces of the narrative, and the storyteller's rhapsody weaves together disparate spaces into a map, which is also the territory, which is another map. And so on, as Kurt Vonnegut liked to say.[40] The structures used to make sense of these spaces are inevitably revealed to be at best provisional and strategic or at worst illusory and unhelpful. The active processes of mapping in literature enfold the mapmaker into the territories mapped. Literary cartography, in combining exploration and presentation, narrative and description, inevitably leads one into a hall of mirrors in which the spaces depicted are irreducibly formed of their own representations, such that there are no "true places" just as there are no "true maps." The fervid dreams of Borges's imperial cartographers reveal a nightmare from which we cannot awaken, since an imperative of literature remains engaging in the impossible task of giving form to this world, whether through the use of realistic or fantastic means. But then Borges's brief narrative on the undesirability of a too-exacting science of mapmaker is itself such a map.

These provisional maps are also the means by which writers and readers *do* make sense of the whole. The fact that there are no true maps does not negate the value of mapping. On the contrary, the inability to produce perfectly mimetic representations of the realities with which we contend is the *Ansatzpunkt* from which the literary cartographer, no longer beholden to a naive or a pseudoscientific perspective, may project alternative spaces and places as befits the contingent, timely, and situated narrative aims. The projection of a coherent map onto a plane of recognition is, like the constellation, an artificial organization of the chaotic elements of an unrepresentable totality, but maps and constellations have indubitably immense value for navigators: Odysseus eventually makes it home to Ithaca, Dante arrives in paradise, and Ahab finds his white whale. More importantly, of course, in the infinitely reflective and projective narratives of world literature, the reader finds innumerable ways, some more effective than others, of imaginatively making sense of the spaces and places of one's experience of *this* world, which is after all what mapping is all about.

Notes

1. Jorge Luis Borges, "On Exactitude in Science," *Collected Fictions*, trans. Andrew Hurley (New York: Penguin, 1999), 325. (As if to highlight his own fastidiousness with respect to the exactitude of historical sciences, Borges cites a fictional source: Suárez Miranda, *Viajes de varones prudentes*, Libro IV, Cap. XLV, Lérida, 1658.)

2. Lewis Carroll, *Sylvie and Bruno Concluded* (London: Macmillan, 1893), 169.

3. Jean Baudrillard, *Simulacra and Simulation*, trans. Sheila Faria Glaser (Ann Arbor: University of Michigan Press, 1994), 1–2.

4. Neil Gaiman, *Fragile Things: Short Fictions and Wonders* (New York: HarperCollins, 2006), xix–xx.

5. Friedrich Nietzsche, "On Truth and Lie in an Extra-Moral Sense," in *The Portable Nietzsche*, trans. Walter Kaufmann (New York: Penguin, 1976), 46–47.

6. Peter Turchi, *Maps of the Imagination: The Writer as Cartographer* (San Antonio, TX: Trinity University Press, 2004), 12.

7. See Georg Lukács, "Narrate or Describe," in *Writer and Critic and Other Essays*, trans. Arthur D. Kahn (New York: Grosset, 1970), 110–148.

8. Yi-Fu Tuan, *Space and Place: The Perspective of Experience* (Minneapolis: University of Minnesota Press, 1977), 161–162.

9. See Charles Olson, *Call Me Ishmael* (San Francisco: City Lights, 1947), 117–119, italics in the original. Olson may be credited with coining the term *Post-Modern*; see Perry Anderson, *The Origins of Postmodernity* (London: Verso, 1998).

10. See Homer, *The Odyssey*, trans. Robert Fagles (New York: Penguin, 1996), Book 9; all references in the text, using book-and-line numbers rather than page numbers, are to this edition. After the invocation to the muse, in fact, the *Odyssey*'s book 1 does begin with a scene depicting the Olympian gods, thus establishing a point of view even beyond their purview.

11. In revealing his name, of course, Odysseus is also telling a story of "the man of twists and turns" (*Odyssey* 1.1).

12. See François Hartog, *The Mirror of Herodotus: The Representation of the Other in the Writing of History*, trans. Janet Lloyd (Berkeley, CA: University of California Press, 1988); see also my *Spatiality* (London: Routledge, 2013), especially 48–50.

13. Hartog, *The Mirror of Herodotus*, 354–355.

14. See Georg Lukács, *The Theory of the Novel*, trans. Anna Bostock (Cambridge, MA: MIT Press, 1971).

15. Aristotle, *The Poetics*, trans. Samuel Henry Butcher (New York: Hill and Wang, 1961), 67. Of course, Homer's *Odyssey* does include the famous "flashback" scene (29.399–466), so

famously analyzed by Erich Auerbach in the opening chapter of *Mimesis,* in which the origin of Odysseus's scar (that is, his wounding on Mount Parnassus) is described. There are various theories as to why Aristotle makes this error, but it is possible that Aristotle did not consider the moment as integral to the plot, given the episodic nature of the "flashback," as the nurse Eurycleia discovers the scar on the stranger's thigh, thus discovering him to be the long-lost Odysseus, home at last; that moment in the "present" Ithaca, and not the distant memory of the fateful hunt years earlier, is perhaps the key point of the plot for Aristotle.

16. Edward W. Said, *Beginnings: Intention and Method* (New York: Columbia University Press, 1985), 43.

17. Lukács, *The Theory of the Novel,* 67.

18. On the distinction between the itinerary and the map, see Michel de Certeau, *The Practice of Everyday Life,* trans. Steven Randall (Berkeley: University of California Press, 1984), especially 115–121.

19. Fredric Jameson, "Modernism and Imperialism," in *The Modernist Papers* (London: Verso, 2007), 167.

20. The classic expression of this argument remains Joseph Frank's influential discussion of spatial form in modern literature. See Joseph Frank, *The Idea of Spatial Form* (New Brunswick, NJ: Rutgers University Press, 1991).

21. Tellingly, what the Sirens' "ravishing voices" say to Odysseus plays on his desire for knowledge: "Come closer, famous Odysseus — Achaea's pride and glory — / moor your ship on our coast so you can hear our song! / Never has any sailor passed our shores in his black craft / until he has heard the honeyed voices pouring from our lips, / and once he hears to his heart's content sails on, a wiser man. / We know all the pains that Achaeans and Trojans once endured / on the spreading plain of Troy when the gods willed it so — / all that comes to pass on the fertile earth, we know it all!" (*Odyssey* 12.200–207).

22. Dante, *The Divine Comedy,* vol. I, *Inferno,* trans. Mark Musa (New York: Penguin, 1984), 307–309; all references in the text, using canto and line numbers rather than page numbers, are to this edition.

23. There are, of course, other delays; the journey features several obstacles, each with its literal and allegorical significance. But here Virgil finds "some way to keep our time from being wasted" (11.14), instructing Dante and the reader in the logic that governs the ordering of the lower circles.

24. Lukács, *The Theory of the Novel,* 68.

25. Fredric Jameson, *Postmodernism, or, the Cultural Logic of Late Capitalism* (Durham, NC: Duke University Press, 1991), 51–54.

26. Ibid., 52.

27. Ibid., 52.

28. Ricardo Padrón, "Mapping Imaginary Worlds," in *Maps: Finding Our Place in the World,* ed. James R. Akerman and Robert W. Karrow Jr. (Chicago: University of Chicago Press, 2007), 265.

29. Ibid., 265.

30. Lukács, *The Theory of the Novel,* 88, 56.

31. See Jonathan Arac, *Impure Worlds: The Institution of Literature in the Age of the Novel* (New York: Fordham University Press, 2011).

32. On *Moby-Dick* as a formal experiment in the literary cartography of the world system, see my *Melville, Mapping and Globalization: Literary Cartography in the American Baroque Writer* (London: Continuum, 2009).

33. Herman Melville, *Moby-Dick* (New York: Penguin, 1992), 221. References to pages in this edition hereinafter cited parenthetically in the text.

34. See Edward W. Soja, *Thirdspace: Journeys to Los Angeles and Other Real-and-Imagined Places* (Oxford: Blackwell, 1996).

35. Edward Said, "Introduction to *Moby-Dick*," in *Reflections on Exile and Other Essays* (Cambridge, MA: Harvard University Press, 2000), 369.

36. See Jonathon Arac, "'A Romantic Book': *Moby-Dick* and Novel Agency," *boundary 2* 17, no. 2 (Summer 1990): 48.

37. Ibid., 46.

38. The very etymology of the word *whale*—and in particular the ones given in the first, unnumbered chapter of *Moby-Dick* titled "Etymology"—suggests an "overwhelming" figure, one that anticipates the final scene of the novel. See my *Melville, Mapping and Globalization*, 54–59.

39. On Ishmael as an ironic reader or misreader, see my *Melville, Mapping and Globalization*, 63–64.

40. Vonnegut suggested that all stories should end with the phrase "ETC" to register the fact that there are no tidy beginnings and endings, which he says partly explains why Vonnegut chooses to "begin so many sentences with 'And' and 'So,' and end so many paragraphs with '. . . and so on.'" See Kurt Vonnegut, *Breakfast of Champions* (New York: Delacorte Press, 1973), 234.

5   The Space of the Novel

With its typically lengthy narrative unfolding across hundreds of pages, the novel is usually considered a profoundly temporal literary form. Duration, if only in terms of the time it takes to read such a large work, is a defining characteristic of the novel. Indeed, as some historians and theorists of the genre have suggested, time or temporality is the true subject of the novel—the modern European novel, at least—which then becomes the principle literary genre or form by which time, its experience, and its effects are explored. The formal correspondences between the novel and historiography, for instance, would seem to confirm the sense that the novel is, as it were, *about* time, and many of the world's most famous novels are presented as fictional (and sometimes even nonfictional) histories, chronicles, biographies, or autobiographies, from *The Tale of Genji* to *Don Quixote*, *Wilhelm Meister's Apprenticeship*, *In Search of Lost Time*, *One Hundred Years of Solitude*, *Beloved*, or *The Brief Wondrous Life of Oscar Wao*. In *The Theory of the Novel*, Georg Lukács pointed out that of all literary genres "only in the novel . . . is time posited together with the form."[1] Unlike the brief poem, whose very appearance on the page, including its spacing, line breaks, and iconography (the verbal icon, the well-wrought urn, etc.), marks it as a distinctively spatial form, the novel's expansive narrative registers its fundamental relationship to time, as it requires an extensive period during which the story will unfold. Even if the narrative takes place in a single day, as *Ulysses*, *Mrs. Dalloway*, or *One Day in the Life of Ivan Denisovich* makes abundantly clear, the experience of time and its passing often occupy a central place in the theory and reading of the novel.

After what has been called the spatial turn in the humanities and social sciences, increasing numbers of scholars are paying attention to the relations among space, place, and the novel.[2] Of course, this is not to say that space or spatiality was ignored previously. Critics obviously paid attention to matters of geography or topography in examining a novel's setting, for example, and regionalism, local color, and national identity have long been standard features of critical inquiry. Even at the level of form, as in Joseph Frank's influential 1945 essay on "Spatial Form in Modern Literature," which demonstrated the suppression of temporality in a number of modernist works, critics have examined the ways in which texts were imbued with spatial relations of their own.[3] Indeed, one could say that matters of space as well as those of time have always been addressed in literary criticism, although time and temporality have, until recently, tended to predominate in studies of the novel or of narrative more generally. In many cases, critical attention to space or spatial relations was often reserved for the areas in which things took place: the setting a mere backdrop or container in which the events unfolded but which itself had little direct consequence. Space or place in this rendering remained rather static and inconsequential, whereas time and temporality appeared to gain significance, whether they be considered in terms of grand historical developments over centuries or an individual's experiences of the passage of the hours in a day.

In recent years critics have asserted the significance of spatiality in the theory of the novel. This spatial turn has been linked to various developments, including postmodernism, with its distinctive "new spatiality,"[4] and postcolonial criticism, which has emphasized the significance of place and territory in cultural studies.[5] In critical theory, structuralist and poststructuralist thought called into question the dominance of time and temporality, as Michel Foucault (among others) identified the present era as "the epoch of space."[6] Although much of the work currently being done under the auspices of geocriticism, literary geography, or the spatial humanities is directly associated with such timely developments within twentieth- and twenty-first-century social or cultural theories, many critics operating in these areas have returned to earlier texts and thinkers whose writings inform the current conversations.[7] As a result of these varied interventions into the theory and history of the novel, the distinctively spatial aspects of that apparently temporal form have been increasingly brought to light and studied.

In this chapter I discuss the space of the novel in terms of both its formal characteristics and its variegated content, and I argue in particular that the novel is a form of literary cartography. The novel projects, describes, and figuratively maps the social spaces depicted and in some sense created in its pages. In a way, the novel is a sort of map, one that enables readers to orientate themselves and the characters, events, settings, and ideas of the novel in the world. Looking at various critics and theorists, I suggest that the novel is a form ideally suited for the project of figuratively mapping the world and our situation and prospects in it.

Space and Place in the Novel

When one thinks of space in relation to the novel, the first consideration is usually the depiction of spaces or places in the text. This is sometimes thought of as the "storyworld," the area in which the events of the novel take place.[8] The storyworld could be entirely imaginary, such as Terry Pratchett's Discworld, whose population, history, and geography are explored over dozens of humorous fantasy novels. Alternatively, the storyworld could closely resemble the geographical spaces of the real world, as with the gritty realism of Raymond Chandler's Los Angeles in *The Big Sleep* and other detective novels. Or it might combine some aspect of the two, as in William Faulkner's Yoknapatawpha County, which undoubtedly resembles in many ways the real Lafayette County, Mississippi, but which has developed its own mythic history and geography over the course of Faulkner's writings. The basic geography and distinctive places in a novel are powerfully effective in orienting the reader and establishing the setting of the fictional world.[9]

But then, no matter how much a given storyworld refers to the spaces of the "real" world, the spaces of a novel are necessarily imaginary, by virtue of being part of that fictional universe. As Virginia Woolf once observed in an essay on the "real" places to be found in Dickens's novels, "A writer's country is a territory within his own brain; and we run the risk of disillusionment if we try to turn such phantom cities into tangible brick and mortar. . . . No city indeed is so real as this that we make for ourselves and people to our liking; and to insist that it has any counterpart in the cities of the earth is to rob it of half its charm."[10] Woolf here insists that the storyworld maintains its own autonomy from the real world and that the reader encounters this geography as a space of the imagination. In some ways this is certainly true. The places and persons in the novel are, by definition, fictional, even if they are closely tied to referents in the real world. *Within* the pages of a novel, the places are certainly "real" enough, even if the place in question is the flying island of Laputa in *Gulliver's Travels* by Jonathan Swift. Nevertheless, one can distinguish fantastic places such as the Land of Oz in Frank Baum's novels from more clearly referential locations such as Fyodor Dostoevsky's Saint Petersburg in *Crime and Punishment*, and indeed such distinctions are often crucial to drawing lines, even those that might occasionally be blurred, between various genres or modes of writing.

The *setting* of a novel is already a spatiotemporal concept. For example, when we say that at the beginning of Mark Twain's *Adventures of Huckleberry Finn* the story is set in Missouri in the 1840s, we identify both a location in space and a moment in time. Setting is often a crucial aspect of the novel, since the history and geography directly affect the way that characters, events, and plots are understood. In the case of *Huckleberry Finn*, much of the humor and the pathos of the novel derives from the regional color of what would still have been thought of as "the old Southwest," the distinctive landscapes along the Mississippi River, and the historical moment, most notably the reality of slavery before the Civil War. But this all takes place at a distance from the place and time of the composition and of the readership's reception, as Twain would have written the novel while living in Connecticut for a largely Eastern US audience in the 1880s, many years after the abolition of slavery. Twain not only sets his novel in a distinctive region, one somewhat removed from the mainstream society of his intended readers, but his prose partakes of a regionalism that makes *Huckleberry Finn* all the more memorable. It is a picaresque novel set among the riffraff of the wild, sometimes beautiful but largely unsophisticated or uncivilized part of the country. The odd vernacular used by Huck (the narrator) and others helps to accentuate the difference between the region of the storyworld and those areas of the country that were more familiar to the reader.

The relevance of space and place to the novel is not limited to the physical or political geography so frequently associated with maps. Other spatial arrangements, such as architecture, interior design, urban planning, or types of spatial organization, invariably have their own effects on a narrative. One need think only of the affective resonances of a word like *home,* which means something rather different from mere abode, apartment, or house. Houses or other buildings can frequently be the main setting for novels, and the layout of the rooms or the relations between the interior and exterior often determine the plot. The haunted house, for instance, has provided a memorable site for mystery or horror from Horace Walpole's gothic *The Castle of Otranto* to Stephen King's *The Shining* or Mark Danielewski's *House of Leaves.* Sometimes the actual location in the "real world" is unknown or irrelevant—Edgar Allan Poe never says in what country or region his House of Usher is located, for instance—but the building itself generates the sense of spatial anxiety. The space aboard a vessel, as in Herman Melville's *Moby-Dick* or Brian Aldiss's *Starship*, can have similar effects. Often the setting has less to do with the geographical location than with the type of place or the arrangement of spaces in the novel.

Rooms or other enclosed spaces offer excellent examples of this. The same basic space means different things, even though the dimensions may be identical, depending on the meanings attached to it. For instance, a bedroom and an office tend to serve rather different purposes and carry quite different senses.[11] Meanings of given spaces vary dramatically across literature as well, as a room could signify comfort to some, confinement to others. Woolf's apparently liberatory "room of one's own" is a far cry from the isolated room occupied by the protagonist of Charlotte Perkins Gilman's "The Yellow Wallpaper," for example. There is an almost limitless number of associations that could be made about a given room, and novelists over time have attempted to represent these in manifold ways.

Indeed, spaces and places in the novel may refer not only to the physical setting of the story or to the layout of the spaces in which the characters move but also to the ideas and thoughts about various spaces and places that emerge in the novel. For example, in Gustave Flaubert's *Madame Bovary*, Emma constantly dreams of Paris, which makes that city a key site in the text; she never actually makes it to Paris (the closest she gets is Rouen), but the dream of Paris colors every aspect of her character and of the plot. Hence, what a character *thinks* about a place is another important way in which place can affect a novel, even if the place in question never appears or is depicted. Such a place, whether real or imaginary, immediately becomes part of the literary geography of the novel, which in turn becomes a space to be mapped.

Spatial Representation

In discussing his approach to composing *The Lord of the Rings*, J. R. R. Tolkien explained that he "wisely started with a map, and made the story fit (generally with meticulous care for distances). The other way about lands one in confusions and impossibilities, and in any case it is weary work to compose a map from a story."[12] Tolkien is referring to an actual, physical map, one that he drew up himself and that allowed him to make visible the spaces and places of Middle-earth. But the plot of Tolkien's novel is itself cartographic, even if one were to set aside the helpful maps included at the beginning of each volume.[13] *The Lord of the Rings* represents a vast space: the imaginary realms of Middle-earth, which features not only a diverse topography and geography (complete with rivers, lakes, seas, mountains, valleys, forests, caves, cities, towns, and so forth) but also a rich, dense historical background that gives these various places a kind of overdetermined significance or surfeit meaning. Each place is not only marked as if on the map but also described, contextualized, interpreted, and woven into a larger geopolitical discourse. Many of the places encountered bear three or four different names, for example, as their geographical or spatial situation is couched in a long history that includes encounters with different races, ethnicities, or linguistic groups. The more or less linear itineraries of the novel's protagonists—notably Frodo and Sam's long journey into Mordor or Merry and Pippen's peregrinations around Fangorn Forest, Isengard, Rohan, and Gondor—are set in relation to a much larger geography and history that make their own personal encounters and discoveries all the more meaningful. The "map" of Middle-earth is not merely the sketched drawing included at the front of the book, designed to aid the reader (like the writer) in following the errant travelers along their way but is primarily formed through the narrative itself. For the imaginary world created by and through *The Lord of the Rings*, the novel itself serves as the map.

It makes sense that a wholly imaginary otherworld such as Tolkien's Middle-earth would call for a cartographic narrative, so that its distinctive spaces and places could be rendered visible in the mind of the reader. Yet the same processes and effects can be found in highly realistic works as well; Charles Dickens's London or Honoré de Balzac's Paris would require the same sort of narrative mapping, regardless of how familiar the reader might be with the underlying "geospace" purportedly represented in the text. In truth, all novels—or more generally all narratives—take part in this sort of literary cartographic project.

Lennard Davis, in *Resisting Novels*, distinguishes between three types of place: the actual (such as the London of Dickens), the fictitious (say, George Eliot's Middlemarch, which is similar to parts of Great Britain but not localizable on a map), and the renamed (F. Scott Fitzgerald's East and West Egg, for instance, which mirror locales on New York's Long Island).[14] But each of these is "ideological" according to Davis, and each therefore partakes in the crisis of representation that lies at the heart of the novel's project: to give form to or make sense of the world. One of the main ways in which novels give form to the world is by orienting readers, whether by reference to places in the readers' "real" world, by reference to distinctive places in the storyworld, or most often by some combination of the two.[15] Eric Bulson has shown how the modern novel employs geographic or spatial information to orient, and sometimes to disorient, the reader, whose imagination must navigate the figural landscapes of the novel's represented space. Bulson demonstrates the degree to which actual maps and guidebooks played a role in novelistic representation.[16] But as with novels depicting imaginary worlds, the actual figured geography plotted on a chart is not required and could even interfere with the literary cartography of a novel. The literary cartography of the novel certainly does relate to the spaces of the real world, but there need not be any one-to-one correspondence between the referential space outside the text and the representations within it.

How does this work? As a form of literary cartography, the novel presents its readers with descriptions of places, situates them in an imaginary geography, even if it is quite similar to familiar places in the extradiegetic sphere beyond the text, and provides points or frames of reference by which they can orient themselves and understand the world in which they live. In this way the novel may also help readers to get a sense of the worlds in which others have lived, currently live, or will live in times to come. From a novelist's point of view, the work provides a way of mapping the spaces encountered or imagined in the author's, the reader's, or a character's experience. Ricardo Padrón has observed that literary works not only "allow us to picture places and spaces, but by telling stories that take place in them, or by sculpting characters associated with them, they give those places life and meaning."[17] The text does not replace the image, nor could the image entirely replace the text, but the novel's *literary* cartography, operating as it must at the level of the imagination and bringing to the fore problems of representation, interpretation, and meaning, makes possible different ways of seeing and thinking of the world, as it appears both inside and apart from the text itself.

In a manner that is not merely metaphorical, the novel both represents space and helps to produce it. The novelist or narrator creates the world depicted in its pages; the narrative makes connections, establishes relations, and emphasizes a given feature, all while surveying the territory in which characters, actions, settings, and events exist, operate, or merely take place. Whether expressly acknowledged, the space and place of the novel at least condition, if not determine, those characters and events so that the "imagined geography," as Edward Said called it, is not simply a backdrop or container. It is also an active force in its own right, a means by which to shape a world, as the plot so often entails descriptions—literal or figurative—of landscapes or domains, connecting discrete elements in order to produce the narrative. Famously multiformal and heteroglossic, the novel brings together remnants of other narratives, depictions of peoples or occurrences, observations, meditations, information gleaned from eyewitness testimony or from secondary reports, scraps of legends, myths, and inventions of the fancy. In stitching together this patchwork representation of a world, the novel or literary map makes possible an image that gives shape to the world and that can become the basis for future surveys, narratives, or maps.

Literary Cartography

The novel is not the only literary genre in which a project of literary cartography could be carried out, and one could certainly see how the practice operates in other literary forms, such as the epic, romance, or lyric, not to mention such genres as travelogue, ethnographic writing, and so on. In fact, one could argue that iconographic poetry or nonnarrative description could appear to be all the more maplike inasmuch as it already appears to be a straightforward representation of space, whether in the form of various spatial arrangements of lines on a page or of depictions of the geographical space exterior to literature. When Joseph Frank referred to the way in which certain modern or modernist works take advantage of a "spatial form," he was in part comparing them to the short poem or vignette, in which all parts are present at once, not extended temporally across the *longue durée* of a typical novel.[18] More specifically Frank was looking at the way modern (or modernist) writers used formal techniques to give a sense of simultaneity, thus disrupting the fluvial progression of time in the narrative and emphasizing events taking place side by side. But the beginning, middle, and end required of all plots in Aristotle's estimation are not only temporal but spatial, and to find oneself thrust *in medias res* refers as much to the geographic milieu or situation as it does to the position within a chronological sequence. A plot itself is spatial, for a plot is also a plan, which is to say, a map. The plot establishes a setting, sets a course, and marks features of an imaginative landscape.

In *Maps of the Imagination*, Peter Turchi argues that every creative writer is a mapmaker. Turchi concedes that his usage is metaphorical, but he notes that an actual map is itself a kind of metaphor, since its representation of the places or spaces of the world can only be figural or figurative. There are no "true maps," in the sense of perfectly mimetic images of the depicted territories. The famous parable from Jorge Luis Borges, "On Exactitude in Science," which describes a map so detailed that it was made coextensive with the territory it was intended to map, warns us against being too fastidious in the cartographic enterprise. But then no one ever truly mistook the map for the territory, the territory for the map. As in the literary cartography produced by a narrative, the matter is necessarily creative, provisional, incomplete, and also extraordinarily useful. Turchi identifies several categories or processes with which every writer and every mapmaker must deal, of which the question of selection or omission might be the most important.[19] To begin with, the writer, not unlike the cartographer, must determine what elements to include in the story or map. This question already implies others, such as the following: What is the function of this story or map? What do I want the reader to get out of it? What counts as a place (or event, character, or theme) worth marking? What can safely be left out? For example, a road map intended for motorists would be expected to depict all available roads, streets, avenues, highways, and so on, but it might be forgiven for omitting pedestrian walkways or trails. Similarly, the novel might include high levels of detail with respect to certain characters, places, or events, while skimming over other features. No map is definitive, but then that merely opens up the possibility of more and better maps, depending on the perspectives of the maps' makers and users.

In a well-known formulation, James Joyce once stated that in *Ulysses* he wanted "to give a picture of Dublin so complete that if the city one day suddenly disappeared from the earth, it could be reconstructed out of my book."[20] *Ulysses* is imagined as a narrative map, even a blueprint, of the city of Dublin. But then one hardly believes that urban planners or developers would agree that the sprawling modernist novel actually provided a feasible blueprint for the cityscape of Dublin. Joyce's stated desire reflects the degree to which a writer's cartographic project is ultimately impossible, doomed to failure in advance, but also capable of failing in interesting ways. The spaces represented in the novel cannot be the same as the "real" space of a city or country. However, the spaces projected and depicted in the novel's literary cartography are not *unreal* either. The imaginary space of the novel and the actual geospace of Dublin are clearly connected, but they do not coincide exactly, and Joyce's comment must be taken to reflect an ironic ambition, no less meaningful for being ironic. The same would hold for the other types of representation mentioned by Davis, since the novelistic description of a renamed place (e.g., Fitzgerald's West Egg) or of an entirely imaginary place (such as China Miéville's New Crobuzon) would still operate differently than would a visual image or drawn map of the place. Nevertheless, the literary cartography developed through the novel, whether it be that of *The Great Gatsby* or *Perdido Street Station*, makes possible new ways of seeing, experiencing, and interpreting the spaces depicted.

The mapping project of a novel is necessarily open-ended, which means that it can only be incomplete, provisional, and tentative, although this characteristic is actually one of its great strengths. For example, as I have discussed elsewhere,[21] in his *Attempt at Exhausting a Place in Paris* (1974), Georges Perec spent three days monitoring a single location in Paris and recording everything he saw. Of course, his literary representation could not "exhaust" the place, owing to the necessary processes of selection and omission that characterize the project of narrative mapmaking. As Bertrand Westphal observed of Perec's experiment, it would have remained incomplete even if he had "camped out in the heart of the Sahara," but "Perec instead chose to engage with the bustling Place Saint-Sulpice," a busy urban locale, where far more was going on than could possibly be noticed, much less narrated or described. "Although he was confined to one location at a specific time, the project was actually boundless."[22] Indeed, merely enumerating the buses that pulled up at the bus stop would quickly become tedious, not to mention describing other vehicles, pedestrian passersby, their clothing and over-all appearance, the dogs or birds, and so on. Moreover, beyond the visual archive, Perec needed to bring the other senses into play, by describing, for example, the feel of the midday sun, the smell of diesel fumes, and the sounds of children cry-ing. Ironically, all this attention to detail and almost indiscriminate recording of information ultimately leads to a failure, not only to "exhaust the place" entirely (which in any case would be impossible) but also to register the uniqueness of the place chosen. After all, when one starts focusing on such apparently insignificant details as a bus passing by, what difference does it make that the author is at Place Saint-Sulpice in Paris, as opposed to some other town in France or elsewhere in Europe or even the world? For all its attention to detail and focus on a single, actual place, the literary cartography of Place Saint-Sulpice is not well served by this exhausting method.

The novelist must select the particulars of a given place or story that will allow the narrative map to be meaningful. A story lacking essential elements or, in contrast, containing too many inessential ones, will fail to deliver the proper "place" to its readers. The author produces the world through the narrative, thereby rendering it meaningful. A failure in this enterprise can be more ser-ious than a mere inaccurate picture, since all maps are technically inaccurate or incomplete. But the failure might lead to the reader or narrative itself becom-ing "lost," which in turn makes the story and its depicted spaces and places less effective.

Spatiotemporality and the Novel

In "Forms of Time and of the Chronotope in the Novel," Mikhail Bakhtin coined the term *chronotope*, literally translated as "time-space," in order to make clearer sense of the relations between historical time and geographical space in litera-ture. Bakhtin focuses especially on early forms of the novel, written well before such "first" novels as *Don Quixote* or *Robinson Crusoe*, which demonstrates the long history of the novelistic chronotopes.[23] As Franco Moretti has pointed out, Bakhtin's essay is "the greatest study ever written on space and narrative," and yet it does not include a single map or diagram, which perhaps demonstrates the degree to which Bakhtin understands this space-time to operate within the language and form of the novel itself, rather than in connection to some other way of visualizing space or place.[24] The chronotope is a way of understanding the "generic techniques that have been devised for reflecting and artistically processing" aspects of time and space. Space and time are inextricably bound together, and the chronotope is "a formally constitutive category of literature."[25] Sharon Marcus observes that the chronotope is the key concept of the entire Bakhtinian theory of the novel, since the ways time and space are represented constitute the force and effectiveness of the form itself. As she puts it,

> Bakhtin argues that the history of the novel is the history of the chronotope, that is, the history of the novel's representation of time and space. While all novels develop chronotopes, different subgenres have different chronotopes, which function as generic markers. The chronotope gives substance to the historically variable ways of experiencing and perceiving space and time, and changes in chronotope also indicate changing relationships between the literary work and historical reality, particularly with respect to such factors as subjectivity, social relations, and knowledge production.[26]

Essential to Bakhtin's concept of the chronotope is its historicity. Chronotopes are not fixed, stable, or static; they develop over time, and they are specific to their times and places.

Bakhtin does not provide a definitive or detailed treatment of the theory of the novelistic chronotope; rather, he allows its terminological flexibility to cover a number of related notions. Hence, at times the chronotope primarily appears to be defined by its respective genre, while in other moments it seems to refer to a particular spatiotemporal figure within a work or genre, such as "the road" as distinctive chronotope. As Bakhtin states, "In the literary artistic chronotope, spatial and temporal indicators are fused into one carefully thought-out, concrete whole. Time, as it were, thickens, takes on flesh, becomes artistically visible; likewise, space becomes charged and responsive to the movements of time, plot and history. This intersection of axes and fusion of indicators characterizes the artistic chronotope."[27] Bakhtin's discussion of the chronotope in the development of narrative forms or genres leads from the ancient romance with its "adventure chronotope" and abstract space, through the ancient Roman novels of Apuleius and Petronius where "space becomes more concrete and saturated with a time that is more substantial," to ancient biography and autobiography whose focus on the time and space of the individual would "exercise enormous influence . . . on the development of the novel."[28] In moving from "the ancient forms of the novel," as he calls them, to the folkloric chronotope, the chivalric romance, and the *carnivalesque* fiction of François Rabelais, Bakhtin identifies a movement in narrative forms similar to the one identified by Lukács in *The Theory of the Novel*, but he does not view the shifting chronotopes or narrative forms as a degradation of some earlier unity or integrated totality visible in the pre-novelistic epic form. Instead, he finds that the proliferation of various voices and the historical "inversions" of myth and history offer moments of democratic or revolutionary potential.

Bakhtin argues that chronotopes are "the organizing centres for the fundamental narrative events of the novel. The chronotope is the place where the knots of the narrative are tied and untied. It can be said without qualification that to them belongs the meaning that shapes narrative."[29] The chronotope is thus a critical element of any literary cartography, for it is through the use of and reference to particular chronotopes that the meaning of the narrative, the shape of the world, is established. However, here it is also certain that the individual writer or mapmaker is not simply making choices, selections or omissions, but is participating, perhaps without his or her knowledge of it, in larger historical and cultural processes by which these moments and places gain greater significance. As Bakhtin concedes, "The represented world, however realistic and truthful, can never be chronotopically identical with the real world it represents, where the author and creator of the literary work is found."[30] These broader and more complex relations among the world, the text, and the literary cartographer point to the supra-individual or historical forms discussed in Lukács's theory of the novel. The chronotope itself develops over time, such that "the road" as it appears in *Don Quixote* is quite different from the one animating Jack Kerouac's narrative in *On the Road*. The changing aspects of this spatiotemporal feature highlight the ways in which spaces and places are themselves both produced and productive of different ways of seeing the world.

In his essay on spatial form in modern literature, Frank argued that while the traditional novel was a fundamentally temporal form, modern literature tended to break up, freeze, or cease the flow of time in the narrative, presenting instead isolated images that appear simultaneously or in a static field.[31] In some respects, this spatialization of time in the modern novel might be viewed as an "epic" maneuver, inasmuch as the writer attempts to reproduce the conditions under which the epic form had thrived: for example, a stable social hierarchy or a strictly delimited, relatively unchanging storyworld. The idea, which draws on a somewhat Romantic tradition, is that the ancient societies that produced such works as the Homeric epic were whole, integrated, and even static social spheres, whereas a breakdown in the social totality along with an increasing sense of anxiety or alienation characterized the modern world. The novel, as the literary form par excellence of open-endedness, indecision, and indeterminacy, will have as its vocation the figurative mapping of a world no longer whole. The novel, like the map, becomes the means by which the fragmented sphere can be imagined, if only provisionally, as a totality.[32]

Space and the Modern Novel

The advent of the age of the novel coincides with the fragmentation of this imagined coherence or totality in the ancient world of the epic.[33] Implicit in this view of space and representation in the epic or novel is the idea that a given social formation will have social and spatial relations proper to it. Put differently, one might say that each society produces its own kinds of space, which then must be addressed in various ways by novel forms of cartographic or other spatial practices. This is partly the argument in Henri Lefebvre's *The Production of Space*, in which he asserts that "every society—and hence every mode of production with its subvariants (i.e., all those societies that exemplify the general concept)—produces a space, its own space."³⁴ The novel as a form of literary cartography develops different techniques, styles, or genres in attempting to map this space. Put another way, the novel provides an opportunity to imagine the world and to see how it is constructed.

Drawing on Lefebvre's theory of the production of space, as well as the insights of economic historians, Fredric Jameson understands that the social and political transformations effected by the capitalist mode of production have also radically transformed spatial relations. In *Postmodernism, or, the Cultural Logic of Late Capitalism*, Jameson argues that "the three historical stages of capital have each generated a type of space unique to it," and that these "are the result of discontinuous expansions or quantum leaps in the enlargement of capital, in the latter's penetration and colonization of hitherto uncommodified areas."³⁵ The first stage, market capitalism, witnessed the homogenization of space, the development of a Cartesian grid-like spatial organization, a geometric space that demystified the earlier, feudal or medieval senses of space and place. In market capitalism the realist novel or realism more generally emerges as the dominant mode of novelistic discourse, as the narrative mapping project attempts to apprehend the experience of this kind of spatial formation. Later, with the emergence of monopoly capital and imperialism, particularly in the late nineteenth and early twentieth centuries, a new sort of national space, already becoming international, emerges. The "realistic" novel no longer captures the experience of such a space, and as the problem of figuration becomes more urgent, so the techniques association with modernism (such as free indirect style, stream of consciousness, montage, collage, and spatial form) may be viewed as attempts to overcome the representational crisis. For Jameson the revolutionary experiments with language and style, including such novel representational techniques as free indirect discourse, stream of consciousness, polyphony, or collage, in modernist texts reflect "an attempt to square this circle and to invent new and elaborate strategies for overcoming this dilemma."³⁶

Edward W. Said makes a similar point in a "note on modernism" in his *Culture and Imperialism*. Said suggests that the new aesthetic forms reflect a growing apprehension of the irony of imperialism. "To deal with this," writes Said, "a new encyclopedic form became necessary." The features of the modernist novel include "a circularity of structure, inclusive and open at the same time," as, for example, in the stream of consciousness of Joyce's *Ulysses* or Faulkner's *The Sound and the Fury*. Such techniques would also include epic and mythic elements, not to mention generic and pop-cultural elements, and an "irony of a form that draws attention to itself as substituting art and its creations for the once-possible synthesis of the world empires." For Said this aesthetic of modernism represents a reaction to the impending breakdown of the imperial system, as the literary artist attempted to hold an imaginary reality together that was no longer feasible in the "real world." As Said concludes, "Spatiality becomes, ironically, the characteristic of an aesthetic rather than of political domination, as more and more regions—from India to Africa to the Caribbean—challenge the classical empires and their cultures."[37]

In the age of globalization or of postmodernity, in which the traditional borders or frames of reference have been redrawn, elided, or exploded, the representational crisis becomes all the more urgent, while the forms of representation (now including media and technologies hitherto unimaginable) struggle to map the seemingly unmappable totality. If in Lukács's view the seventeenth- or eighteenth-century novel attempted to map societies in "a world abandoned by God," then the scope of the novel today extends to a scale of the global system itself, as might be witnessed in such recent works as Amitav Ghosh's magnificent Ibis trilogy (*Sea of Poppies*, *River of Smoke*, and *Flood of Fire*), whose multicultural cast of characters range globally from China and India to Mauritius and beyond during the nineteenth-century Opium Wars. The result is a "world picture" tied to specific historical events but crucially informing our own image of the twenty-first-century world system.

Although the social and spatial conditions for its emergence as a cultural form were quite different from those in place today, the novel seems particular well suited to represent the human experience, social relations, and the world more generally in an age of globalization. In its multiformal style, heteroglossia, and attention to ever-changing chronotopes, the novel is expansive enough to attempt to comprehend this vast space and the myriad forces operating within it. No novel or set of novels could lay claim to completeness or perfection, but in their impurity and audacity, novels attempt to map the system. Even in the case of novels that seem to operate on a much smaller spatial scale—focusing, for example, on a single person, a small area, or a limited series of events—the "world" mapped in this literary cartography takes shape and takes on meanings that then serve as the basis for other, perhaps more powerful literary maps. The space of the novel thus involves the constant mapping and remapping of the real and imaginary spaces of the world.

Notes

1. Georg Lukács, *The Theory of the Novel*, trans. Anna Bostock (Cambridge, MA: MIT Press, 1971), 122.

2. See, e.g., Barney Warf and Santa Arias, *The Spatial Turn: Interdisciplinary Perspectives* (London: Routledge, 2008); Peta Mitchell, *Cartographic Strategies of Postmodernity: The Figure of the Map in Contemporary Theory and Fiction* (London: Routledge, 2007); Michael Dear, Jim Ketchum, Sarah Luria, and Doug Richardson, eds., *GeoHumanities: Art, History, Text at the Edge of Place* (London: Routledge, 2011); and Robert T. Tally Jr., *Spatiality* (London: Routledge, 2013).

3. See, e.g., Raymond Williams, *The Country and the City* (Oxford: Oxford University Press, 1973); Joseph Frank, "Spatial Form in Modern Literature," in *The Idea of Spatial Form* (New Brunswick, NJ: Rutgers University Press, 1991), 1–68.

4. Fredric Jameson, *Postmodernism, or, The Cultural Logic of Late Capitalism* (Durham, NC: Duke University Press, 1991), 418; see also Edward Soja, *Postmodern Geographies: The Reassertion of Space in Critical Social Theory* (London: Verso, 1989).

5. See, e.g., Edward W. Said, *Orientalism* (New York: Vintage, 1978) and *Culture and Imperialism* (New York: Knopf, 1993); Gayatri Chakravorty Spivak, *In Other Worlds* (London: Routledge, 1987); and Homi Bhabha, *The Location of Culture* (London: Routledge, 1994).

6. Michel Foucault, "Of Other Spaces," trans. Jay Miskowiec, *Diacritics* 16 (Spring 1986): 22.

7. See, e.g., Sharon Marcus, "Space," in *The Encyclopedia of the Novel*, ed. Paul Shellinger (Chicago: Fitzroy Dearborn Publishers, 1998), 1259–1262.

8. See Mieke Bal, *Narratology: Introduction to the Theory of Narrative*, trans. Christine van Boheemen (Toronto: University of Toronto Press, 1985), 93–99; see also Marie-Laure Ryan, Kenneth Foote, and Maoz Azaryahu, *Narrating Space / Spatializing Narrative: Where Narrative Theory and Geography Meet* (Columbus: Ohio State University Press, 2016), 16–43.

9. See Alberto Manguel and Gianni Guadalupi, *The Dictionary of Imaginary Places*, rev. ed. (New York: Harcourt, 1999).

10. Virginia Woolf, "Literary Geography" [1905], in *Books and Portraits: Some Further Selections from the Literary and Biographical Writings of Virginia Woolf*, ed. Mary Lyon (New York: Harcourt, Brace, Jovanovich, 1977), 161.

11. See Gaston Bachelard, *The Poetics of Space*, trans. Maria Jolas (Boston, MA: Beacon Press, 1969).

12. J. R. R. Tolkien, *The Letters of J. R. R. Tolkien*, ed. Humphrey Carpenter (Boston, MA: Houghton Mifflin, 2000), 177.

13. See Tom Shippey, *The Road to Middle-Earth: How J. R. R. Tolkien Created a New Mythology* (Boston, MA: Houghton Mifflin, 2003), 94.

14. Lennard J. Davis, *Resisting Novels: Ideology and Fiction* (London: Routledge, 2014), 55.

15. See Ryan, Foote, and Azaryahu, *Narrating Space / Spatializing Narrative*, 19–20.

16. See Eric Bulson, *Novels, Maps, Modernity: The Spatial Imagination, 1850–2000* (New York: Routledge, 2006).

17. Ricardo Padrón, "Mapping Imaginary Worlds," in *Maps: Finding Our Place in the World*, ed. James R. Akerman and Robert W. Karrow Jr. (Chicago: University of Chicago Press, 2007), 258–259.

18. Frank, "Spatial Form in Modern Literature," 18.

19. Peter Turchi, *Maps of the Imagination: The Writer as Cartographer* (San Antonio, TX: Trinity University Press, 2004), 25.

20. Frank Budgen, *James Joyce and the Making of* Ulysses, *and Other Writings*, ed. Clive Hart (Oxford: Oxford University Press, 1989), 69.

21. See my *Spatiality*, 53–54.

22. Bertrand Westphal, *Geocriticism: Real and Fictional Spaces*, trans. Robert T. Tally Jr. (New York: Palgrave Macmillan, 2011), 150; see Georges Perec, *An Attempt at Exhausting a Place in Paris*, trans. Marc Lowenthal (Cambridge, MA: Wakefield Press, 2010).

23. On novels in the Greek and Hellenistic traditions, among others, see Alexander Beecroft, *An Ecology of World Literature: From Antiquity to the Present Day* (London: Verso, 2015).

24. Franco Moretti, *Graphs, Maps, Trees: Abstract Models for a Literary History* (London: Verso, 2005), 35.

25. Mikhail Bakhtin, "Forms of Time and the Chronotope in the Novel," in *The Dialogic Imaginations: Four Essays*, ed. and trans. Caryl Emerson and Michael Holquist (Austin: University of Texas Press, 1981), 84.

26. Marcus, "Space," 1260.

27. Bakhtin, "Forms of Time and the Chronotope in the Novel," 84.

28. Ibid., 120, 146.

29. Ibid., 250.

30. Ibid., 256.

31. See Frank, "Spatial Form in Modern Literature."

32. See Lukács, *The Theory of the Novel*, 60; Mikhail Bakhtin, "Epic and Novel," in *The Dialogic Imaginations*, 16.

33. On "the age of the novel," see Jonathan Arac, *Impure Worlds: The Institution of Literature in the Age of the Novel* (New York: Fordham University Press, 2011).

34. Henri Lefebvre, *The Production of Space*, trans. Donald Nicholson-Smith (Oxford: Blackwell, 1991), 31.

35. Jameson, *Postmodernism*, 410.

36. Ibid., 411.

37. Said, *Culture and Imperialism*, 189–190.

6 *Theatrum Geographicum*

THE NOVEL MAY be viewed as a form of spatiotemporal mapping that produces a literary cartography of a world system that it simultaneously represents and constructs. The novel, like the map, is a form of knowledge, registering accumulated information and experience, shaping data into an intelligible array, and projecting potential future formations. The novel thus makes possible a visualization of the world system, as with the classic atlases (such as Abraham Ortelius's *Theatrum Orbis Terrarum*), except that the "theater" stages historical as well as geographical knowledge, which in turn must include the social, political, and economic forces that give form to the world system as it discloses itself in the novel. Formal techniques and narrative conventions help to define the world's "spaces." Correspondingly, from the reader's perspective, matters of scale affect the perception and the interpretation of space and place, while the subject's position within these different scalar diagrams affects her or his ability to recognize their significance. The history and theory of the novel offers so many glimpses into the ever-changing atlas of world literature and its protean literary cartographies. The novel's *theatrum geographicum* sets the stage for a broader consideration of the literary cartography of the world system, a sort of cognitive mapping by which writers and readers achieve a sense of place and hence make meaning in their lives.

Regarding the Map

There is a moment in *Don Quixote* in which the hero and his squire board an enchanted ship, in reality a small rowboat lacking oars, and set forth toward "such longinquous ways and regions" as it may carry them. After floating a few yards downstream, the knight feels certain that they must have traveled at least two thousand miles. "If I only had an astrolabe here with which to take the height of the pole," he says, "I would tell you how far we have gone; though if I know anything, we have passed, or soon shall pass, the equinoctial line which divides and cuts the opposing poles at equal distance." In response to Sancho Panza's question about this "noxious line," Don Quixote cites Ptolemy and observes that Sancho knows nothing of "colures, lines, parallels, zodiacs, ecliptics, poles, solstices, equinoxes, planets, signs of the zodiac and points, which are the measures of which the celestial and terrestrial spheres are composed." In lieu of this scientific body of knowledge, the knight proposes another surefire test: "That according to the Spaniards and those who embark at Cadiz to go to the East Indies, one of the signs by which they know that they have passed the equinoctial line I mentioned is that the lice die on everyone about the ship." Don Quixote entreats Sancho to check his person for lice, and the squire determines with absolutely certainty that they must not have yet crossed the equator, "not by many a long mile."[1]

As so often occurs in this novel, the humor of the scene lies in the sometimes-violent disjunction between reality and appearance, where rowboats can become enchanted ships, roadside inns take the form of grand palaces, or windmills in the shape of giants menace wayfarers with their mighty arms. But the comedy is heightened in this instance by the dual systems of knowledge invoked and used to perceive and analyze the putative "reality" in question. That is, Don Quixote's reference to Ptolemaic geography and cosmography, complete with an entire vocabulary of scientific terms and concepts, is ultimately supported by what would appear to be a folkloric myth or sailor's fantasy about the disposition of vermin at a certain latitude. The grand abstractions of geometric figures and astrological signs yield to the visceral, earthly experience of lice on a peasant's thigh.

These two modes, the abstract and the experiential, could be said to reflect the narrative modes of the novel itself, which projects in its totality a vast map of the world it simultaneously presents and represents, while also carefully tracing the trajectories of its peregrinating protagonists, whose adventures give flavor—indeed, meaning—to the places and spaces laid out in this literary cartography. This is not just the case in *Don Quixote*, which has long served historians and theorists of the novel as an exemplary model of the form. Arguably all novels, if not all narratives, are engaged in one type of mapping project or another, and the literary cartographies produced in them combine abstract or speculative models with concrete or experiential knowledge. The maplike projection of a wide world combined with the meticulous description of persons, places, and things frequently characterize the form of the novel, and these descriptive practices fruitfully interact with the narrative exploration and movement of the plot. Together these constitute a spatiotemporal novelistic discourse that serves as a form of knowledge, giving the reader a more or less detailed understanding of the world as it is presented, but the novel also serves as a form that troubles systems of knowledge, insofar as its imaginative and figurative language can, at times, serve to delegitimize or corrupt official discourses. In its heteroglossia and multiplicity of styles or forms, which Mikhail Bakhtin famously identified as the determining features of novelistic discourse,[2] the novel directly addresses basic concerns of epistemology, while also undermining its own findings.

Ortelius's 1570 atlas, titled *Theatrum Orbis Terrarum* (literally "the theater of the earthly orb," but more simply a "world map"), is among the most influential works of Renaissance art and science. One of the first atlases, collecting and binding in one volume some 70 maps, later expanded to include 167, the *Theatrum* quite literally defined the space of the world for generations. Along with Gerardus Mercator's 1569 world map, which had employed Mercator's innovative projection, the Ortelius world map gave form to the continents and seas in a new way, exaggerating the spaces furthest from the equator, while condensing those spaces closest to the line. The resulting misrepresentation of space has had notorious ideological uses and abuses, as the Global South could be diminished while the northern territories swell in size and purported value. (Mark Monmonier, in *How to Lie with Maps*,[3] observed that the cartographers and navigators of the British Empire embraced the "flattering" Mercator projection, with its use of Greenwich as the center and its enlargement of Canada, especially.) Ortelius was also the first popular world map to give the continents of the Western Hemisphere the label *America*, thus solidifying the legacy of Amerigo Vespucci in this name over and against such rival toponyms as Columbia, New India, and so on. Above all, the new world map depicted the world as a political and geographical system, one that could be synoptically presented by the mapmaker and taken in by the user. The whole world was brought before one's eyes in a single, theatrical moment.

When Ortelius's *Theatrum Orbis Terrarum* was first published, Miguel de Cervantes Saavedra was a soldier, freshly inducted into the Infantería de Marina, the Spanish Navy Marines, although the phrase is quixotically suggestive of walking on water. It is not clear whether he was able to test the louse-at-the-equator theory personally, but he would take part in the Battle of Lepanto in Greece, pitting a "Holy League" against the expanding Ottoman Empire. Cervantes was wounded in battle and spent time convalescing in Italy, then he continued fighting elsewhere in the Mediterranean over the next few years. Sometime afterward, he was taken hostage by pirates and enslaved for five years in Algiers before returning to Spain. Even if it limited itself to this period, Cervantes's biography already makes for the stuff of adventure novels or romances. His own trajectory from Spain to Italy, thence to the Greek isles and northern Africa, traced a personal itinerary through a key part of the emergent world system: the Mediterranean of Fernand Braudel's "geohistory" and Immanuel Wallerstein's sixteenth-century European "core."[4] Even before he began writing his own works, Cervantes's adventures placed him squarely on the map, while indubitably highlighting the crucial differences in the specific places, languages, and cultures of the various stops along his journeys. The "big picture" vision of the world figured on Mercator's and Ortelius's maps undoubtedly influenced the novelist's perspective on the new world into which the heroes of his own novels would move, but his own peripatetic movements, characterized by a good deal of peripety, certainly colored his understanding of those spaces.

The experience of place, as the geographer Yi-Fu Tuan has repeatedly observed, comes down to this fluctuating mixture of movement and rest. Tuan has said that "space is transformed into place when it has acquired definition and meaning," at which point it becomes the subject of interpretation, the traditional purview of literature.[5] Yet the more abstract conception of space, as a largely undifferentiated zone in which the subject moves without awareness or identification of discrete places is also crucial to literary discourses, since the distinction Tuan makes requires a sort of symbolic or representational activity whereby the individual subject connects his or her direct experience to a broader system or structure that, in various ways, gives form to or makes sense of that experience. As Fredric Jameson has argued persuasively, narrative is itself a socially symbolic act by which the writer coordinates the subjective or existential experience with the broader social totality, a national allegory or world system, that makes possible the "truth" of that experience.[6]

The grand world maps and atlases of Ortelius and Mercator were both representative and productive of the age of exploration that witnessed the rise of cartography. One tends to think of mapmaking as an innate, universal, and even "natural" aspect of human understanding of the world, and undoubtedly certain forms of primitive geographical sketches, along with the portolan charts and the medieval T and O maps, existed long before the fifteenth century. However, the explosion of ever more elaborate maps and charts in this age indicated that a revolution, not only in geography but also in the arts, sciences, and culture more generally, was under way. As Tom Conley has pointed out, "At the beginning of the fifteenth century, maps were practically non-existent, whereas only two centuries later they were the bedrock of most professions and disciplines."[7] The advent of this new age of cartography literally transformed the way we see the world and ourselves in it.

Recent scholarship on the theory and history of the novel has troubled the ease with which critics formerly named *Don Quixote* the first modern "novel" or identified the "rise of the novel" with sixteenth- and seventeenth-century literature,[8] but one may still observe that the novel form rapidly became a dominant genre in both European and world literature during this epoch. Philosophers as diverse as Georg Lukács and Michel Foucault have identified *Don Quixote* as the turning point, and the emergence of the novel as the aesthetic form expressing mankind's "transcendental homelessness" brings to the fore the fundamentally literary cartographic project of the novel. For Lukács, "The novel is the epic of a world that has been abandoned by God."[9] Whereas the ancient and medieval epic had somehow assumed a clear connection between human experience and the world at large, a metaphysical unity essentially guaranteed by divine providence, the modern condition demands a form that attempts, and likely fails, to make those connections, to project that "archetypal map," as Lukács calls it.[10] The rise of the novel, not surprisingly, corresponds to the rise of cartography.

In *The Order of Things*, Foucault asserts that "*Don Quixote* is the first modern work of literature,"[11] which he explains by distinguishing the novel's epistemology from a Renaissance episteme characterized by similitude. In the Renaissance world not yet abandoned by God, resemblances in nature could disclose the Almighty's signature; thus the natural world could be read like any other text. As Foucault explains, however,

> *Don Quixote* is the negative of the Renaissance world; writing had ceased to be the prose of the world; resemblances and signs had dissolved their former alliance; similitudes have become deceptive and verge upon the visionary or madness; things still remain stubbornly within their ironic identity: they are no longer anything but what they are; words wander off on their own, without content, without resemblance to fill their emptiness; they are no longer the marks of things; they lie sleeping between the pages of books and covered with dust. Magic, which permitted the decipherment of the world by revealing the secret resemblances beneath its signs, is no longer of any use except as an explanation, in terms of madness, of why analogies are always proved false. The erudition that once read nature and books alike as parts of a single text has been relegated to the same category as its own chimeras: lodged in the yellowed pages of books, the signs of language no longer have any value apart from the slender fiction which they represent. The written word and things no longer resemble one another. And between them, Don Quixote wanders off on his own.[12]

After this moment, the novel will have as its vocation the attempt to give some sort of reasonable shape to a world no longer guaranteed of its recognizable contours by a transcendent reality. Like the modern map, which uses figuration, exaggeration, and distortion in attempting to "realistically" represent the spaces on its surface, the novel cannot simply hold a mirror to reality, but shapes and molds the images, characters, events, and places it represents.

The novel is what Lukács calls "a form-giving form," which also suggests its epistemological role, since the natural or social world it presents cannot simply be known objectively. Knowledge had to become the province of the knower, and the writer cannot be expected merely to reveal the truth, but like the reader must interpret the world. Hence, the novel is an essentially epistemological form, and like the map it is a form of knowledge as well as an attempt to know. Bakhtin makes this very point in contrasting the epic and the novel. Whereas in the epic or ancient literature in general "it is memory, and not knowledge, that serves as the source and power for the creative impulse," writes Bakhtin, "the novel, by contrast, is determined by experience, knowledge and practice (the future)." Bakhtin concludes by saying that when "the novel became the dominant genre, epistemology became the dominant discipline."[13]

The epistemological or scientific impulse underlying cartographic and novelistic practice should not be taken in a strictly empirical sense. The will to knowledge in such work confronts a persistence of ambiguity that ultimately frustrates, but at the same time sustains, the project. As it becomes apparent that there can be no "true maps," as Jameson noted in a "digression on cartography," since there can be no perfectly mimetic representation of the spaces depicted on them, "it also becomes clear that there can be scientific progress, or better still, a dialectical advance, in the various historical moments of mapmaking."[14] The knowledge to be gained or advanced through these practices thus will remain provisional, tentative, incomplete, and therefore ultimately erroneous, but this means that the epistemic efforts can be directed at producing better maps or narratives, with the understanding that what counts as "better" may vary from time to time and place to place. As I have put it elsewhere, "If failure is inevitable, the goal must be to fail in interesting ways."[15]

A more recent novel, Daniel Kehlmann's *Measuring the World* (2005), explicitly takes up the epistemological and cartographic projects of the modern novel. *Measuring the World* is not exactly a historical novel, but by interweaving the fictional and real lives of mathematician Carl Friedrich Gauss and geographer Alexander von Humboldt, Kehlmann evokes the intellectual fervor of the Goethezeit and its aftermath in Germany and elsewhere. The plot involves the crucial distinction between the scientific methods of these giants as they go about their revolutionary work, each measuring the world, thereby changing it forever, but in vastly different ways. Gauss rarely left his home in Göttingen, conducting the occasional experiment and consulting his telescope, but for the most part his labors involved speculation and deduction. Humboldt famously traveled to the Americas, scaling mountains and descending into volcanoes, exploring the Amazon, interviewing indigenous peoples, and always taking special care to measure everything and record his finding. The abstract mathematical speculation is thus contrasted with the physically intensive empirical exploration. (Somewhat-lesser characters in the novel, like Gauss's son Eugen who wishes to study languages or Humboldt's gifted brother Friedrich, the philologist and philosopher, provide the barest glimpse of other, critical forms by which we measure our world.) The two approaches, so different yet entirely complementary to the impossible project of the novel's title, also represent the two discursive modes of literary cartography, as the speculative or totalizing abstraction of the map provides the necessary framework for the experiential perambulations of the itinerary, which in turn gives shape, texture, color, and other characteristics to the places and figures on the map.

In the end, this mapping affects the territory, which itself conditions the possible way in which its maps can be imagined, and so on. Late in *Measuring the World*, Kehlmann's Gauss thinks about this very thing, only he does so while he is engaged in his own wanderings, and he realizes that the mapping project forever alters the landscapes.

> In the afternoon he [Gauss] took long walks through the woods. Over time
> he'd ceased to get lost, he knew this area better than anyone, he'd fixed every

detail of it on the map. Sometimes it was as if he hadn't just measured the region, but invented it, as if it had only achieved its reality through him. Where once there had been nothing but trees, peat bogs, stones, and grassy mounds, there now was a net of grades, angles, and numbers. Nothing someone had ever measured was now or could ever be the same as before. Gauss wondered if Humboldt would understand that. It began to rain, and he took shelter under a tree. The grass shivered, it smelled of fresh earth, and there was nowhere else he could ever want to be but here.[16]

Gauss's surmises, punctuated by the sensual pleasure and homeliness of the sylvan scene, bring the abstract and the experiential back into amenable relationship to one another.

The realism of a novel, as with the basic practicality of a map, can lead one to miss the intensively figurative, imaginative function of the form. For all their epistemological value, the novel and the map are far better at reminding us of the artificiality of representation, of the trickiness associated with languages and images, and of the potential for these forms to create radically alternative visions of the world. "While the map is never the reality," the great geographer J. B. Harley once observed, "it helps us to create a different reality."[17] The various anecdotes and examples of this essay suggest the ways in which novels and maps, two exceedingly powerful forms of knowledge, give form to or make sense of the world system presented in and by them. Together they disclose a *theatrum geographicum* in which the places and spaces of our world are made meaningful.

Spatiality and *The Theory of the Novel*

Although it is strange to put it this way, particularly given the prominence of his later critique of the ideology of modernism, Lukács's magnificent "historico-political essay on the forms of great epic literature" strikes me as a profoundly modernist work, drawing on a vast array of cultural resources in response to the feelings of generalized anxiety and uncertainty associated with the historical moment of its emergence. Indeed, one might say that *The Theory of the Novel*, first published in 1916 (the same year that James Joyce's *Portrait of an Artist as a Young Man* appeared in book form), *is* a sort of modernist novel. In Lukács's words (from the 1962 preface), "It was written in a mood of permanent despair over the state of the world," particularly in response to the outbreak of the First World War and its well-nigh universal acclaim among so many Europeans.[18] The text itself is vividly experimental, even though Lukács had at first imagined an even more bizarre presentation, a *Decameron*-like dialogue among "a group of young people withdraw[ing] from the war psychosis of its environment."[19] The finished product, ostensibly a more straightforward essay (*Versuch*) on the ways in which the epic and novel forms of literature give shape to human experience and to the world, is a still-remarkable and eccentric exploration. In its attempt to map out the history of those form-giving forms and, more implicitly, the history of the present situation of Western civilization in the early twentieth century, *The Theory of the Novel* represents both a study and an example of literary cartography.

Was there ever a more striking, evocative opening to a work of literary theory, history, or criticism?

> Happy are those ages when the starry sky is a map of all possible paths—ages whose paths are illuminated by the light of the stars. Everything in such ages is new and yet familiar, full of adventure and yet their own. The world is wide and yet it is like a home, for the fire that burns in the soul is that of the same essential nature as the stars; the world and the self, the light and the fire, are sharply distinct, yet they never become permanent strangers to one another, for fire is the soul of all light and all fire clothes itself in light. Thus each action of the soul becomes meaningful and rounded in this duality: complete in meaning—in *sense*—and complete for the senses; rounded because the soul rests within itself even while it acts; rounded because its action separates itself from it and, having become itself, finds a centre of its own and draws a closed circumference round itself. "Philosophy is really homesickness," says Novalis: "it is the urge to be at home everywhere."[20]

Lukács's initial reference to this stellar cartography is, of course, metaphorical, but then so is cognitive mapping or, indeed, any form of mapping. Figuration is a necessary part of the project itself. It is precisely in the figurative discourse of *The Theory of the Novel* that what I refer to as his "literary cartography" is at its most forceful, since the image of the literal map is somewhat confusing under the circumstances. Literary cartography is not a literal form of mapmaking, after all; rather it involves the ways and means by which a given work of literature functions as a figurative map, serving as an orientating or sense-making form. In this sense, I would argue that Lukács's project in *The Theory of the Novel*, which is so often rightly considered a historical or temporal project, also involves a profound sense of spatiality. *The Theory of the Novel* is an early and influential study of the processes and forms underlying literary cartography.

Crucial to Lukács's theory of the epic and the novel, form-giving forms by which human beings make sense of their world and invest it with meaning is the relationship between the individual subject and the milieu in which he or she is situated. Although Lukács does not directly emphasize the particularly spatial aspects of this condition, it is clear that what Lukács refers to poetically as "transcendental homelessness," the disorientation and angst associated with living in a "world abandoned by God," has many aspects in common with what Derek Gregory has referred to as the "cartographic anxiety" of modernity.[21] In his attention to the way in which the subject makes sense of and gives form to his world through narrative, Lukács's theory resonates well with Fredric Jameson's conception of cognitive mapping, insofar as the individual subject attempts to project a maplike figure, a tentative, contingent, and provisional image of the unrepresentable space (for Jameson, the social totality or perhaps even history itself).[22] Similarly, but with respect to narrative in particular, literary cartography requires the projection of a figural map through which individual or collective perception and experience may be coordinated with a larger social and spatial totality in meaningful ways. If, as Lukács would have it, "the task of true philosophy" is "to draw that archetypal map,"[23] establishing a connection between subjective experience and objective existence, then the narrative forms of the epic and novel operate as examples of differing modes for engaging in literary cartography.

Jameson develops the concept of cognitive mapping in relation to his reflections on the postmodern condition, yet the origins of its practice lay in narrative analysis more generally. As I note in my study of his work,[24] Jameson was already using the metaphor of the map (and not *merely* metaphorically, it should be pointed out) as early as 1968. In a brief essay published that year, "On Politics and Literature," Jameson asserts that the would-be political writer in the United States "has to make something of a map," by which he or she can

> coordinate two different zones of experience and bring them into a coherent relationship to each other. On the one hand he has to do justice to his own lived experience, to the truth of the individual life, of the monad, to the domain if you like of psychology and of the psychological problem. But that isn't enough: then he has to situate that subjective dimension with respect to the objective, he has to bring the point in relation to the coordinates of the map, he has to give a picture of the objective structure of society as a whole and deal with matters that ordinarily have nothing to do with my own subjective experience, my own psychology, but which are rather ordinarily dealt with in political science textbooks, sociological or economic studies—all those basic questions about how the country is organized, what makes it do what it does, who runs it, and so forth—things I may *know* about intellectually but which I can't translate into the terms of my personal experience. The opposition is between subjective and objective, between mere abstract knowledge and lived experience; and the problem for the political writer—perhaps well-nigh impossible to solve—is to find some kind of real experience in which these two zones of reality intersect. But such experiences are very rare: and generally they are only abstract, or allegorical, or somehow symbolic. . . . Basically, the only way we can think our own individual lives in relationship to the collectivity is by making a picture of the relationship. The notion of a map was such an image, or picture, or the image of an airplane from which you can look down and see masses of life, of houses and cities, disposed out below you like a map.[25]

How different is this idea from Lukács's sense of a "transcendental homelessness" in a "world abandoned by God"? Projecting a maplike image of a totality that is not or is no longer accessible through any individual's lived experience, the storyteller fashions a narrative that can somehow approximate in figurative form the absent totality. In Lukács's view, of course, this follows from a fundamental breakdown in the relationship of the individual subject to his or her social totality (or *Lebenstotalität*), which in the "integrated" civilizations of the great Homeric epic is taken to be unified and which in the "problematic" civilizations of the modern novel is viscerally rent. Again, the language is not especially spatial or spatiotemporal, but the phenomenon under consideration is not unlike that spatial confusion or sense of being at sea in the world, which Jameson emphasizes in his analysis of postmodern hyperspace.

Jameson's use of this spatial analogy indicates the degree to which he was already concerned with a recognizably cartographic anxiety of the late modern (or postmodern) existential condition, but the figure of cognitive mapping is particularly relevant to his understanding of realism, and hence one can find in Lukács's writings—from *The Theory of the Novel* to *Realism in Our Time* and beyond—clear precursors to the distinctively Jamesonian concept. For example, Jameson acknowledged that his 1977 article "Class and Allegory in Mass Culture," an essay ostensibly on the grittily realist crime drama *Dog Day Afternoon*, was an earlier attempt at illuminating the processes of a cognitive mapping, *avant la lettre*.[26] And Jameson's first use of the phrase "cognitive mapping" arguably appeared in connection to realist narrative in *The Political Unconscious*, in which he observes that "realism . . . unites the experience of daily life with a properly cognitive, mapping, or well-nigh 'scientific' perspective."[27] Yet for all its value to forms associated with realism, modernism, and perhaps especially postmodernism, cognitive mapping as a figure for what Jameson elsewhere calls "the desire for narrative" can be viewed in retrospect as a critical element of the representational project that Lukács investigates in *The Theory of the Novel*.[28]

Lukács's cultural history imagines three distinctive moments or periods, beginning with the "closed" (*geschlossene*) or integrated civilization represented by the Homeric epic, moving toward the more problematic relationship between individuals and the *Lebenstotalität* visible in the medieval epic form of Dante's *Commedia*, and on to the more or less modern condition of abstract idealism in a "world abandoned by God" so well rendered in the novel form of *Don Quixote*. In the aftermath of Quixote's peregrinations, the modern novel registers the distinctive break between self and world, a unbridgeable chasm between subjective and objective reality that will require a new kind of literary map—the novel itself—best suited to give form to, or make sense of, this condition. In the latter half of his book, Lukács examines the ways in which this works itself out in Goethe, Balzac, Flaubert, and Tolstoy, before declaring that we have not entirely exited the stage of the "romanticism of disillusionment" and coyly suggesting that Fyodor Dostoevsky's work lies outside the scope of the study, for he "did not write novels" and only time will tell whether he is "already the Homer or Dante" of a new world or merely one voice among many that will herald its arrival.[29]

Lukács establishes a fundamental opposition between the "age of the epic," that happy era in which the starry sky is the map of all possible paths, and the age of the novel, in which the breakdown of subjective experience and objective reality—a phenomenon Lukács will not be able fully to theorize until he writes his monumental essay on reification in *History and Class Consciousness* a few years later—necessitates a new form. The Homeric epic, which Lukács also refers to as "strictly speaking" the only true epic form,[30] typifies the condition of this ancient Greek "integrated" civilization. The *oikoumene* made visible in Homer's narratives is part of a historical plenum, a literary world filled with stories to be woven together in various ways and with various effects, but which all appear to fit within a cognizable totality.

This epic indifference to hierarchical order is reflected in what Joseph Frank famously identified as the genre's "spatial form."[31] Among other effects of this spatiality, Lukács observes that both character and narrative form are relatively static. "Nestor is old just as Helen is beautiful or Agamemnon mighty."[32] After all, in Lukács's view, since the epic world is already an integrated totality, the narrative need not project or organize the world's disparate elements into a totality. One might say that a map is fixed in the mind beforehand, and it is not necessary to create new ones. This is Lukács's point about the age of the epic having "no philosophy," since there is no need for that "archetypal map." Mikhail Bakhtin, in an essay on the distinction between epic and novel, makes a similar assertion: "The epic past is absolute and complete. It is as closed as a circle; inside it everything is finished, already over. There is no place in the epic world for any openendedness, indecision, indeterminacy."[33] For these critics, the contours of the ancient map are more or less fully established prior to the epic's representation of these spaces, so the Homeric epic is not required to organize the elements of this world into a sensible totality but merely has the duty to present the already-constituted portions of the map or of the history in various, interesting ways.

As I have discussed elsewhere, for Lukács as for Jameson, the desire for such maps arises only when accompanied by that uncanny sense of alienation that could be literalized in the feeling of being lost.[34] The key transition between the epic epoch and the age of the novel for Lukács is represented by Dante's *Commedia*, itself an epic but also a form that is developing toward a more novelistic or *romantische* form, perhaps typified in its dramatic opening lines in which the pilgrim finds himself literally and figuratively "lost" in a dark forest (*selva oscura*), the first sign of a large, symbolic system operating at a level beyond that of the individual subject.[35] As Lukács argues,

> The totality of Dante's world is the totality of a visual system of concepts. It is because of this sensual "thingness," this substantiality both of the concepts

themselves and their hierarchical order within the system, that completeness and totality can become constitutive structural categories rather than regulative ones: because of it, the progression through the totality is a voyage which, although full of suspense, is a well-conducted and safe one; and, because of it, it was possible for an epic to be created at a time when the historico-philosophical situation was already beginning to demand the novel.[36]

Dante's world is structured according to rigid principles, and yet it is also—as Erich Auerbach so forcefully argued—a profoundly "worldly world" (*die irdische Welt*), powerfully connecting the abstract moral geography of an Aristotelian or Thomist variety with a human, physical, and visceral experience.[37] In canto 11 of the *Inferno*, for example, the canto in which Virgil explains to Dante just how the lower circles of Hell are organized according to this moral geography, one also notes that the pilgrims are forced to pause because of the irrepressible stench emanating from below. No matter how abstract or idealistic the philosophy, Dante nevertheless situates his hero in the most materially substantial conditions, even in the otherworldly realms.

The abstract yet corporeal experience of the *Commedia* suggests a sort of dialectical advance in the literary cartography of the epic. Whereas the already well-known tales of Odysseus's wanderings furnished the raw materials for the Homeric bard to weave into a new whole, Dante's itinerary is largely restricted by the predetermined, logical structure of the otherworldly territories through which he travels. Literary mapmaking now relies on an impersonal, supraindividual, or even objective body of knowledge to determine its "truth." In Lukács's history of epic forms, this represents a powerful break from the earlier epic tradition and a distinctive move in the direction of modern novel. As he puts it,

> Dante is the only great example in which we see the architectural clearly conquering the organic, and therefore he represents a historico-philosophical transition from the pure epic to the novel. In Dante there is still the perfect immanent distancelessness and completeness of the true epic, but his figures are already individuals, consciously and energetically placing themselves in opposition to a reality that is becoming closed to them, individuals who, through this opposition become real personalities. The constituent principle of Dante's totality is a highly systematic one, abolishing the epic independence of the organic part-unities and transforming them into hierarchically ordered, autonomous parts.[38]

Ironically, perhaps, for such an important religious poem, this is not unlike the technological or scientific developments in the history of cartography, whereby the subjective attempts to orientate oneself in a given space (such as Dante's *selva oscura*) must embrace supra-individual or nonsubjective means in order to achieve a more accurate representation.

As I have been arguing throughout this book, the novelist is a kind of cartographer insofar as she or he must coordinate the various elements of human experience and the world in order to form a new unity, however provisional it may be. For Lukács, this would entail the artful piecing together of various fragmented or disparate elements into a new, artificial, yet meaningful ensemble. To borrow a word from Claude Lévi-Strauss, this narrative mapping must involve *bricolage*—that is, working with whatever materials come to hand in a provisional but no less intentional project aimed at forming a new whole. "The novel is the epic of an age in which the extensive totality of life is no longer directly given, in which the immanence of meaning in life has become a problem, yet which still thinks in terms of totality."[39] But, as Lukács insists a bit later, the "organic whole" into which the novelist has fused "heterogeneous and discrete elements" is "abolished over and over again."[40] Or to put it more positively, this uncertain situation also makes possible infinitely new and different maps.

From this perspective, the advent of the age of the novel coincides with the fragmentation of this imagined, ancient coherence or totality. Whereas the epic could reflect the integrated civilization of the ancient Greeks, the novel will have as its vocation the projection of an imaginary, perhaps provisional and contingent, totality, since there is no longer one that we can simply assume. In Lukács's evocative phrasing, "The novel is the epic of a world that has been abandoned by God."[41]

Lukács's image of the unified totality of the ancients is both romantic, inasmuch as it posits a lost organic wholeness for which we moderns yearn in vain, and largely erroneous, since it is certain that the ancient world also required surveying spaces, knitting these spaces together, and projecting a world.[42] But it really does not matter whether Lukács—or Georg Hegel or Novalis, for that matter—is "correct" about this historical moment. As Franco Moretti has observed, this is mostly a matter of periodization, of establishing the parameters of a modern world in which meaning is itself the problem. In Moretti's words, notwithstanding the vast amount of knowledge to be found in the book, "The *Theory [of the Novel]* is not after knowledge: it is after *meaning*."[43] The novel for Lukács is above all a form-giving form, whose fundamental vocation is to make sense of, find meaning in, the world and our experience of it. Lukács's romantic notion of the novel form as an expression of "transcendental homelessness" is of direct relevance to much of the more directly spatial discourse in twentieth-century philosophy and literary theory. Whether from a strictly existential perspective or from a more broadly historical and philosophical point of view, this sense of homelessness occasions the need for a kind of mapping, which is also the purpose of a literary cartography.

Mapping New Worlds

The artistic forms associated with literary cartography undoubtedly derive their force and their desirability from the general unease with respect to our sense of place, what Lukács would have likened to a loss of a sense of totality: "Art, the visionary reality of the world made to our measure, has thus become independent: it is no longer a copy, for all the models have gone; it is a created totality, for the natural unity of the metaphysical spheres has been destroyed forever."[44] The representation of reality in a world abandoned by God relies on a cartographic imperative, by which the novelist projects a figurative map that can, if not restore a sense of transcendental homeliness (assuming that were even desirable at this stage in historical development), at least allow one to become more accustomed to and familiar with the life in exile. Hence, one can see the profound modernism of *The Theory of the Novel*, less in its nostalgia for the premodern unities than in its embrace of the utopian possibilities of a new world to be mapped and remapped. But above all the map fosters interpretation and exploration, making it more suited to narrative than to epistemological ends.

In spite of its close association with postmodernism and postmodernity, Jameson has conceded that cognitive mapping is ultimately a "modernist strategy," for it "retains an impossible concept of totality whose representational failure seemed for the moment as useful and productive as its (inconceivable) success."[45] Unlike the more properly postmodern celebration of the fragmentary or of the incessant play of difference, the necessarily representational project of cognitive mapping cannot help but shore these fragments on modernity's ruins, and thus it cannot help but also involve a distinctively utopian dimension.[46] The value of the novel form's literary cartography lies in a similarly utopian, and perhaps therefore impossible, project, since it must constellate the disparate stars that in themselves offer no sure map of any possible paths into a meaningful ensemble that we may use to make our own way in the world. Here, utopia is not the ideal state to be realized but—as Jameson has stated in various places—a boundary by which we come to comprehend our own imaginative limits,[47] a frame for the map that we create and re-create in various moments along the way. The novel as form thus exceeds epic, since the latter had a kind of transcendent reality to be represented, whereas the novel's literary cartography generates its own territories as it allows us to explore them. Lukács's warning about art's inability to transform the world—"the great epic is a form bound to the historical moment, and any attempt to depict the utopian as existent can only end in destroying the form, not in creating reality"—is well taken, but the final word of *The Theory of the Novel* offers the barest hope of a new world resistant to "the sterile power of the merely existent."[48] In a characteristically modernist and Marxist formulation, then, we see the dialectic of modernity played out in the literary forms of its age. The maps are no longer revealed in the firmament before our eyes, but the promise of new, different, and hitherto unimaginable cartographies impels us to give form to, and make sense of, those radically alternative spaces and places that we will ineluctably occupy and attempt to represent.

Notes

1. Miguel de Cervantes, *Don Quixote*, trans. J. M. Cohen (New York: Penguin, 1950), 657–659.

2. See Mikhail Bakhtin, "The Discourse of the Novel," in *The Dialogic Imagination: Four Essays*, trans. Caryl Emerson and Michael Holquist (Austin: University of Texas Press, 1981), 368.

3. Mark Monmonier, *How to Lie with Maps* (Chicago: University of Chicago Press, 1991), 94–99.

4. See Fernand Braudel, *The Mediterranean and the Mediterranean World in the Age of Phillip II*, trans. Siân Reynolds (New York: Harper & Row, 1972); Immanuel Wallerstein, *The Modern World-System*, 3 vols. (New York: Academic Press, 1974).

5. Yi-Fu Tuan, *Space and Place: The Perspective of Experience* (Minneapolis: University of Minnesota Press, 1977), 136.

6. See Fredric Jameson, *The Political Unconscious: Narrative as a Socially Symbolic Act* (Ithaca, NY: Cornell University Press, 1981); see also, Jameson, *Postmodernism, or, the Cultural Logic of Late Capitalism* (Durham, NC: Duke University Press, 1990), especially 410–418.

7. Tom Conley, *The Self-Made Map: Cartographic Writing in Early Modern France* (Minneapolis: University of Minnesota Press, 1996), 1.

8. See, e.g., Alexander Beecroft, *An Ecology of World Literature: From Antiquity to the Present Day* (London: Verso, 2015); see also Franco Moretti's enormous editorial project, *Il Romanzo*, a five-volume collection of essays reconstellating the theory and history of the novel in a global context. It appears in English in two volumes as *The Novel, Volume 1: History, Geography, and Culture* and *The Novel, Volume 2: Forms and Themes* (Princeton, NJ: Princeton University Press, 2007).

9. Georg Lukács, *Theory of the Novel*, trans. Anna Bostock (Cambridge, MA: MIT Press, 1971), 88.

10. Ibid., 31.

11. Michel Foucault, *The Order of Things: An Archaeology of the Human Sciences*, trans. anon. (New York: Vintage, 1973), 48.

12. Ibid., 47–48.

13. Bakhtin, "Epic and Novel," in *The Dialogic Imagination*, 15.

14. Jameson, *Postmodernism*, 52.

15. See my "Translator's Preface: The Timely Emergence of Geocriticism," in Bertrand Westphal, *Geocriticism: Real and Fictional Spaces*, trans. Robert T. Tally Jr. (New York: Palgrave Macmillan, 2011), xi.

16. Daniel Kehlmann, *Measuring the World*, trans. Carol Brown Janeway (New York: Vintage, 2006), 229.

17. J. B. Harley, *The New Nature of Maps: Essays in the History of Cartography*, ed. Paul Laxton (Baltimore, MD: Johns Hopkins University Press, 2001), 168.

18. Lukács, *The Theory of the Novel*, 12.

19. Ibid., 11–12.

20. Ibid., 29.

21. See Derek Gregory, *Geographical Imaginations* (Oxford: Blackwell, 1994), especially 70–75.

22. See Jameson, *Postmodernism*, 51–54.

23. Lukács, *Theory of the Novel*, 29–30.

24. See Robert T. Tally Jr., *Fredric Jameson: The Project of Dialectical Criticism* (London: Pluto, 2014), 100–102.

25. Fredric Jameson, "On Politics and Literature," *Salmagundi* 2, no. 3 (Spring–Summer 1968), 22–23.

26. Fredric Jameson, *Signatures of the Visible* (London: Routledge, 1990), 54.

27. Fredric Jameson, *The Political Unconscious: Narrative as a Socially Symbolic Act* (Ithaca, NY: Cornell University Press, 1981), 104.

28. Fredric Jameson, "Introduction," *The Ideologies of Theory: Essays, 1971–1986*, vol. 1, *Situations of Theory* (Minneapolis: University of Minnesota Press, 1988), xxviii.

29. Lukács, *Theory of the Novel*, 152–153.

30. Ibid., 30.

31. See Joseph Frank, *The Idea of Spatial Form* (New Brunswick, NJ: Rutgers University Press, 1991).

32. Lukács, *Theory of the Novel*, 121.

33. Bakhtin, "Epic and Novel," 16.

34. See Robert T. Tally Jr., *Spatiality* (London: Routledge, 2013), 1–7.

35. As Jonathan Arac points out, citing Friedrich Schlegel's "Letter on the Novel," the German word *romantische* could be translated either as "romantic" or "novelistic," and hence referring to a work as a "romantic novel" (a potentially oxymoronic expression for some English readers) would seem almost a tautology—that is, a "romantic romance" or a "novelistic novel"—in German. See Jonathan Arac, "'A Romantic Book': *Moby-Dick* and Novel Agency," *boundary* 2 17, no. 2 (1990): 44.

36. Lukács, *Theory of the Novel*, 70.

37. See Erich Auerbach, *Dante: Poet of the Secular World*, trans. Ralph Mannheim (New York: NY Review of Books, 2001).

38. Lukács, *The Theory of the Novel*, 68.

39. Ibid., 56.

40. Ibid., 84.

41. Ibid., 88.

42. See, e.g., François Hartog, *The Mirror of Herodotus: The Representation of the Other in the Writing of History*, trans. Janet Lloyd (Berkeley: University of California Press, 1988).

43. Franco Moretti, "Lukács's Theory of the Novel: Centenary Reflections," *New Left Review* 91 (January–February 2014), 41.

44. Lukács, *Theory of the Novel*, 37.

45. Jameson, *Postmodernism*, 409.

46. See, e.g., Robert T. Tally Jr., *Utopia in an Age of Globalization: Space, Representation, and the World System* (New York: Palgrave Macmillan, 2013).

47. See, e.g., Fredric Jameson, *Archaeologies of the Future: The Desire Called Utopia and Other Science Fictions* (London: Verso, 2005), 232–233.

48. Lukács, *Theory of the Novel*, 152–153.

PART III

FANTASY AND THE SPATIAL
IMAGINATION

7 Adventures in Literary Cartography

ADVENTURE OFFERS A particularly tantalizing theme for a discussion of literary cartography, particularly inasmuch as adventures are by their nature exploratory, representational, and projective, three attributes that are also characteristic of the narrative and mapmaking enterprises. Any discussion of the adventures in literary cartography would undoubtedly include some consideration of the work undertaken by various writers in order to map the real and imagined, and what Edward W. Soja has called the "real-and-imagined," spaces of the world depicted in, and to a certain extent created and shaped by, the text.[1] The literary cartographer is, in a sense, already an adventurer, setting forth to explore territories mapped in the narrative and connecting disparate elements or events in an effort to fabricate a larger ensemble or totality. The adventure tale as a genre or narrative mode frequently involves a wayfaring hero who explores strange places and undergoes novel experiences, only to return, either to tell the tale or to be the exemplary figure in some other writer's story. In their charting of exotic lands, peoples, and phenomena, adventures seem especially well suited to the project of literary cartography, although one could certainly argue that all narratives partake of the cartographic imperative.

In this chapter I approach the adventures in literary cartography by examining the ways that adventure stories illustrate and enact the project of narrative mapping by foregrounding in their own aesthetic projects the exploratory, representational, and projective or speculative modes of cartographic theory and practice. I am speaking quite generally, of course, but my sense is that the adventure—my primary example here comes from J. R. R. Tolkien's 1937 fantasy adventure *The Hobbit*, but the argument applies to other works in the genre—affords a privileged vantage from which to view these characteristic elements. Moreover, the broader project of literary cartography reveals itself to be a sort of adventure, insofar as its activity requires the meticulous coordination of different registers, from the individual subject's subjective experience of spaces and places to the vaster, abstract, or even scientific apprehension of a spatial and historical constellation of forces.[2] Hence, in their dynamic spatiotemporality, the adventurer and the literary cartographer find that their vocations intertwine and that the resulting narratives and maps offer rich resources for further adventures in literary cartography.

The Return of the Adventurer

What is an adventure? The term *adventure* is common enough, but there is an oddly contranymic quality to the word as it is commonly used. For the word *adventure* denotes, simply enough, an arrival, an "advent," or a "coming to" a place or event. The etymology, from the French and Latin, is quite clear on this matter. However, in common parlance, the word *adventure* has long carried the sense of a "setting forth," a departure, or a venturing outward. To go adventuring is to leave one's home. True, any setting forth from one place also leads to an arrival somewhere, whether at another place entirely or a return to the original point of departure, but in common parlance, an adventure is not generally associated with the arrival at that destination. The word *adventure* is freighted with other meanings as well, including the sense of the extraordinary, of risk and reward, and of matters of chance (here, the term *adventitious* shows its family resemblance). But the sense of motion, of movement in space, and of explorations of other places seems to lie at the core of the word's significance, particularly as it is used in literature. When someone is said to be going on an adventure, it is normally understood that he or she is not arriving, but rather departing, notwithstanding the etymology. A paradox, perhaps.

Let us consider a very popular and famous adventure story, J. R. R. Tolkien's *The Hobbit*. The novel begins with the wandering wizard Gandalf the Grey "looking for someone to share in an adventure I am arranging," as he tells Bilbo Baggins, who responds that hobbits "have no use for adventures. Nasty disturbing uncomfortable things! Make you late for dinner!"[3] Naturally, the humorous scene is merely a prelude to a charming adventure in which the bourgeois Bilbo leaves the comforts of home, travels over hill and under hill, across rivers, valleys, forests, mountains, and lakes, all while accompanying dwarves and encountering trolls, elves, goblins, wolves, eagles, a sort of werebear, lake-men, and, of course, a dragon. But after all of these adventures, the final scene of the novel portrays Bilbo sitting with Gandalf in his cozy little home at Bag End in Hobbiton, sharing the tobacco jar with the wizard, who tells him that, notwithstanding the role he has played in the great world-historical events of the Third Age of Middle-earth, "You are a very fine person, Mr. Baggins, and I am very fond of you; but you are only quite a little fellow in the wide world after all," to which Bilbo assents, "Thank goodness!"[4]

Is it any surprise that, when he writes the narrative of this adventure, Bilbo chooses to name it "There and Back Again"? If we were to characterize the adventure story as a distinctive literary genre, we might conclude that the adventure is only accomplished at this point, with the return (or advent) of the wandering hero— that is, the narrative becomes an *adventure* only when this ultimate arrival, often a homecoming, takes place. Indeed, it cannot be entirely accidental that Tolkien's much grander adventure story, *The Lord of the Rings*—with its much larger geopolitical and historical range of reference, its exponentially greater number of characters, toponyms, and plots—nevertheless ends in the humble homecoming of an adventuring hero. The sequel to *The Hobbit* (which had concluded with an altogether homey or domestic scene) also ends with a hobbit (Sam) returning to the comforts of hearth and home, ending with these words: "Well, I'm back."[5]

Structurally then, the adventurer sets forth, but only to come home again, and this homecoming lends color to all that had come before. As in the greatest adventure of the classical antiquity, *The Odyssey*, Homeric narrative of Odysseus's postwar travels—now unavoidably mediated by Max Horkheimer and Theodor Adorno's astonishing reconsideration of it in the *Dialectic of Enlightenment*—the most memorable scenes contain bizarre, exotic, or otherworldly phenomena and locales, but the bourgeois gentleman's arrival and reclamation of his domicile establishes the ultimate stability, or we might even say, in a Foucauldian key, the "epistemic regularity," of the world depicted in the adventure.[6] At this point, perhaps, one is capable of envisioning a map of the world, charting one's knowledge of the places visited and peoples encountered, projecting an overarching diagram of use for further reflection and exploration. The narrative of adventure thus becomes a map, a literary cartography of its own world system.

In fact, the adventure does have an epistemic or scientific quality as well: the protagonist, who is also an observer, sets forth into exotic or unknown lands, and his or her account brings such places into the register of geographical and historical knowledge, which can then be brought to bear on further study, exploration, and potentially colonization or domination of disparate territories of the periphery by the forces at the metropolitan center or core, to invoke Immanuel Wallerstein's famous formulation in *The Modern World-System* volumes.[7] We see this quite clearly in many nineteenth-century adventures, some of which are also nonfiction personal narratives or travelogues, in which the narrator departs for whatever reason from the world of mainstream or familiar experience, enters—or rather, as it would commonly be viewed by contemporary readership, *descends*—into some unfamiliar, exotic, or primitive cultural space, only to return and deliver the goods about these experiences for a reading public based in the central and likely privileged zone of civilization. As Jonathan Arac has put it, looking specifically at personal narratives written in the United States in the 1840s, "Personal narratives characteristically have the circular shape of descent and return—a touching of ground, even a humiliation before the return to the elevation of ordinary, civilized life."[8]

This structure makes possible a related spatiotemporal engagement of the reader with the details of the narrative. In Arac's view, "A generic appeal of personal narratives in their time and since is their registration of what seems a more archaic way of life, a virtual past achieved by travel in space rather than in time, but from the perspective of a narrator who is, like the readership, part of the modern world, making contact with that 'other' world and transforming it while integrating it. Personal narratives may act thereby to colonize places and kinds of experience, which are then appropriated into national narrative."[9] Hence, regardless of the author's intent, adventure stories have frequently participated, wittingly or otherwise, in a sort of imperialist project as they serve to explore, identify, and incorporate foreign spaces and experiences, ineluctably forcing them into the general reservoir of knowledge and power in the metropolitan center. In the case of late-nineteenth-century writers such as Rudyard Kipling, H. Rider Haggard, and other well-known authors of adventure stories in that epoch, the complicity with or even celebration of the British colonial project and its "civilizing mission" is written on the surface of the tales; others, such as Joseph Conrad, may be more ambivalent about the politics, even if the narrative form and cultural effects are similar, as Edward Said's *Culture and Imperialism* so effectively demonstrated. The geocritical analysis of such tales discloses their connection to a network of power-knowledge relations that, in its micropolitical functions or effects, gives form to the modern world system in its emergence.[10]

As we know, such narratives also played a role in the burgeoning science of modern geography, as the stories of individual travelers helped to fill in the vast white spaces still on the map. In Joseph Conrad's *Heart of Darkness*, Marlow speaks of his boyhood love of map gazing, a love that was animated primarily by the "big, white spaces" of mystery and promise. As Marlow explains, "I had a passion for maps. . . . At that time there were many blank spaces on the earth, and when I saw one that looked particularly inviting on a map (but they all look that) I would put my finger on it and say, 'When I grow up I will go there.'"[11] Elsewhere, Conrad praises modern scientific cartography for its "honest" maps and their blank spaces, in contrast to the "fabulous geography" of old, which populated the unknown regions with sea monsters and the like. For Conrad, the "blankness," rather than the dragon, was the call to adventure, which must now in part be understood as the scientific quest to fill in spaces that were hitherto blank. Marlow points out that much of the map of Africa "had ceased to be a blank space of delightful mystery—a white patch for a boy to dream gloriously over. It had become a place of darkness."[12] Or rather, as he puts it later, the map had been filled with many colors, each indicating the sort of activity to be found there: "All the colours of a rainbow. There was a vast amount of red—good to see at any time, because one knows that some real work is being done in there, a deuce of a lot of blue, a little green, smears of orange, and, on the East Coast, a purple patch, to show where the jolly pioneers of progress drink the jolly lager-beer."[13] The irony of the "pioneers of progress" reference is acute, but underlying this observation is the tacit, or perhaps even unconscious, critique of the mapmaking enterprise in which the geographical and political pioneers are also engaged. Just as some persons on the ground may imbibe lager, bringing the comforts of home to their outposts of progress,[14] the cartographer organizes the elements and colors of the map to make things intelligible, familiar, and generally known to the viewer, here Marlow.

In Conrad's novel, as in Tolkien's, the itinerary of the protagonist—or the narrative of that protagonist's itinerary—gives form to the overall geography, filling in "spaces that before were blank," creating or adding significance to places previously marked, and helping to render comprehensible the entire imaginary space of the work. The result is a more or less fully formed cartography of the world depicted in the adventure story. The exotic zones depicted in the narrative are incorporated into an overall system of geographic, historical, cultural, and other knowledge for which the map itself is an entirely apt figure. The remarkable itinerary helps to trace the contours of the narrative map of that world, and the homecoming perhaps offers the frame-like closure of a projected artistic space. The adventure, in this way, fashions a certain kind of literary cartography, which is formed through the combination of the itinerary-like tracing of lines by the adventuring protagonist or narrator and the maplike overview afforded by the completed adventure.

The Contours of the Map

By this term *literary cartography*, I merely want to indicate the practice by which writers figuratively represent, or attempt to represent, the social space of the narrative or text, as well as the relationship of the individual or collective subject to a larger spatial, social, and cultural ensemble.[15] Literary cartography is a form of mapping, but one that certainly goes beyond the attempt to faithfully reproduce in diagrammatic fashion the places of the putatively "real-world" geospace. (But then neither does literal mapping faithfully reproduce the "real" world.) Literary cartography, in my view, is thus part of any narrative project and not a technical term for a certain type of interdisciplinary practice limited to the combining methods used in literature and geography, although there are clearly useful ways in which such overlapping artistic and scientific programs would come to address matters relevant to any discussion of literary cartography.

The figure of the "map" here is metaphorical, but only *just so*, since I also believe that a sort of cartographic anxiety animates the desire for narrative itself, which is necessarily a socially and spatially symbolic activity by which the subjective and objective modes are bound in inextricable, tense, yet productive relation. As a practical matter, this anxiety reflects not only one's sense of *being* lost, unable to locate oneself in space existentially, but also the quasi-scientific angst of feeling unable to map one's place and one's surroundings in a meaningful way: a crisis of representation. These two aspects of the cartographic anxiety align roughly with what might be considered the two phases, subjective and objective, of the narrative mapping project. The adventure of literary cartography will likewise involve the personal, experiential knowledge of given places and spaces, as well as the more abstract or philosophical projection of a maplike totality.[16]

In many ways telling a story is like drawing a map and vice versa. The adventure story, which traces the trajectory of the individual hero or a group of characters across the time and space of their adventures, is also a map of the world depicted in the narrative. Ultimately, the narrative as a whole not only represents the places depicted in it but also shapes them, giving form to the imaginary world in the text while also projecting a "world" that can be apprehended all at once. The adventure story, more often than not, operates like a world map.

Returning to *The Hobbit* for a moment, we see that that the starting point for this particular adventure story is an actual map, which Tolkien supplies in his own hand and which has a crucial diegetic function as a motive force for the adventure itself: Thrór's Map, the artifact that leads Thorin and Company on their quest. The map not only lays out the geography of the Lonely Mountain and its surroundings but also reveals a secret doorway into the mountain, a sine qua non of the Quest for Erebor. Of course, stepping outside of the narrative, the map is also helpful to the reader, who is able to orient himself or herself within the fantasy world Tolkien is creating. Indeed, the now-dominant marketing genre of fantasy practically requires maps, it seems; in any case many fantasy novels include maps, which—and I hope this is clear—are not the same as, or even necessarily correlative with, the literary cartography produced in their narratives.[17] The map in *The Hobbit* is thus simultaneously an element of the plot and a tool for making sense of that plot. Moreover, the map itself tells a story while also projecting a spatial diagram, and similarly the narrative of Bilbo's adventures figures forth a geography, imbuing the places depicted in it with meaning. Thus, the discovery of Thrór's Map makes possible the adventure in which the literary cartography of Middle-earth is rendered visible, but that hand-drawn map is itself an element of the strictly *literary* mapping undertaken by *The Hobbit*.

This is the nature of literary cartography, which is always characterized by a productive tension between two related but sometimes antagonistic registers: the narrative trajectory and the descriptive geography. For example, in his beautifully illustrated and compelling book, *Maps of the Imagination: The Writer as Cartographer*, Peter Turchi identifies two distinct but overlapping activities that together make possible an effective "map" for the reader. These are *exploration*, understood as "some combination of premeditated searching and undisciplined, perhaps only partly conscious rambling," and *presentation*, the deliberate creation of "a document meant to communicate with, and have an effect on, others."[18] Turchi, a creative writing professor, is thinking specifically about the writer's approach to a given work, but the tensions between exploration and presentation can be seen as typical of any number of literary productions.

Drawing from the history of mapmaking as well as from Fredric Jameson, Michel de Certeau, and others, I have suggested that the distinction between the *itinerary* and the *map* offers a useful way of dramatizing this tension, but we could easily imagine a roster of parallel binaries, whose elaboration and deconstruction could be productive of some engaging spatial criticism and theory. Such a list might include Georg Lukács's famous distinction between *narrative* and *description* in his powerful essay on European realism and naturalism, "Narrate or Describe."[19] Or perhaps we might consider the illuminating if not always stable distinction made by the Russian formalists between *fabula* and *sjuzhet*, except that the discursive form of the latter can be conceived as a plot in the spatial sense, of surveying a field or plotting a course, for example. Erich Auerbach's elegant reading of the remarkable differences in narrative representation between the Homeric epic and the book of Genesis in the opening chapter of *Mimesis* hints at this narrative tension as well. Furthermore, we might look to Mikhail Bakhtin's distinction between the epic and novelistic modes as further evidence of a complex spatiotemporal antagonism in the text, which is only partially resolved by reference to a literary chronotope.[20]

Behind these various distinctions we might discern the old rivalry between text and image, between the verbal and the iconic, and between storytelling and painting, for instance. (Here I am purposefully omitting any discussion of music, the third wheel of Roland Barthes's *Image-Music-Text*,[21] which seems to lie outside of this particular argument but which could offer another way of addressing these spatiotemporal phenomena, particularly since the literary cartography inevitably involves an aspect of polysensoriality.) The verbal narration and the visual diagram, while thoroughly compatible, do seem to stand as rival representational forms, each taunting the other over the ultimate futility of their respective quests.

The possible antagonism between media is worth considering, although I remain focused here on how these different modes or registers of experience, knowledge, and imagination play out in the *literary* text. Some people have noticed that I never include any maps, diagrams, or images of any kind in my own writings. This is not because I believe that such imagery is not useful, and I am a great admirer of many scholars who do employ actual maps and other figures in their work. But I do think that literary cartography, as I imagine it, has to be able to be practiced without recourse to nonliterary means. In other words, the mapping project implicit in many if not all narratives is not reliant on the use of actual maps. Indeed, arguably, maps could interfere with or confound such a project.

However, the rivalry between these two registers in the end is not a winner-take-all affair, since neither can definitively conquer the other, nor would either wish to do so, so we ought best view them, à la Baruch Spinoza, as *non opposita, sed diversa* (not opposed, but different). In any event, literary cartography is a form that necessarily combines, often in unforeseen or unexpected ways, both narrative and description. The interplay between the two animates and gives shape to the figurative map produced thereby. Any literary cartography must navigate between the need to advance the elements of a plot or story, thus acceding to a temporal register, and the equally pressing imperative to pause, to explain matters, to "paint a picture" or describe a scene, or—if I can draw upon the cinematic idiom for a minute—to pull back and offer "long" shots, figuring forth some imagined sense of overview.

This process not only allows the literary cartographer to represent, if only provisionally, the spaces and places under consideration but also, in the view of geographer Yi-Fu Tuan, actually calls into existence the "place" itself, making it subject to apprehension, interpretation, and exploration—that is, a place does not become a "place" at all until it has distinguished itself from the undifferentiated and abstract space of which it is a part. Furthermore, places are invested with significance only by being recognized as places "in the first place," which necessarily leads back into a narrative framework.[22] Tuan expresses a phenomenological notion of place as a "resting of the eyes," a pause that gives meaning, which he elaborates in both *Topophilia* and *Space and Place*. Tuan's conception reminds us that place and space are not interchangeable, yet they cannot be so categorically distinguishable at all times either. In resting one's eyes on—or, here, directing the reader's attention to—a given place, we observe that this portion of the spatial array in which we are ourselves embedded or enfolded becomes, if only temporarily and situationally, meaningful. This places it within the bailiwick of literary criticism as something to be interpreted or analyzed. Within the narrative, these pauses offer the reader a chance to consider or interpret the place in question and the narrative as a whole.

This topophrenia is essential for establishing the contours of the literary map, as well as the entire affective geography and history that emerges from the narrative. In the adventure story, one finds this dramatized in the well-nigh constant back and forth between the adventurer's dynamic adventures, explorations of exotic lands and experiences, and the narrative's almost static moments of description or "still life" in which the places are rendered more fully visible. (Goethe referred to these moments in Homer's *Odyssey* as "retarding elements" of the story.) *The Hobbit*, in its rather episodic form, appears to combine these in somewhat dramatic ways, as each "scene" nearly stands on its own, many taking place during a moment of rest or pause, which is thus a break from the overall narrative trajectory of "there and back again." Each of Bilbo's isolated adventures—for example, confounding the trolls, riddling with Gollum, fighting spiders, or escaping from the Wood Elves—takes place at various "stops" along the road. Yet as in Tuan's example, these pauses are crucial not only for the narrative's more general meaning, but also for lending significance to these places, which can now appear on the narrative map. Bilbo Baggins's individual adventures are therefore only a small part, albeit an essential part, of Tolkien's broader literary cartography. In order for the literary cartography of Middle-earth to emerge from the story of *The Hobbit*, the existential or phenomenological registers must be supplemented with a more abstract, theoretical, or speculative project. The sense of imaginary overview achieved by the narrative map helps to reinscribe both the experience of the characters and the topographical features of the imaginary world into a larger geopolitical and historical system, a system that in turn makes meaningful those discrete phenomena encountered along the way.

Structural Coordinates

Earlier I mentioned the distinction between the itinerary and the map. In Jameson, the reference comes from his famous discussion of cognitive mapping in his original, influential 1984 essay "Postmodernism, or, the Cultural Logic of Late Capitalism," a slightly revised version of which became the first chapter of his 1991 book of that name. Jameson argues that the dramatic permutations of lived space occasioned, if not entirely caused, by the radical restructuring of the world system in an era of late capitalism had produced a sort of postmodern hyperspace with which individual subjects are not physically (and certainly are not politically) equipped to deal. The result is a novel form of existential alienation and political impasse, an aporia that now stifles even our capacity for imagining potential alternatives. Analogizing the spatial bewilderment of an individual subject attempting to move about in an unmappable postmodern space—famously, it was the 1982 MLA convention held at the Bonaventure Hotel in Los Angeles that provided the exemplary *selva oscura* for so many postmodern Dantes—Jameson argues that a form of cognitive mapping is a necessary prerequisite for any future political and aesthetic practice in the era of globalization.

Jameson's first use of the phrase "cognitive mapping" actually appeared in a discussion of literary realism in *The Political Unconscious*, although the idea had clearly been taking shape over many years.[23] In the now canonical version, Jameson presents cognitive mapping as a blend of Kevin Lynch's urban studies and Louis Althusser's reconception of ideology as "the representation of the subject's Imaginary relationship to his or her Real conditions of existence."[24] In *The Image of the City*, Lynch had argued for a type of cognitive mapping—he does not use this term—when he refers to a city space's inherent "imageability" in connection with the urban pedestrian's practice of "wayfinding." In an alienated or alienating urban environment, the individual subject struggles to imagine the social space and to navigate within it, hence the need for some sort of cognitive mapping.[25] As Jameson summarizes it, "Disalienation in the traditional city, then, involves the practical reconquest of a sense of place and the construction or reconstruction of an articulated ensemble which can be retained in memory and which the individual subject can map and remap along the moments of mobile, alternative trajectories." In Jameson's view this cognitive mapping coincides with Althusser's theory of ideology, in which an individual may form a "situational representation" of the individual subject in relation to "that vaster and properly unrepresentable totality which is the ensemble of society's structures as a whole."[26]

At this point Jameson indulges in what he calls a "digression on cartography," for he recognizes that Lynch's model is more like an *itinerary* than a map, properly speaking. That is, Lynch's maps are really "diagrams organized around the still subject-centered or existential journey of the traveler, along which various significant key features are marked." Jameson compares this to the ancient portolan charts. Later developments, such as the technologies of the compass and the sextant, altered the process, such that mapping "comes to require the coordination of existential data (the empirical position of the subject) with unlived, abstract conceptions of the geographical totality." Finally, with the globe and the Mercator projection, Jameson notes that the properly representational crisis of modern cartography comes to the forefront, and "it becomes clear that there can be no true maps," but "at the same time it also becomes clear that there can be scientific progress, or better still, a dialectical advance, in the various historical moments of mapmaking." Jameson concludes this digression by returning to the problem of ideology, noting that "we all necessarily also cognitively map our individual social relationship to local, national, and international class realities."[27] Jameson later conceded that "'cognitive mapping' was in reality nothing but a code word for 'class consciousness'," albeit a class consciousness of a hitherto undreamed-of kind, with a consideration of the "new spatiality implicit in the postmodern."[28] For Jameson, such a figurative map—the projection of an imaginary cartography that can somehow make sense of the social totality—is the necessary-if-impossible prerequisite for any meaningfully utopian political or artistic program today.

My conception of the aesthetic practice of literary cartography draws upon this vision of cognitive mapping, which, truth be told, is in Jameson's own work a kind of supercharged metaphor for something like narrative itself. The "desire for narrative," as he once wrote, functions as a way of mapping our own, existential spatiotemporal finitude onto an alternative system of space and time, that of the great economic cycles, natural history, or just history itself.[29] The conflicting but not ultimately incommensurable registers of individual subjective perception and experience on the one hand and an abstract, totalizing or systemic theorizing on the other are maintained in the literary cartographic project. The itinerary informs the map, which in turn makes possible the significance of all those points encountered along the way. Just because one cannot represent the totality does not mean that one cannot try; in fact, as Jameson would point out, we do so all the time, whether we are aware of it or not. And the effort to map the totality is, in part, what underwrites the more limited sense-making or form-giving practices of storytelling itself.

Let me return to my poor, unadventurous little hobbit for a moment. Bilbo Baggins, although loathe to undertake any adventures when we meet him at the beginning of *The Hobbit*, was very intrigued by the history and geography of the wider world; in this, he was apparently unlike most of his fellow Shire folk, who preferred the comfort of a rather narrow, largely ignorant Weltanschauung. Like a young Joseph Conrad, Bilbo was partial to map gazing, and he delighted in stories of elves, dragons, and other mythlore—that is, after all, why Gandalf selects him. The wizard knows that in this otherwise unassuming person lies a consciousness equipped to countenance the ineluctable ruses of history, even if he himself does not know it yet. The final lines of the book, which I quoted above—"you are only a very little fellow in a wide world" and "Thank goodness!"—remind us of the humble origins of Bilbo's personal adventure, but they also advert to the vaster spatiotemporal adventure that exceeds any individual's personal experience. (As a side note, the presence of immortal beings complicates this somewhat, since characters such as Elrond and Galadriel vividly recall events that took place thousands of years before, but even among such persons, the overarching geohistory appears to be beyond anyone's individual ken.) As we later learn from *The Lord of the Rings* and from the immense backstory provided in *The Silmarillion* and other posthumously published writings,[30] Tolkien's little bourgeois burglar participates in what we can now see is but a brief episode of a much longer epic, extending backward into prehistory and anticipating further adventures that manifest themselves only in some dimly descried future. But then such is the nature of all of our adventures.

What emerges from these narratives, even those that follow closely the itinerary of a wandering protagonist, is a sense of overview, not very unlike the projection of a map. The bird's-eye view—or maybe I should say the dragon's-eye view—makes possible a kind of mapping that can empower otherwise bewildered or alienated agents to act, if only tentatively, and based on provisional and transitory information. Amid the apparently chaotic and incomprehensible forces and relations affecting us, the adventurers, on this shifting, unstable terrain, the clarifying overview of a maplike figure is frequently needed. Like Oedipa Maas in Thomas Pynchon's *The Crying of Lot 49*, alone in the planetarium and utterly bewildered by the circumstances in which she finds herself, we might well decide to "project a world"; as she concludes, "Anything might help."[31]

The map, as so many politically engaged critics have correctly observed, is itself a tool that can be wielded by powerful interests against the powerless, and geography—like other sciences and arts—has undoubtedly been complicit in various regimes of domination, from straightforwardly imperialist appropriations of territory to more subtle redistributions of power and knowledge relations across an array of social institutions and spaces. For these reasons, some have found the map form to be inherently repressive. Michel de Certeau suggests as much in his famous analysis of "Walking in the City," in which he finds the urban itineraries of the pedestrians, postmodern variants on Charles Baudelaire's flaneurs, to be free, liberatory, or revolutionary activities, resistant to the panoptic, ultimately static vision of the map, the view from above from some "Solar Eye." The view from above, in Certeau's reckoning, freezes the fluid mobility of the pedestrians below, forming a static image or map that, operating somewhat like Foucault's panoptic disciplinary mechanism, locates and distributes bodies in space according to an apparently retrogressive regime of power and knowledge.[32]

But what is missing from this analysis is the degree to which maps, however bound up in potentially baleful power-knowledge relations, remain inescapably useful to the persons on the ground. The itinerary of the flaneur might seem to follow no set path, as she or he creates shortcuts within officially sanctioned spaces or idly strolls along carefully planned avenues of commercial activity, but the urban pedestrian or the wandering adventurer cannot help but project maps, whether we think of them in terms of Lynch's imageability and wayfinding or in terms of a more abstract cartographic projection of an entire world. The maps produced from the imaginary bird's-eye view are, like all maps, provisional, and in their very mutability such schemes or plots necessarily resist complete capture by a static or stable image. Like Deleuzian nomads, the itinerant subjects map and remap, transforming spaces even as they occupy or traverse them. However, I do not mean to suggest that there is anything inherently revolutionary in the nomadic cartographies, for as Gilles Deleuze and Félix Guattari have cautioned, smooth spaces alone will not save us.[33] In this case, the itinerant pedestrians are not so much subverting some panoptic mapping scheme as they are informing the creation and re-creation of multiple cartographies.

As Jameson has put it, with respect to cognitive mapping, "My thesis . . . is not merely that we ought to strive for it, but that we do so all the time without being aware of the process."[34] This thesis has been restated, in a way, with great timeliness in Alberto Toscano and Jeff Kinkle's recent book, *Cartographies of the Absolute*, which notes that "one of the first products of a genuine striving for orientation is disorientation, as proximal coordinates come to be troubled by wide, and at times overwhelming vistas."[35] Combining these insights, I might say that the cartographic imperative compels us to try to produce a map even as we remain experientially limited in our itineraries, but one of the more common results of this cognitive mapping is a completely different, perhaps unforeseen, or previously unimaginable image. It may sound odd to say it this way, but literary cartography partakes of estrangement. Arriving back from where we had set forth on an adventure, the world may well look suddenly strange and new.

The End of the Adventure

The mapping project of narrative frequently discloses the pitfalls or downright failures associated with it, as the attempt to give form to the vast, shifting spaces of any world system, and of its untranscendable horizon of history, inevitably frustrate the earnest literary cartographer. But then that is part of the adventure, and the mapmaker's rough drafts prove to be the foundations on which subsequent efforts are based. "True" maps, after all, are impossible, but that merely ensures the possibility of better maps.

In this, we might say, the work of art maintains its utopian dimension in the projection of an alternative reality that, like the map itself, both depicts a discernible space and bodies forth a distorted vision of it. In telling a story, one necessarily traces an itinerary and projects a map, and both of these aspects of storytelling in turn give form to the world as it becomes narratable or knowable. The rivalry between text and image, narrative and description is thus shown to be both false and inevitable, as the literary cartographers simultaneously create and represent the territories as they map them.

The adventure of literary cartography conjures up these various aspects of exploration, representation, and projection. An adventure ineluctably combines the inner and outward journeys of a subject situated in, moving through, and conditioned by space and place.[36] These adventures in literary cartography—adventures *as* literary cartography—make possible new ways of imagining the world, as well as new ways of imagining the text today. For critics whose job is to interpret these maps, the adventure begins anew with each reading, and the maps formed and reformed over many adventures in literary cartography yield fresh ways of seeing, not to mention thinking, the world we inhabit.

Notes

1. See Edward W. Soja, *Thirdspace: Journeys through Los Angeles and Other Real-and-Imagined Places* (Oxford: Blackwell, 1996).

2. See Bertrand Westphal, *The Plausible World: A Geocritical Approach to Space, Place, and Maps*, trans. Amy D. Wells (New York: Palgrave Macmillan, 2013).

3. J. R. R. Tolkien, *The Hobbit* (New York: Del Rey, 1982), 4.

4. Ibid., 305.

5. J. R. R. Tolkien, *The Return of the King* (New York: Del Rey, 1986), 340.

6. See Max Horkheimer and Theodor W. Adorno, *Dialectic of Enlightenment: Philosophical Fragments*, trans. Edmund Jephcott (Palo Alto, CA: Stanford University Press, 2002); see also Michel Foucault, *The Archaeology of Knowledge*, trans. A. M. Sheridan Smith (New York: Pantheon, 1972).

7. Immanuel Wallerstein, *The Modern World System*, 3 volumes (New York: Academic Press, 1974).

8. Jonathan Arac, *The Emergence of American Literary Narrative, 1820–1860* (Cambridge, MA: Harvard University Press, 2005), 77.

9. Ibid.

10. See Edward W. Said, *Culture and Imperialism* (New York: Knopf, 1993); see also my "Introduction: The World, the Text, and the Geocritic," in *The Geocritical Legacies of Edward W. Said*, ed. Robert T. Tally Jr. (New York: Palgrave Macmillan, 2015), 1–16.

11. Joseph Conrad, *Heart of Darkness* (New York: Bantam Books, 1969), 10–11.

12. Ibid., 11; see also Joseph Conrad, "Geography and Some Explorers," in *Last Essays* (London: J. M. Dent, 1926), 1–31.

13. Conrad, *Heart of Darkness*, 14–15.

14. See Joseph Conrad, "An Outpost of Progress," in *Tales of Unrest*, ed. Allan H. Simmons and J. H. Stape (Cambridge: Cambridge University Press, 2012), 75–100.

15. See, e.g., Barbara Piatti, *Die Geographie der Literatur: Schauplätze, Handlungsräume, Raumphantasien* (Göttingen: Wallstein Verlag, 2008).

16. On "cartographic anxiety," see Derek Gregory, *Geographical Imaginations* (Oxford: Blackwell, 1994).

17. In a 1989 foreword to his humorous and loving send-up of the fantasy genre, *The Color of Magic* (New York: Harper, 1989), Terry Pratchett feels the need to explain why this novel *does not* include maps of his fictional Discworld: "There are no maps. You can't map a sense of humor. Anyway, what is a fantasy map but a space beyond which There Be Dragons? On the Discworld we know that There Be Dragons Everywhere. They might not all have scales and forked tongues, but they Be Here all right, grinning and jostling and trying to sell you souvenirs."

18. Peter Turchi, *Maps of the Imagination: The Writer as Cartographer* (San Antonio, TX: Trinity University Press, 2004), 12

19. See Georg Lukács, "Narrate or Describe," in *Writer and Critic*, trans. Arthur D. Kahn (New York: Grosset, 1970), 110–148.

20. See Erich Auerbach, *Mimesis: The Representation of Reality in Western Literature*, trans. Willard R. Trask (Princeton, NJ: Princeton University Press, 1953); see also Mikhail Bakhtin, *The Dialogic Imaginations: Four Essays*, ed. and trans. Caryl Emerson and Michael Holquist (Austin: University of Texas Press, 1981).

21. See Roland Barthes, *Image-Music-Text*, trans. Stephen Heath (New York: Hill and Wang, 1977).

22. See Yi-Fu Tuan, *Space and Place: The Perspective of Experience* (Minneapolis: University of Minnesota Press, 1977) and *Topophilia: A Study of Environmental Perception, Attitudes, and Values* (New York: Columbia University Press, 1990).

23. See Fredric Jameson, *The Political Unconscious: Narrative as a Socially Symbolic Act* (Ithaca, NY: Cornell University Press, 1981), 104. Jameson has noted that his 1977 essay "Class and Allegory in Mass Culture" was an attempt to illuminate those processes he later associated with cognitive mapping; see Fredric Jameson, *Signatures of the Visible* (London: Routledge, 1990), 54. As early as 1968, Jameson had used the figure of the map to describe the political challenges faced by the American artist at that time; see Fredric Jameson, "On Politics and Literature," *Salmagundi* 2, no. 3 (Spring–Summer 1968), 22–23.

24. Fredric Jameson, *Postmodernism, or, the Cultural Logic of Late Capitalism* (Durham, NC: Duke University Press, 1991), 51.

25. Kevin Lynch, *The Image of the City* (Cambridge, MA: MIT Press, 1960).

26. Jameson, *Postmodernism*, 51.

27. Ibid., 52.

28. Ibid., 418.

29. Fredric Jameson, introduction to *The Ideologies of Theory: Essays, 1971–1986*, vol. 1, *Situations of Theory* (Minneapolis: University of Minnesota Press, 1988), xxviii.

30. See J. R. R. Tolkien, *The Silmarillion* (New York: Del Rey, 2002).

31. Thomas Pynchon, *The Crying of Lot 49* (New York: Harper and Row, 1966), 82.

32. Michel de Certeau, *The Practice of Everyday Life*, trans. Steven Randall (Berkeley: University of California Press, 1984).

33. Gilles Deleuze and Félix Guattari, *A Thousand Plateaus*, trans. Brian Massumi (Minneapolis: University of Minnesota Press, 1987), 500.

34. Fredric Jameson, *The Geopolitical Aesthetic: Cinema and Space in the World System* (Bloomington and London: Indiana University Press and the British Film Institute, 1992), 2.

35. Alberto Toscano and Jeff Kinkle, *Cartographies of the Absolute* (Winchester, UK: Zero Books, 2015), 25.

36. See, e.g., Andrew Thacker, *Moving through Modernity: Space and Geography in Modernism* (Manchester: Manchester University Press, 2003).

8   In the Suburbs of Amaurotum

UTOPIAE INSULAE FIGURA, an illustration included in the original 1516 publication of Thomas More's *Utopia*, depicts the rough form of More's fanciful but ideal nation-state. In this woodcut, Utopia's capital city, Amaurotum, is placed in a suitably central position, but even more prominent in the foregrounding is a ship at anchor, presumably the one that brought Raphael Hythlodaeus to the island. A sailor stands on the deck and appears to be gazing off at the Utopian landscape, and one could argue that this figure represents the position of More's own readers, who vicariously take part in a travel narrative, exploring the spaces of this strange country.[1] It is a peculiarly modern image, and the careful ordering of its elements reflects the rational order of Utopian society, which in turn discloses a perhaps unconscious desire for order, symmetry, and reason in early modern European societies as well. The mere historical and geographical accident of Hythlodaeus's discovery of Utopia is duly compensated for in the methodical, logical, and rational organization of the society. More's *Utopia* supplies a fantastic vision of how a society can reorganize itself, spatially and socially, as a thoroughly modern state.

Utopia, as well as the genre it helped to establish and the mode of thought it exemplifies and popularized, represents a critical node at which conceptions of fantasy, spatiality, and modernity intersect. In this vision of the utopian place (or *no place*),[2] More enacts a reorganization of social spaces that anticipates the changing spatiality of the Baroque epoch and the project of Enlightenment rationality, thus forming a certain image of modern social organization. If, as Phillip E. Wegner has convincingly argued,[3] utopia is inextricably tied to the spatial histories of modernity, then More's literary cartography of the ideal *insula* might be seen as a prototype for the imaginary maps of modern societies. These are fundamentally fantastic, at least as much as the imaginary community of Utopia is, since they are both fictional and imaginary. However, the term *fantasy* has often been freighted with unfavorable associations and must overcome critiques from at least two fronts: the somewhat scientific or philosophical bias toward a kind of narrative realism on the one hand and the politically charged critique of fantasy as an "escapist" genre on the other. Traditionally, the critical discourse of modernity has envisioned a demystification of the world, such that the repression or elimination of those elements deemed fantastic has appeared to be almost an imperative of a distinctly modern worldview, as in that archetypical narrative of Western modernity, *Don Quixote*, in which the fantasies promulgated by chivalric romances and embraced as facts by the mad knight are repeatedly and humorously shown to be false in the face of an all-too-realistic real world. But because all utopias are necessarily always fantastic inasmuch as they project an entirely imaginary and by definition not (or not yet) real place, utopian discourse has itself at various times been dismissed as unrealistic, impractical, or romantic, perhaps most famously by Karl Marx and Friedrich Engels in *The Communist Manifesto*. From the perspective of a sober realism, both works of fantasy and utopia might be dismissed as fanciful, if not also childish or silly. Yet a number of antifantasy critics have embraced utopia and granted special status to this particular form of fantasy, owing to its cognitive, quasi-scientific projection of a rational order.[4] In this view utopia is the progressive, future-oriented, and modern genre or mode par excellence, while fantasy appears as backward-looking, nostalgic, or anti-modern.

However, viewed from the perspective of a *longue durée*, the experience of modernity has also been imbued with a profoundly fantastic content—whether in the sense of a utopian projection of idealized societies or later by a sort of Gothic return of the repressed (perhaps best emblematized by Francisco Goya's famous "Sleep of Reason")—the speculative projection of alternative futures or places in what emerges as the genre of science fiction, or the historical vision of radically different pasts or presents in the fantasy genre. The dialectic of mimesis and fantasy in literature, as Kathryn Hume has analyzed in some detail, does not resolve itself as a simple victory for one mode or the other, but both continue to inform works of the imagination.[5] This dialectic has undoubtedly played itself out in narrative throughout history, but many scholars have observed an increasing tendency toward the fantastic in the past century, as even the most high-minded of serious literature (such as *Ulysses* or *One Hundred Years of Solitude*) has drawn on myth, magic, or other apparently unrealistic modes of discourse in their production. Although readers and scholars differ as to the merits of fantasy as a literary genre, there is little question that, as Tom Shippey has put it, "the dominant literary mode of the twentieth century has been the fantastic."[6] Between More's *Utopia* of the early sixteenth century and what China Miéville has called the "fiction of alterity" in the twenty-first century, a persistent if discontinuous line of fantastic thought runs through modern literary history.

Realism itself, one could argue, is not exempt from fantasy's influence. Even for those whose aim is to produce a pragmatic and realistic representation of the people, events, and spaces under consideration in a given work, the fantastic mode has become a necessary part of any literary cartography. If narratives are among the principal means by which writers and readers project imaginary maps of their world, these may or may not also be utopian, and the degree to which their representational techniques may be deemed realistic or unrealistic may vary wildly from work to work. However, the basic grounding in a certain mode of alterity makes possible the innovative and critical apprehension of reality itself, as I discuss below. Unlike in More's canonical version or even in the modern utopias of the industrial age (such as Edward Bellamy's *Looking Backward*, William Morris's *News from Nowhere*, or H. G. Wells's *A Modern Utopia*), the utopian imagination in the age of globalization is not concerned with discovering a hidden island or future ideal state in the world; rather, it involves a figurative projection and representation of the world itself. Yet these earlier versions share with the more recent productions a fundamentally fantastic approach to the reality they seek simultaneously to represent and to transform. Utopias such as More's, then, might be said to provide fantastic maps in which the given social system's other spaces—those liminal and hybrid zones in which the strange, seemingly fantastic, but possibly liberating elements of this world make themselves visible—may be discerned. No less than a writer interested in a realistic depiction of the society in which the narrative takes place, the utopian or fantasist addresses the condition of the "real" world but does so with the possibility in mind that the improbable might be true. In these otherworldly spaces the radical alterity associated with the fantastic mode establishes a conceptual and affective break with the present state of things. The city of Amaurotum, whose name is etymologically suggestive of shadows or dreams, offers one kind of fantasy for imagining the social spaces of modernity, but in the mist-enveloped realms of fantasy, we may discover some of modernity's other spaces as well.

Utopian Spatiality

More's fictional Utopia establishes an ideal image of how social spaces are to be organized in a modern nation-state. Among the many marvelous scientific and social achievements in this country that is at once a no place (*ou-topia*) and a good place (*eu-topia*), urban planning must be counted near the top. "There are fifty-four splendid big towns on the island, all with the same language, laws, customs, and institutions. They're all built on the same plan, and, so far as the sites will allow, they all look exactly alike."[7] Such standardization of the Utopian urban space is part of what makes it utopian: "Let me tell you some more about the towns. Well, when you've seen one of them, you've seen all of them, for they are as nearly identical as local conditions will permit. So I'll just give you one example—it doesn't matter which. However, the obvious choice is Amaurotum," obvious because it is the capital city.[8] The centrality of this imaginary city and its role in the idealized state accord it some privilege in the world of imaginary places. The fantastic metropolis of Amaurotum appears as a representative space of modernity.

In projecting this rational, standardized space of the capital city, More and the utopians who followed in his wake anticipate the massive social and spatial transformations associated with the emergence of the modern nation-state.

The rationalization of social space he envisions partakes of the same sorts of revolutionary spatial transformations that have been famously described and analyzed in Michel Foucault's archaeologies of the medical "gaze" or genealogy of disciplinary societies. Sounding a good deal more ominous than the utopians, Foucault describes the "disciplinary mechanism" that this political reorganization of social space establishes: "This enclosed, segmented space, observed at every point, in which the individuals are inserted in a fixed place, in which the slightest movements are supervised, in which all events are recorded, in which an uninterrupted work of writing links the centre and the periphery, in which power is exercised without division, according to a continuous hierarchical figure, in which each individual is constantly located, examined, and distributed among the living beings, the sick and the dead—all this constitutes a compact model of the disciplinary mechanism."[9] The plague-stricken, late seventeenth-century society Foucault describes in *Discipline and Punish* would seem to be rather far removed from the humanistic ideals of More's Utopia, yet Foucault concludes that "the plague-stricken town . . . is the utopia of the perfectly governed city."[10] In Foucault, the shadows of an Amaurotum appear a good deal darker.

More's idealized description of the social ordering of Utopia anticipates the revolutionary reorganizations of power and knowledge in the Enlightenment.[11] This new spatial order of the modern urban geography, which increasingly extends its conceptual reach to the national and international spatiopolitical ensembles as well, has been historically associated with a philosophical discourse of modernity connected to the multimodal phenomenon of *Aufklärung,* which for Kant entailed mankind's emancipation from a childish or minor status and which itself cannot be wholly separated from the material basis in the transformations of political economy or in other words the capitalist mode of production.[12] The capitalist reorganization of time had a tendency to spatialize the temporal mode through what Marx understood as the fetishism of the commodity, in which (subjective) labor time congealed into the (objective) form of the physical commodity. "Thus," according to Georg Lukács in his famous meditation on reification, "time sheds its qualitative, variable, flowing nature; it freezes into an exactly delimited, quantifiable continuum filled with quantifiable 'things' (the reified, mechanically objectified human personality): in short, it becomes space."[13] From a more general, philosophical point of view, the Enlightenment project is also characterized by a sort of spatialization of experience, such that every aspect of human and inhuman existence could somehow be ordered into a rational and orderly diagram.

Max Horkheimer and Theodor W. Adorno in *Dialectic of Enlightenment* notoriously observed that the crucial aspect of Enlightenment rationality was the meticulous coordination and classification of the elements of existence, which extends to its apprehension of geographical space, obviously, in rationalizing the spaces of the world with new geometric and geographic precision. But it also tends to spatialize knowledge itself, making everything increasingly measurable and mappable. Referring to the bizarrely resonant conceptual parallels between Immanuel Kant's transcendental aesthetic and the Marquis de Sade's gymnastic sexual concatenations, Adorno and Horkheimer argue that "what Kant grounded transcendentally, the affinity of knowledge and planning, which impressed the stamp of inescapable expediency on every aspect of a bourgeois existence that was wholly rationalized, even in every breathing-space, Sade realized empirically."[14] Not only space but all human activity becomes measurable, quantifiable, and ordered, such that even the extravaganzas of Sadean pornography can appear as dully categorical as the periodic table of elements. But in terms of the Enlightenment's great modern injunction, *Sapere aude!*—enunciated by Kant himself in his answer to the question, "What is Enlightenment?"—such drily methodical ordering is a sign of mankind's maturity. It is evidence that humankind, having overcome the chimeras of superstition and affiliated phantasmagoria, can now embrace the coolly rational understanding of the world.[15] This is itself a utopian vision, reflecting the aspirations of a rationalist thinker whose optimism with respect to humankind's self-emancipation from religious or political charlatans would be sorely tested in the coming years and centuries.

More's perfectly laid out social spaces and standardized cities, the Baroque reorganization of social space in terms of mathematical precision or the Cartesian grid, the ordering of spaces according to the exigencies of a disciplinary society à la Foucault's genealogy of power, the transformation of time and experience into a spatial framework in a capitalist mode of production, the Enlightenment project of rationalization, and the desacralization of the world: all of these are themselves the real-world results of what may well be considered, ironically or otherwise, a fantastic mode of thought. The dream of a perfectly rational organization of social space, like utopia itself, is after all a fantasy, and the utopian philosophical order, political policies, economic processes, or urban planning that attempt to realize these fantasies are in some ways also fantastic. The literary or figurative mappings produced by such processes disclose fantastic spaces.

The paradigm shifts associated with the advent of a modern social organization require the imaginative projection of an almost mathematical order that is quite unreal, bringing the chaotic and vicissitudinous elements of nature, culture, and society into an orderly whole that cannot but be artificial. The utopian project of modern philosophy and science is to imagine an alternative reality in which reason and order prevail, if only provisionally, or as a means of making more sense of our own, intransigently irrational or disorderly experience of the world. In this manner, one could liken the utopian project to that of cartography itself, which imposes an obviously artificial order, often in the form of a Cartesian grid, complete with coordinates and trajectories, on a space that in one's "real-world" experience frequently resists the map's logical order, as smooth spaces become striated, deterritorialized and reterritorialized.[16] The distinctive spatiality of this modern vision is marked in the figure of the map itself, which is inherently modern while also exceeding its own attempts to confine the spaces it represents to the limits of its frame. Although some sort of orienting or mapping activity seems essential to the human condition, the rise of cartography in Europe during the Age of Discovery is far from coincidental. As Tom Conley points out in *The Self-Made Map*, aside from the portolan charts used by Mediterranean navigators to help locate harbors, "At the beginning of the fifteenth century, maps were practically nonexistent, whereas only two centuries later they were the bedrock of most professions and disciplines."[17] There is something simultaneously fantastic and real about the map, particularly the world map, in which an abstract representation of an impossibly vast space—the world itself—is to be grasped in almost banally practical terms, as a mere tool for navigation, or in a more sublime sense, as a work of art. The map then, like the fantastic vision of an ideal social organization, is itself utopian.

The Need for Fantasy

One might argue that the fantastic, broadly conceived as a mode but also encompassing the literary genre of fantasy, a genre that would include utopian writing as a subset,[18] is constitutive of the "unfinished project" of modernity itself.[19] That is, the attempt to apprehend critically the diverse spaces in which we live requires a fantastic literary or figurative cartography. Such a project concerns both the daily, lived experience of individuals in modern societies and the broader structural totality, the mode of production or the spaces of the world system, which lie beyond the ken of the individual subject but which may be figured forth in the aesthetic sphere. The practical value of fantasy lies in its ways of simultaneously making sense of the world and imagining alternatives to it.

However, since "fantasy" is frequently used to dismiss whatever it purports to represent, any aesthetic or critical project in the fantastic mode must address the stringent critiques of those who oppose fantasy in all of its forms.[20] Even more so than with the often maligned *utopia*, a word and concept that continues to need to be defended against those forces that militate in favor of the sociopolitical status quo, *fantasy* is freighted with a rather pejorative sense in modern criticism and theory. Fantasy is opposed not only to mimetic realism in literature or art but also to reality itself at times. Fantasy's apparent rejection of the real, the possible, and even the probable is perhaps reason enough for some to reject it outright. Moreover, as noted above, fantasy also finds enemies from within the realm of nonmimetic or antirealistic literature and criticism. Some of its most influential and vocal foes today are critics who themselves embrace utopia and science fiction but who argue that the estrangements of fantasy are politically suspect: at best offering mere escapism, worse reinforcing the status quo, or worst of all actively supporting reactionary politics. Following Darko Suvin's influential notion of "cognitive estrangement" in science fiction, such theorists as Fredric Jameson, Carl Freedman, and others have dismissed fantasy as a genre (taken to be distinct from science fiction and utopia) on the grounds that it is characterized by irrational, noncognitive, or mythic estrangement, which then leaves it open to the potentially reactionary politics of nostalgia or romanticism.[21]

While a number of spatially oriented critics have embraced utopia, many of these same critics have been openly hostile to fantasy. For example, Fredric Jameson has long defended utopian thinking against those, both within a leftist intellectual tradition and outside of it, who would use the term *utopia* to defame cultural projects intended to imagine radical alternatives to the present social or political system. Referring particularly to the utopianism of Herbert Marcuse in the 1960s and defending it against the charges of Marx's own anti-utopian arguments, Jameson contends that, whereas "in the older society (as in Marx's classic analysis) Utopian thought represented a diversion of revolutionary energy into idle wish-fulfillments and imaginary satisfactions, in our own time the very nature of the Utopian concept has undergone a dialectical reversal. Now it is practical thinking which everywhere represents a capitulation to the system itself, and stands as a testimony to the power of that system to transform even its adversaries into its own mirror image."[22] If practical thinking, perhaps including a certain philosophical or literary realism, has become the enemy of the imagination—the faculty that resists the gravitational force field of the merely actual in favor of speculative projections of the distantly possible, virtual, or even impossible—then one might argue for the necessity of fantasy for rethinking the world. Yet Jameson joins Suvin, Freedman, and a number of other prominent utopians in rejecting fantasy. Indeed, in his own extensive statement on "the desire called utopia," Jameson condemns any confusion between the generic modes of utopia (here understood as a "socio-economic subset" of science fiction) and fantasy by stating that "we must now lay this misunderstanding to rest."[23] Here then the antagonism is not between fantasy and some favored form of realism but between fantasy and a still-preferable but nonrealistic form, that of utopia or more generally science fiction.

Although the fantasy-versus-SF antagonism, with its strident partisans and passionate arguments, undoubtedly antedates academic criticism on the subject, a key point of departure for scholars remains Suvin's trailblazing 1979 study, *Metamorphoses of Science Fiction*. In that book, Suvin both champions and carefully analyzes the broad-based and expansive genre of science fiction, while also establishing the terms by which fantasy would be dismissed. Drawing on the Brechtian concept of "estrangement," Suvin argues that science fiction is a genre of "cognitive estrangement," whereas fantasy relies on irrational, mythic, or metaphysical estrangement. Suvin finds that fantasy as a genre is fundamentally anti-scientific, using religious themes, magic, and other fanciful elements to project a different world, but one that has little direct bearing on the world in which we live. As such, fantasy is less useful for those who wish to *think* the world, and much less so for those who wish to change it.[24] Fantasy is thus "escapist" and reactionary, as the world into which the reader is expected to escape is often that of a mythical, often pastoral, past. For example, Michael Moorcock has argued that "since the beginnings of the Industrial Revolution, at least, people have been yearning for an ideal rural world they believe to have vanished—yearning for a mythical state of innocence. . . . This refusal to face or derive any pleasure from the realities of urban industrial life, this longing to possess, again, the infant's eye view of the countryside, is a fundamental theme in popular English literature."[25] Fantasy thus is deemed either useless or harmful for any progressive political project.

It probably does not help that the most inescapable figure in twentieth-century fantasy literature, J. R. R. Tolkien, whose own political views were not exactly revolutionary, defended fantasy precisely *as* an escapist practice. Complaining that readers opposed to fantasy have confused "the escape of the prisoner with the flight of the deserter," Tolkien asks: "Why should a man be scorned if, finding himself in prison, he tries to get out and go home? Or if, when he cannot do so, he thinks and talks about other topics than jailers and prison-walls?"[26] (In response, Moorcock has observed that jailers most certainly do not hate *escapism*; what they hate is actual escape.[27]) Indeed, Tolkien goes so far as to claim that the world outside this prison is just as "real," whether the prisoner can see it or not, which suggests a view of fantasy as an imaginative method for apprehending the "real world" rather than a means of escaping from it—that is, in imagining an otherworld like Middle-earth and populating it with histories, persons, events, and so on, fantasists such as Tolkien provide readers with the means of making sense of their all-too-real worlds in a manner consistent with the most realistic of fiction but also going beyond the merely realistic. The literary cartography of Middle-earth can aid us in giving shape to our own views of this world, drawing on the lessons of the fantastic narratives that may not be accessible or even possible in strictly mimetic representations of "real" everyday life.

Coming from an entirely different political and philosophical tradition, China Miéville has also defended fantasy against its detractors on both the right and the left. A committed socialist and activist, as well as an important author of fantasy and science fiction (a distinction he does not think is very useful), Miéville has said some rather mischievous things about Tolkien, most famously, that the Oxford professor's influential presence was "a wen on the arse of fantasy literature," although he has repented of this view in recent years.[28] Miéville is undoubtedly opposed to the retrogressive politics of such fantasists as Tolkien or

C. S. Lewis, but he finds in the Marxist critique of capitalism evidence for fantasy's critical value. Indeed, Miéville asserts that fantasy offers a better approach than even realism for getting at the truth of the "real world" under capitalism. After discussing Marx's analysis in *Capital* of the fetishism of the commodity and the hidden social relations embedded in it, Miéville explains that "'real' life under capitalism *is a fantasy*: 'realism,' narrowly defined, is therefore a 'realistic' depiction of 'an absurdity which is true,' but no less absurd for that. Narrow 'realism' is as partial and ideological as 'reality' itself."[29] Furthermore, Miéville insists, the "apparent epistemological radicalism of the fantastic mode's basic predicate," namely that "the impossible is true," makes it well suited to the task of an oppositional or critical project.[30] It should be noted, however, that Miéville quite rightly does not claim that fantasy is itself a revolutionary mode or "acts as a guide to political action."[31] The value of fantasy lies less in its politics, which could fall anywhere along the political spectrum, than in its imaginative encounter with alterity. As Miéville concludes, "The fantastic might be a mode peculiarly suited to and resonant with the forms of modernity. . . . Fantasy is a mode that, in constructing an internally coherent but actually impossible totality— constructed on the basis that the impossible is, for this work, *true*—mimics the 'absurdity' of capitalist modernity."[32] That is, where the so-called real world of capitalist modernity is in fact false, masking the underlying social relations of production, the fantastic mode, precisely because it calls this so-called real world into question from the start, makes possible novel, imaginative, and radically different representations.

Miéville decries the attitude that has allowed "generations of readers and writers to treat, say, faster-than-light drives as science-fictional in a way that dragons are not, despite repeated assurances from the great majority of physicists that the former are no less impossible than the latter."[33] Against the anti-fantasy sentiments of the spaceship enthusiasts or dragon detractors, Miéville files all of these genres—science fiction, utopia, and fantasy—within a larger but perhaps more helpful category that he terms the literature of alterity. This intensive regard for otherness, whether presented in terms of the past or future, the earthly or the interstellar, the monstrous or the alien, is shared by all forms of the fiction of estrangement, including some, such as *Moby-Dick*, that are inexpressibly "strange" even while they present absolutely realistic (or at least possible) persons, places, and events. The conception of a "fiction of estrangement" enables the fantastic mode to exceed the boundaries of its more tightly circumscribed genre. The supreme value of fantasy lies in its meditation on the impossible, which can enable a radically different vantage point from which to view reality. As Miéville puts it, "We need fantasy to think the world, and to change it."[34]

In this sense Miéville's defense of fantasy as a critical mode with which to map the world connects neatly with the argument of one of the leading utopian theorists of the past century. Herbert Marcuse saw in the power of the imagination and specifically in the products of the aesthetic sphere an opportunity to "refuse" the limitations of the spatiotemporal conditions of modern life: "The Great Refusal is the protest against unnecessary repression, the struggle for the ultimate form of freedom—'to live without anxiety.' But this idea could be formulated without punishment only in the language of art. In the more realistic realm of political theory and even philosophy, it was almost universally defamed as utopia."[35] Of course, Marcuse does not intend this last word as a pejorative but acknowledges the way in which utopia, like fantasy, is normally dismissed by those with a vested interest in the "reality principle" or the sociopolitical status quo. But, as Marcuse concludes, "In its refusal to accept as final the limitations imposed on freedom and happiness by the reality principle, in its refusal to forget what *can be*, lies the critical function of phantasy."[36] Here utopia and fantasy come together as a single theoretical practice in the service of a literary cartography of both the existing world system and potential alternative formations.

Conclusion: *Plus Ultra*

The value of this fantastic effort seems to be confirmed in the imaginative endeavor involved in mapping our own "real world," particularly the postmodern world system in which the traditional guideposts are no longer trustworthy or desirable. "Happy are those ages when the starry sky is a map of all possible paths," writes Lukács of the age of the epic, using language that sounds not much different from Tolkien's: "The world is wide and yet it is like a home."[37] Today, the celestial charts are not so reliable or *heimlich*, and the literary cartography of the present world system has to be, in some ways, otherworldly. In theory and in practice, the alterity of fantasy makes possible new ways of seeing, and thus of interpreting and perhaps even changing, the world in which we actually live, for better and for worse. In the era of globalization, an age that has witnessed a remarkable resurgence of fantasy in the arts and literature, perhaps not coincidentally, the world system forms what Jameson, following Sartre, has called the "untranscendable horizon" of any critical project, such that "all thinking today is *also*, whatever else it is, an attempt to think the world system as such."[38] This global space requires a sort of abstraction and imaginative projection that makes a literature of estrangement the form potentially best suited to the present condition. The fantastic mode allows us, among other things, to see the world anew and to imagine different approaches to representing and otherwise engaging with it. As Miéville asserts pointedly, "Fantasy . . . is *good to think with*."[39]

In More's case, the "discovery" of the island of Utopia signaled the possibility, if only in the form of satire or social critique, of a radically transformed society, even if the main thrust of the narrative is less prescriptive than critical. New spaces are possible, if only they can be imagined. Famously, More's island nation was not originally an island. Before it could function as an ideal society, the conqueror-king Utopus had ordered a fifteen-mile-wide trench to be dug in order to separate the nation from the mainland. The radical break, of course, becomes symbolic of the spatiotemporal rupture that signals the emergence of the modern state. That is, it involves both the delineation of a distinctive national space, with all the concomitant ideological freight of borders and boundaries, enclosure, subdivisions, and so on, and the marked disjunction between the viscerally experienced present and a soon-to-be-forgotten or romanticized past.[40] It is a spatiotemporal metaphor for what Marcuse would call "the scandal of qualitative difference."[41] More's capital city and prototype of the modern state are imaginary, but their effects are all too real. The utopian space to be found in the organization of Amaurotum is perhaps quintessentially modern, fit for the world system emerging in the wake of voyages of discovery, ordered and rational, and, above all, sensible. But the fantastic or otherworldly spaces to be found in the suburbs of Amaurotum are where we might see glimmers of another modernity or a postmodernity. In the troubled waters surrounding Utopia on the map,[42] we might discern the old warning, *hic sunt dracones*.[43] But that is a zone where the modern imaginary grapples with an unrepresentable real, where bureaucrats and monsters jostle each other, and the fantastic mode of mapping such fictional spaces may disclose an image of the world we live in and, perhaps, of other worlds not yet visible on the horizon.

Notes

1. In a subsequent, more detailed illustration attached to the 1518 edition of *Utopia*, the sailor is looking out toward the viewer, rather than at the island. In the foreground, Hythlodaeus lectures a man (More himself, who stands in for the reader) while gesturing toward the island nation in the distance.

2. Famously, More's coinage of the word *utopia* from Greek roots involved a homophonic pun, combining in the same pronunciation the *eu*-topos (good place) and the *ou*-topos (no place).

3. See Phillip E. Wegner, *Imaginary Communities: Utopia, the Nation, and the Spatial Histories of Modernity* (Berkeley: University of California Press, 2002).

4. Darko Suvin's influential conception of science fiction—of which utopia is a "socio-economic subset"—as a genre of "cognitive estrangement" accounts for part of this reaction to fantasy as a genre or mode. In Suvin's view, the estrangements of fantasy are noncognitive, irrational, or specifically "metaphysical," and therefore retrogressive. See Darko Suvin, *Metamorphoses of Science Fiction: On the Poetics and History of a Literary Genre* (New Haven, CT: Yale University Press, 1979), 4. Carl Freedman offers an updated and somewhat more nuanced account, but he also embraces the distinction, dismissing the estrangements of fantasy as "irrationalist" and therefore "theoretically illegitimate"; see Freedman, *Critical Theory and Science Fiction* (Middletown, CT: Wesleyan University Press, 2000), 17. But see also China Miéville's response to this notion in "Cognition as Ideology: A Dialectic of SF

Theory," in *Red Planets: Marxism and Science Fiction*, ed. Mark Bould and China Miéville (Middletown, CT: Wesleyan University Press, 2009), 231–248.

5. See Kathryn Hume, *Fantasy and Mimesis: Responses to Reality in Western Literature* (New York: Methuen, 1984).

6. T. A. Shippey, *J. R. R. Tolkien: Author of the Century* (Boston, MA: Houghton Mifflin, 2000), vii.

7. Thomas More, *Utopia*, trans. Paul Turner (New York: Penguin, 2003), 50.

8. Ibid., 52, translation modified.

9. Michel Foucault, *Discipline and Punish: The Birth of the Prison*, trans. Alan Sheridan (New York: Vintage, 1977), 197.

10. Ibid., 198.

11. The timeline is not as important as the development and dissemination of ideas and practices, such that the early modern transformations of both abstract (Cartesian) and social space may be seen as part of the radical reordering of urban spaces in the Baroque and later epochs, along with the restructuring of social spaces along evermore striated, segmented, and coordinated lines.

12. See Immanuel Kant, "What Is Enlightenment?" in *On History*, ed. and trans. Lewis White Beck (Indianapolis, IN: Bobbs-Merrill, 1963), 3. Here one might also mention the sociological interventions of Max Weber and Georg Simmel, whose work established the relations between rationalization and social spaces long before the definitive work of Henri Lefebvre in *The Production of Space*, among other writings.

13. Georg Lukács, *History and Class Consciousness: Studies in Marxist Dialectics*, trans. Rodney Livingstone (Cambridge, MA: MIT Press, 1971), 90.

14. Max Horkheimer and Theodor W. Adorno, *Dialectic of Enlightenment*, trans. John Cumming (New York: Continuum, 1987), 88.

15. Kant, "What Is Enlightenment?," 3.

16. On the distinction between smooth and striated space, see especially Gilles Deleuze and Félix Guattari, *A Thousand Plateaus*, trans. Brian Massumi (Minneapolis: University of Minnesota Press, 1987), 361–362.

17. Tom Conley, *The Self-Made Map: Cartographic Writing in Early Modern France* (Minneapolis: University of Minnesota Press, 1996), 1.

18. See Miéville, "Cognition as Ideology," 243–244.

19. See Jürgen Habermas, *The Philosophical Discourse of Modernity: Twelve Lectures*, trans. Thomas McCarthy (Cambridge, MA: MIT Press, 1987).

20. For example, in 2015, Ursula K. Le Guin criticized Kazuo Ishiguro for apparently belittling fantasy in explaining that his novel *The Buried Giant* merely used "surface elements of fantasy" but was not itself a work of fantasy. Le Guin defended fantasy as "probably the oldest literary device for talking about reality," and she noted that the presence or absence of "surface elements" is not what constitutes fantasy. Rather, "Literary fantasy is the result of a vivid, powerful, coherent imagination drawing plausible impossibilities together into a vivid, powerful and coherent story." See Ursula Le Guin, "95. 'Are They Going to Say This Is Fantasy?'" *Ursula K. Le Guin's Blog* (March 5, 2015), accessed March 27, 2016, http://www.ursulakleguin.com/Blog2015.html.

21. See note 4 above; see also Suvin, *Metamorphoses of Science Fiction*, 4.

22. Fredric Jameson, *Marxism and Form: Twentieth-Century Dialectical Theories of Literature* (Princeton, NJ: Princeton University Press, 1971), 110–111.

23. Fredric Jameson, *Archaeologies of the Future: The Desire Called Utopia and Other Science Fictions* (London: Verso, 2005), 56. The chapter in which Jameson attempts to distinguish science fiction definitively from fantasy is titled, aptly enough, "The Great Schism"; see Jameson, *Archaeologies of the Future*, 57–71.

24. See Suvin, *Metamorphoses of Science Fiction*, 4.

25. Michael Moorcock, *Wizardry and Wild Romance: A Study of Epic Fantasy* (London: Victor Gollancz Ltd., 1987), 126.

26. J. R. R. Tolkien, "On Fairy-Stories," in *The Tolkien Reader* (New York: Ballantine Books, 1966), 79.

27. Quoted by China Miéville, "Tolkien—Middle-earth Meets Middle England," *Socialist Review* 259 (January 2002), accessed August 13, 2017, http://socialistreview.org.uk/259/tolkien-middle-earth-meets-middle-england.

28. See China Miéville, "There and Back Again," *Omnivoracious* blog, guest post (June 15, 2009), accessed September 14, 2012, http://www.omnivoracious.com/2009/06/there-and-back-again-five-reasons-tolkien-rocks.html.

29. China Miéville, "Editorial Introduction," Symposium: Marxism and Fantasy, *Historical Materialism* 10, no. 4 (2002): 42.

30. Ibid., 42–43.

31. Ibid., 46.

32. Ibid., 42.

33. Miéville, "Cognition as Ideology," 234. Compare Tolkien's comment in "On Fairy-Stories," 81: "The notion that motor-cars are more 'alive' than, say, centaurs or dragons is curious; that they are more 'real' than, say, horses is pathetically absurd."

34. Miéville, "Editorial Introduction," 48.

35. Herbert Marcuse, *Eros and Civilization: A Philosophical Inquiry into Freud* (Boston, MA: Beacon, 1966), 149–150.

36. Ibid., 148–149.

37. Georg Lukács, *The Theory of the Novel*, trans. Anna Bostock (Cambridge, MA: MIT Press, 1971), 19.

38. See Fredric Jameson, *The Geopolitical Aesthetic: Cinema and Space in the World System* (Bloomington and London: Indiana University Press and the British Film Institute, 1992), 4.

39. Miéville, "Editorial Introduction," 46, emphasis in the original.

40. In More's Utopia, the past is not romanticized.

41. Herbert Marcuse, "The End of Utopia," in *Five Lectures: Psychoanalysis, Politics, and Utopia*, trans. J. Shapiro and S. Weber (Boston, MA: Beacon Press, 1970), 69.

42. See Antonis Balasopoulos, "'Utopiae Insulae Figura': Utopian Insularity and the Politics of Form," *Transtext(e)s/Transcultures: Journal of Global Cultural Studies* 3 (2008), 22–38.

43. *Hic sunt dracones* has its own fantastic backstory. Despite its influence on the popular imagination, the phrase "Here be dragons" appeared on no known historical world maps (except the Hunt-Lenox Globe, perhaps); see my *Utopia in the Age of Globalization: Space, Representation, and the World System* (New York: Palgrave Macmillan, 2013), 95–96.

9 Beyond the Flaming Walls of the World

The planet is in the species of alterity, belonging to another system; and yet we inhabit it . . .

—Gayatri Chakravorty Spivak, *Death of a Discipline*

IN HIS INFLUENTIAL 1827 essay "On the Supernatural in Fictitious Composition," Sir Walter Scott extols the beauty and power of E. T. A. Hoffmann's writing but criticizes "the wildness of Hoffmann's fancy," declaring that the German Romantic's taste and temperament have "carried him too far 'extra moenia flammantia mundi,' too much beyond the circle of not only the probable but the possible."[1] Scott is concerned that the "fantastic" mode is only acceptable to the degree that "it tends to excite agreeable and pleasing ideas." In his use of the Latin phrase, borrowed from Lucretius, Scott evokes a spatial metaphor to make a broader point. By venturing "beyond the flaming walls of the world," the fantasy author indulges, in Scott's view, in an "extravagant" aesthetic practice that evokes horror, or even disgust, a radical alterity that defamiliarizes the homely and aggrandizes the horrible.[2] Not stated directly by Scott but implied in his mild critique is the degree to which this outré sensibility disrupts the conventions and expectations of a national literature. In addition to providing a more limited national space for a particular country's native authors, such a literature must somehow represent the recognizably national character of or in its narratives, a character that must above all be familiar to readers. In other words, extravagant fantasy subverts an aesthetic standard of beauty by becoming "grotesque" and "arabesque." Such fiction also undermines a national vocation of literature by its estrangement—that is, by its imaginative flights away from familiar landscapes, customs, events, and so on. Or, to put it another way, a national literature tends to domesticate the strange elements and represent them in a comfortable, recognizable pattern.[3] A romantic realism of the sort found in Scott's own historical novels offers a fitting mode for such a national narrative, as the foundational legends and myths can be incorporated into a calm, more quotidian, and rather familiar culture. By contrast, the fantastic mode exceeds the national and cultural boundaries, drawing the narrative out into the world and beyond by positing a radical alterity from the outset.

Today's planetary turn in literary and cultural studies may be associated with a number of interrelated historical phenomena that have forcefully asserted the intertwined matters of spatiality, fantasy, and postnationality into the critical discussion. Above all, the multiform processes now aggregated under the rubric of globalization, including those practices in the aesthetic or cultural spheres sometimes called postmodern, have occasioned the diminution of the national in favor of the global, the elevation of space above (or at least to the level of) time, and the interrogation of representational modes linked to the nation-state. In sum, most of the formerly recognizable modes are deemed no longer suitable for making sense of the present, dynamic world system. As numerous artists, critics, philosophers, and social scientists have observed, the revolutionary social transformations throughout the world in the postwar era have fundamentally altered the effectiveness of sense-making systems of past epochs, be they scientific, religious, or, as is my concern here, literary-cultural. Narrative fiction, for example, may no longer operate as it had in Scott's day, when the "form-giving form" of the historical novel (to use Georg Lukács's expression) could organize an ostensible totality (*Lebenstotalität*) in which the individual could locate him- or herself within a cognizable world system.[4] Scott's historical novels attempted to shape the diffuse passions, partisan interests, and different spaces into a distinctively national imaginary geography, and, as Jonathan Arac has pointed out, these novels were essential precursors to national narrative in American literature.[5] However, in the twentieth century the postmodern crisis of representation is part of an existential crisis akin to being lost in space; it is an utterly alienating experience, evoking an anxiety that Martin Heidegger had associated directly with the uncanny, the *unheimlich* or "unhomely," the *Nicht-zu-hause-sein* ("not-being-at-home").[6] But then the loss of a sense of "home" is also a recognition of the disruptions of "domestic" or national space caused by forces of globalization. Fredric Jameson's call for a "cognitive mapping on a global scale," as both the solution to the crisis of representability and as the vocation of postmodern art, emphasizes the spatial anxiety and postnationality of such a cartographic project.[7]

I would propose that this enterprise is incomplete unless it is also speculative, figurative, and, in a broad sense, *fantastic*. Unlike the naively mimetic maps of an earlier epoch, the literary cartography of the postnational world system has to be, in some ways, otherworldly. Such, at least, is my argument here. Although there is no question about the value of myth, folklore, or "national fantasy" in establishing national narrative,[8] in the present world-historical moment, the radical alterity of fantasy is well positioned to foster a postnational literary perspective. I am not speaking of fantasy as a genre, although I am interested in the potential of what Jameson has called "generic discontinuities" in narratives as part of the overall undertaking of literary cartography.[9] Rather, I am thinking of fantasy as a discursive mode, one that is marked by its fundamental attention to otherness or otherworldliness. Fantasy, of which science fiction and utopia may be considered subsets, enables a figurative mapping of the (so-called) real world but using the (so-called) unreal or impossible as its means. In theory and in practice, the alterity of fantasy makes possible new ways of seeing—and thus interpreting and perhaps changing—the world system that forms the untranscendable horizon of all thinking today.[10] Somewhat like the earlier local, regional, or national space but far more so, the planetary space that subsumes contemporary thought in the age of globalization requires a sort of abstraction and imagination that makes "the literature of estrangement," to use China Miéville's phrase, the form potentially best suited to our postmodern and postnational condition. As Miéville asserts pointedly, "Fantasy . . . is *good to think with*."[11] For, to be sure, the fantastic mode allows us, among other things, to see the planet anew, to visualize our world in novel ways, and to imagine different approaches to representing and otherwise engaging the world system. In "constellating" and working through the various intersecting forces affecting the existential experience of life on the planet at this historical moment, we may venture—like the wayward imagination of Hoffmann in Scott's analysis—beyond the flaming walls of the world in order to discover, in a more meaningful sense, the real world after all. In this *postnational constellation*, as Jürgen Habermas has called it in another context, the principal vocation of literary and cultural work may be to project novel cartographies and alternative trajectories by which to navigate this increasingly unrepresentable, even unrecognizable *Lebenswelt*. After the planetary turn, in the context of a true *world literature* whose representative space is neither regional nor national but global, the postnational constellation may be an apt figure for the present world system, and a fantastic mapping of the planetary space we occupy may constitute an urgent project of contemporary critical theory and practice.

Imagining the Planet

One of the past century's most famous photographs, widely known as "Earthrise," depicts a distinct, blue-and-white planet emerging in the distance over the barren gray-white surface of the moon. Taken by Apollo 8 astronauts in lunar orbit on December 24, 1968, the iconic image became a worldwide sensation when it appeared on televisions and in newspapers on Christmas morning. Humans have been using their vision and imagination to make sense of the world throughout their history, yet never before had such a vista been available to them, as for the first time they ventured beyond the boundaries of the terraqueous globe and looked back upon it as outsiders. From this new perspective, viewers of the "Earthrise" photograph were almost literally repositioned in the universe. Now able to achieve a critical distance from their own planet, they were no longer cosmopolitan citizens comfortably at home in the world but witnessed their world as a strange otherworld. Arguably, in the contemplation of this image and of its ramifications, a planetary consciousness emerged.[12]

This is certainly how American poet Archibald MacLeish envisioned the import of the event. Writing in the *New York Times* only hours after the first appearance of the photograph, MacLeish considered the moment an epochal shift in man's relationship to the world. Referring first to Dante's geocentric universe, then to its waning and ultimate collapse after the Copernican Revolution and the advent of modern physics, which had rendered the earth a metaphysically meaningless ensemble of violent forces that could bring about the slaughter of millions in absurd world wars and nuclear destruction, MacLeish announced that "Now, in the last few hours, the [planet] notion may have changed again. For the first time in all of time men have seen it not as continents or oceans from the little distance of a hundred miles or two or three, but seen it from the depth of space; seen it whole and round and beautiful and small."[13] As MacLeish explained on that Christmas morning,

> The medieval notion of the earth put man at the center of everything. The nuclear notion of the earth put him nowhere—beyond the range of reason even—lost in absurdity and war. This latest notion may have other consequences. Formed as it was in the minds of heroic voyagers who were also men, it may remake our image of mankind. No longer that preposterous figure at the center, no longer that degraded and degrading victim off at the margins of reality and blind with blood, man may at last become himself.
>
> To see the earth as it truly is, small and blue and beautiful in that eternal silence where it floats, is to see ourselves as riders on the earth together, brothers on that bright loveliness in the eternal cold—brothers who know now they are truly brothers.

This somewhat grandiose interpretation of an astronaut's timely snapshot indicates the extent to which a kind of planetary turn in poetry, philosophy, and the arts and sciences as a whole was not only already under way but also deeply longed for by so many of the inhabitants of that "small and blue and beautiful" orb.[14]

The image of the planet captured in and promoted by "Earthrise," which functioned simultaneously as an aesthetic, scientific, ideological, and utopian work of art, occasions a powerful rethinking of the relations among space, narrative, geopolitics, and the world system. Ironically, perhaps, the repercussions of the "Earthrise" phenomenon led not to the extension or intensification of the space age but to a "return to Earth," as it were, with more scientific- and humanities-based attention being paid to this planet and far less to Mars, Jupiter, and the great beyond. As Robert Poole observes in *Earthrise: How Man First Saw the Earth*, the postwar period had been dominated by rockets and space travel whose proponents could proclaim, with Wernher von Braun, that the party who conquered space would control the planet. This notion certainly inspired a great deal of military and political enthusiasm for space research. Along the same lines, science fiction frequently depicting space exploration would dominate popular culture in various media throughout the 1950s and 1960s. Obviously, astrophysics, technology, science fiction, and interplanetary expeditions remain salient today, but they no longer have the cultural cachet they had achieved in the early 1960s. After "Earthrise," the fevered imaginations of the populace turned back to planet Earth. As one writer put it, "The significance of the lunar expeditions was not that men set foot on the Moon, but that they set eye on the Earth."[15]

Time magazine used the photograph as the cover of its final issue of 1968, with the one-word caption (*Dawn*) as if to emphasize the image's liminal and inaugural role in marking the transition to a new stage of world history. Given the turbulence of that year, what with the assassinations, riots, and political turmoil in the United States, the revolutions and repression in Prague, Paris, and elsewhere in Europe, and the warfare and violence of Vietnam, South America, and Africa, the "Earthrise" image, when couched as a "dawn," acquires a poignant, optative, and utopian nuance. Where the future had previously been determined as a "space race" among antagonistic, destructive superpowers, this austere, beautiful vision of a small, fragile, and isolated planet reoriented the very idea of spatiotemporal progression. For many like MacLeish, this image was itself a sign that national boundaries and ideological differences were no longer of any great importance. The time had come to view the earth and its inhabitants as a single people occupying a single global space.

What I want to suggest in dwelling on these pictures is that the moment of this global self-image constitutes a nexus through which several important aspects of the planetary turn in the arts, sciences, and humanities intersect. Significantly, this literal turn back toward the planet from the outermost reaches of human space exploration is representative of an aesthetic planetary turn whereby the entire earth is for the first time seen in its global totality.[16] This moment coincides with tumultuous geopolitical events, most spectacularly visible in the wars of Southeast Asia and the Middle East, in the anticolonial national movements in Africa, in the revolutions in Latin America, and in the internal conflicts throughout Europe and the United States, to name but a few. Also, although this would come into focus more clearly only later, with the collapse of the Bretton Woods agreement, the rise of multinational capital and transnational economies are making the older colonial and mercantile financial systems obsolete around this time, which paves the way to widespread financialization and globalization.[17] The boom in so-called Third World literature complements and supplements the innovations in fiction and poetry in the West, while an emerging aesthetic of postmodernism in fiction, cinema, visual art, and especially architecture alters the way space and culture are perceived. In any event, the widely distributed "Earthrise" image of the planet, which unquestionably changed the way the planet's inhabitants looked at the world, emerged at a time of radical transformation worldwide.[18] Once again, amid so much real-world activity, something quite otherworldly—the earth itself—appeared.

To be sure, this "Earthrise" photograph conveyed a striking reality; indeed, its photographic realism was literal, and grasping its import is crucial to understanding its influence and effect in imagining the planet anew. But the image was also the stuff of the most extremely *outré* science fiction: the fantastic voyage beyond the moon. Parodied in Lucian's *True History* and celebrated by Georges Méliès in *Le Voyage dans la Lune*, with hundreds of lunar fantasies occupying the spectrum in between, this sort of cosmic travel made possible the discovery of hitherto unknown or unimagined realities. The fantastic nature of the worldview afforded from outer space might be said to have inspired a wholly different way of thinking on the surface of the little green-blue sphere. National, regional, and local concerns and conflicts, for instance, may look trivial in the face of a suddenly more salient global space. Thus, the rivalries that animated the geopolitical *Weltanschauungen* of the era seemed petty and absurd from this postnational and supracontinental perspective, and the more optimistic of commentators dared to imagine a united and harmonious future for humankind that formerly only the most wide-eyed dreamers could envision. As Poole points out in a reference to the Apollo 8 mission that produced the "Earthrise" photograph, "The mightiest shot in the Cold War turned into the twentieth century's ultimate utopian moment."[19] And utopia, like the planet itself, is a figure of radical alterity. As Gayatri Chakravorty Spivak has put it in her discussion of planetarity and world literature, the planet's "alterity, determining experience, is mysterious and discontinuous—an experience of the impossible."[20]

A Meditation on the Impossible

Utopia is a favored topic among many spatially oriented critics at present, including Jameson and David Harvey.[21] In some respects, it represents a paradigmatically modern genre or discursive mode, with major literary works such as Thomas More's 1516 genre-establishing *Utopia* (1516) or Tommaso Campanella's *The City of the Sun* (1602) emerging during the Age of Discovery and the European voyages to the "New World"[22] and another wave of utopianism finding its voice and audience amid the nineteenth century's Industrial Age uncertainties with such schemes as Charles Fourier's phalansteries, Edward Bellamy's "nationalism," and William Morris's "news from nowhere." But as I have argued elsewhere,[23] a sort of utopian mode has reasserted itself most strenuously in the postmodern world of our globalization era, paradoxically a world in which utopian alternatives to the status quo seem utterly impossible, even inconceivable. Jameson has famously observed that it seems easier today to imagine the end of the world than the breakdown of late capitalism; often forgotten, however, is Jameson's indispensable follow-up to this remark: "perhaps this is due to some weakness in our imaginations."[24]

An empowered imagination, one that would set out to map a planetary space rather than limit itself to its local or national subsets, would have to come to grips with the radical alterity of the world, specifically with the fantastic otherworldliness emerging in conjunction with an altogether unfamiliar perspective, such as the view from outer space. Obviously, this imaginative project would have to exceed the limits of the real and the known; it would involve not only a consideration of the possible but also "a meditation on the impossible."[25] In my view, this meditation on the impossible is part of the cartographic efforts of fantasy itself, as the projection of imaginary spaces becomes an essential aspect of our engagement with the all-too-real world system after the spatial or planetary turn. Yet the term *fantasy* itself presents a problem. Numerous spatial critics have embraced utopian discourse as a means of conceiving radical alternatives to the status quo, but many of these have been openly hostile to fantasy as a mode or genre on the grounds that fantasy is an escapist, politically reactionary, and backward-looking practice. A case in point is Darko Suvin's groundbreaking 1979 science fiction study, which dismissed fantasy as anti-rational and metaphysical. And in his own extensive statement on utopia, Jameson condemns any confusion between fantasy and science fiction ("We must now lay this misunderstanding to rest ..."), referring to their distinction as "The Great Schism."[26] Nor does it help that the most inescapable figure in the genre of fantasy literature, J. R. R. Tolkien, who was himself relatively conservative in his political views, actively defended fantasy precisely as "escapist" practice. Complaining that anti-fantasy critics have confused "the escape of the prisoner with the flight of the deserter," Tolkien asks: "Why should a man be scorned if, finding himself in prison, he tries to get out and go home. Or if, when he cannot do so, he thinks and talks about other topics than jailers and prison-walls?"[27] Indeed, Tolkien goes so far as to claim that the world outside this prison is just as "real," whether the prisoner can see it or not, which suggests a view of fantasy as an imaginative method for apprehending the "real world" rather than a means of escaping from it.

It is perhaps ironic, then, that a similar argument has been made by Miéville in his spirited defense of fantasy in the face of Marxist and utopian critics' antipathy toward it. As a Marxist, Miéville represents, of course, nearly the political antipode of Tolkien. Yet even though he comes from such a different perspective, Miéville contends that fantasy is superior to realism when it comes to getting at the truth of the "real world." After discussing Marx's own analysis in *Capital* of the fetishism of the commodity and the hidden social relations embedded in it, Miéville offers that "'real' life under capitalism *is a fantasy*: 'realism,' narrowly defined, is therefore a 'realistic' depiction of 'an absurdity which is true,' but no less absurd for that. Narrow 'realism' is as partial and ideological as 'reality' itself."[28] Further, Miéville insists, the "apparent epistemological radicalism of the fantastic mode's basic predicate," namely that "the impossible is true," makes it well suited to the task of an oppositional or critical project.[29] As Miéville concludes, "The fantastic might be a mode peculiarly suited to and resonant with the forms of modernity. . . . Fantasy is a mode that, in constructing an internally coherent but actually impossible totality—constructed on the basis that the impossible is, for this work, *true*—mimics the 'absurdity' of capitalist modernity."[30]

Both Tolkien's and Miéville's positions respond to the perception that works written in the fantastic mode are not only inferior to more realistic works but also morally or politically suspect. Tolkien famously quarreled with fellow conservative C. S. Lewis over whether it was immoral for a Christian to embrace myth, which Lewis disparaged as "lies breathed through silver."[31] And as a practicing fantasist as well as a socialist activist in his own right, Miéville is forced to defend fantasy from those on the Left who have objected to its escapism, nostalgia, or ideological incorrectness. Thus, even when the opposition to fantasy is less morally or politically charged, the prevailing view is that realism, with its familiar and recognizable world presumably uncontroversially presented and shared by reader and writer, is the preferred mode.

This is, after all, Sir Walter Scott's objection to Hoffmann in "On the Supernatural in Fictitious Composition." In considering Hoffmann's work to be both *grotesque* and *arabesque*—the very terms Edgar Allan Poe readily adopted to refer to his collected stories, although it is noteworthy that he had intended to name the revised and expanded collection *Phantasy Pieces*—Scott does not hide a certain disdain for the otherworldly, which here covers the merely exotic (as the term *Arabesque* makes clear) as well as the twisted or horrible. His essay offers a foundational text for the debate concerning the suitable proportion of fantasy and reality in literature during the nineteenth century. This polemic also famously includes Nathaniel Hawthorne's apologia for "romance" as opposed to the more strictly realistic "novel," which "is presumed to aim at a very minute fidelity, not merely to the possible, but to the probable and ordinary course of man's experience."[32] And as we have seen, this argument about how much fantasy is acceptable in serious literature, what Kathryn Hume has succinctly named the "fantasy versus mimesis" controversy, continues to elicit heated responses.[33] Yet again it is important to reiterate that it is Scott who casually delineates the contours of the battlefield. To do so, he first quotes a paragraph of Hoffmann's *The Entail*, in which a frightfully supernatural occurrence culminates in a calm, somewhat revelatory, but still eerie explanation. Scott then elaborates as follows:

The passage which we have just quoted, while it shows the wildness of Hoff-mann's fancy, evinces also that he possessed power which ought to have miti-gated and allayed it. Unfortunately, his taste and temperament directed him too strongly to the grotesque and fantastic,—carried him too far "extra mœnia flammantia mundi," too much beyond the circle not only of probability but even of possibility, to admit of his composing much in the better style which he might easily have attained. The popular romance, no doubt, has many walks, nor are we at all inclined to halloo the dogs of criticism against those whose object is merely to amuse a passing hour. It may be repeated with truth, that in this path of light literature, "tout genre est permis hors les genres ennuyeux," and of course, an error in taste ought not to be followed up and hunted down as if it were a false maxim in morality, a delusive hypothesis in science, or a heresy in religion itself. Genius too, is, we are aware, capricious, and must be allowed to take its own flights, however eccentric, were it but for the sake of experiment. Sometimes, also, it may be eminently pleasing to look at the wild-ness of an Arabesque painting executed by a man of rich fancy. But we do not desire to see genius expand or rather exhaust itself upon themes which cannot be reconciled to taste; and the utmost length in which we can indulge a turn to the fantastic is, where it tends to excite agreeable and pleasing ideas. We are not called upon to be equally tolerant of such capriccios as are not only star-tling by their extravagance, but disgusting by their horrible import.[34]

Neither a naive realist nor an advocate of a strictly mimetic narrative art, Scott is willing to forgive literature that extends "beyond the flaming walls of the world" so long as it can "excite agreeable and pleasant ideas." Thus, he introduces a prag-matic and moral dimension into the discussion of literary aesthetics. That is, the question is less about what constitutes fantasy and more about how such fantastic elements will be used.

The French maxim that Scott paraphrases is Voltaire's assertion that "all genres are good except boring genres." However, the Latin expression comes not from literary fiction, whether fantastic or realistic, but from philosophy, specif-ically Lucretius's first-century BCE treatise *De Rerum Natura* (*On the Nature of Things*). In the original, the expression *extra mœnia flammantia mundi* does not carry a negative connotation. On the contrary, in fact, for Lucretius the phrase signifies a great achievement, a sign of the intellectual courage of the scientific or philosophical mind willing to go beyond the superstitious chimeras of religion in order to seek the truths that lie "beyond the flaming walls of the world." The famous line refers to Epicurus, the atomist and materialist Greek philosopher whose "victory," according to Lucretius, brought religion under our feet and placed human beings on a level with heaven.[35] It is also worth noting that, in this original Epicurean context, the movement "beyond the flaming walls of the world" is not considered an attempt to escape from the real world into a false one but rather a brave discovery of precisely that more truly real world that had been hidden and veiled by the false realities of superstition and religion. In its oddly tortuous philological journey from the first century BCE to the nineteenth century, the phrase as used by Scott had developed a meaning nearly opposite to what Lucretius had intended. However, in what might be considered one more turn of the screw or yet another dialectical reversal, one can argue that Scott's own use of the expression as a means of criticizing fantasy actually reveals the power of fantasy as a device for social and literary critique.

Indeed, one could suggest that Lucretius's defense of the materialist thought of Epicurus against the superstitions of religious belief finds modern and postmodern counterparts in Jameson's pro-utopian argument against so-called practical thinking and also in Miéville's defense of fantasy against its Marxist detractors, including, of course, such science fiction enthusiasts as Jameson himself. In either case, a theorist inveighs against the prejudices and barriers to thinking that predominate in his place and time. As noted in the last chapter, Jameson has acknowledged the anti-utopian positions of Karl Marx and Friedrich Engels in the nineteenth century, but he argues that by the 1960s a "dialectical reversal" had occurred and made visible the renewed desirability of utopian thought. Where "practical thinking . . . represents a capitulation to the system itself," utopianism "keeps alive the possibility of a world qualitatively distinct from this one and takes the form of a stubborn negation of all that is."[36] Along similar lines, utopian theorist Russell Jacoby has maintained that "any effort to escape the spell of the quotidian . . . is the sine qua non of serious thinking about the future—the prerequisite of *any* thinking."[37] In this sense, the more realistic, practical, or feasible position becomes antithetical to the necessarily fantastic, critical project of meditating upon the impossible.

Change and form go hand in hand here. What Jameson has said of the dynamic of utopia applies equally well to the notion of fantasy as the literature of defamiliarization or otherness: "Utopia as a form is not the representation of radical alternatives; it is rather the imperative to imagine them."[38] Truly radical alterity would, in a somewhat literal sense, be unrepresentable, since in the apprehension of the novel otherworld and in its incorporation into our own mental databases—that is, our intellectual archives housing all that we currently can imagine the world itself to be and contain—this representation *refamiliarizes* this otherness and in one way or another domesticates the estrangement. As Jameson notes elsewhere, "Insofar as the Utopian project comes to seem more realizable and more practical, it turns into a practical political program in our world, in the here-and-now, and ceases to be Utopian in any meaningful sense."[39] Or on the flipside of the same argument, "The more surely a given Utopia asserts its radical difference from what currently is, to that very degree it becomes, not merely unrealizable but, what is worse, unimaginable."[40] Hence, we are left once more with a tenebrous conception of radical alterity as a meditation on the impossible rather than as a viable otherworld in which to dwell.

Nevertheless, the value of this fantastic effort seems to be confirmed in the imaginative endeavor involved in mapping our own "real world," particularly the postmodern world system in which the traditional guideposts are no longer trustworthy or desirable. "Happy are those ages when the starry sky is a map of all possible paths," writes Lukács of the age of the epic. "The world is wide and yet it is like a home."[41] In our world system, the celestial cartography is not so homey, and the existential and critical paradigm coming on the heels of the planetary turn may require the speculative or fantastic extension beyond the world's flaming walls in order to chart, albeit provisionally and tentatively, both our location and our available courses of action.

Shall I Project a World?

The planetary space and fantastic mode of apprehending it find their nexus in a speculative critical activity I have been associating with literary cartography and geocriticism. I have been particularly interested in the ways that narratives map a postnational space that cannot easily fold itself into the ideological and geographical atlases of an earlier configuration.[42] I do not mean to say that the existential mapping of one's *Lebenswelt* (à la Martin Heidegger and Jean-Paul Sartre, or even with Lukács's "transcendental homelessness" as a model) emerges only with the postmodern condition but that this kind of cartography reflects the profoundly different spatial and cultural anxieties of a postnational world system in which former certainties are made uncertain and familiar codes lose their meaning. Ironically, in the postnational constellation the insights of a prenational *Weltanschauung* might offer clues to a speculative, fantastic geocriticism adapted for the critical exigencies of the current moment of globalization.

The "prenational" view I have in mind is a variation of the medieval conception of the world, a vision described by Erich Auerbach in "Philology and *Weltliteratur*" in the immediate aftermath of World War II, at what might be thought of as the incipient stage of postmodernity. In this essay Auerbach maintains that the national (and nationalist) traditions of literary study, however valuable in the past two centuries, were no longer suitable for understanding the world. "To make men conscious of themselves in their own history," the critic reflects, "is a great task, but the task is small—more like a renunciation—when one considers that man not only lives on earth, but that he is in the world and in the universe."[43] Auerbach asserts that "our philological home is the earth; the nation it can no longer be. . . . We must return, in admittedly altered circumstances, to the knowledge that prenational medieval culture already possessed: the knowledge that the spirit [*Geist*] is not national."[44] Auerbach then quotes the words of a medieval thinker, Hugo of St. Victor (or Hugh of Saint Vincent), who taught that "the man who finds his homeland sweet is still the tender beginner; he to whom every soil is as his native one is already strong; but he is perfect to whom the entire world is as a foreign land." By invoking this (*mundus totus exilium est*) as his motto, Auerbach turns on its head the wisdom of a medieval Christian, who cautions against attaching oneself to the earthly world; as Auerbach explains, "Hugo intended these lines for one whose aim was to free himself from a love of the world. But it is a good way also for one who wishes to earn a proper love for the world."[45]

The perspective of the exile, one who *cannot* be "at home" in the world, is embraced by Edward Said in his reading of Auerbach and in his own work. In "Reflections on Exile," Said argues that "seeing 'the entire world as a foreign land' makes possible originality of vision."[46] This originality of vision or critical distance is, I would add, not altogether dissimilar from that which obtains through a fantastic or otherworldly vantage, such as the one achieved by the Apollo 8 photographers who witnessed the planet Earth rising above the horizon of the moon. Both Auerbach's plea for a postnational approach to world literature and Said's conviction that the condition of exile affords one a paradoxically privileged position as an observer suggest that the exile is the exemplary figure for the critic in the age of globalization.[47]

This is not to say that the perspective of the exile, even if it captures the situation of the contemporary critic, is a comfortable one.[48] The new vista afforded by finding oneself in an unfamiliar situation is more likely to be bewildering than liberating. Amid the spatial anxieties and temporal confusions of the postnational condition, the artist or critic is called on to come to grips with things as best as one can. As I have proposed, this may require an exercise in the fantastic, a speculative and perhaps even unrealistic practice, but one that can produce a map, albeit a provisional one, by which to make sense of the world system.

Lending itself to such mapping or reading is, to take just one example, a key scene in Thomas Pynchon's 1966 novel *The Crying of Lot 49*. The protagonist, Oedipa Maas, finds herself inexplicably entangled within a global conspiracy, surrounded by bizarre characters, and lost in the confusion of competing, often inscrutable interests while she is attempting to sort out the complex details of a dead man's estate. At her wit's end and thoroughly frustrated by her predicament, Oedipa resolves to reread Pierce Inverarity's will in an effort to gain a clearer sense of things. Thus, she imagines herself as a "dark machine in the center of the planetarium" that can "bring the estate into pulsing stelliferous Meaning" and writes the following in her memorandum book: "*Shall I project a world?* If not project then at least flash some arrow on the dome to skitter among the constellations and trace out your Dragon, Whale, Southern Cross. Anything might help."[49]

"Projecting a world" seems a perfectly appropriate task for both the artist and the critic after the planetary turn, and Pynchon's astronomical metaphor offers another intriguing trope for aesthetic and critical maneuvers. The constellation is at once utterly fantastic, inasmuch as the tracings drawn in the night sky are thoroughly imaginary, and also terrifically real, insofar as travelers and navigators have been able to reliably locate themselves and chart courses in the world based upon these fantastic celestial drawings. With few exceptions, constellations are completely artificial, human made, and even arbitrary. As anyone who has tried to identify and memorize the constellations will concede, their names are not particularly descriptive and rarely fit the images purportedly sketched in the skies. Canis Minor, for instance, which comprises only two stars, looks more like a line than a small dog. In a recent, only somewhat tongue-in-cheek article titled "Starry Blight: How a Bunch of Mesopotamian Peasants Ruined the Night Sky," Daniel Engber refers to these constellations as "a smog of Bronze Age graffiti."[50] Yet in antiquity as in the modern world, such imaginary lines, fantastically projected from human stargazers situated on the surface of this planet, have helped one make sense of one's place in the world, serving as points of reference in a broadly defined terrestrial cartography, as well as operating in a quite practical way to help humans navigate the "real world" below the heavens. Here is a clear example, among many others, of the real-world effects of fictions produced in a fantastic mode.

If the present world system lacks traditional guideposts or reveals such markers to be less than helpful, then the fantastic project of "projecting a world," of "constellating" the various forces, places, and events in the global space in such new ways that we can better understand and engage with the world, seems fitting. One of the formerly indispensable "guideposts" to be challenged or superseded in this effort is the nation-state itself. Although this spatiopolitical ensemble retains immense power even in the postnational constellation, and even though it tenaciously maintains its influence over literary and cultural studies (particularly in university curricula), its effectiveness is waning amid the overwhelming, trans- or supranational forces of the world system.[51] With the term *postnationality*, I refer specifically to the current condition, in the era of globalization, in which the nation-state is no longer the *locus classicus* or *primum mobile* of culture, of the economy, or even of politics. As Habermas has observed, in the past the "phenomena of the territorial state, the nation, and a popular economy constituted within national borders formed a historical constellation in which the democratic process assumed a more or less convincing institutional form. . . . Today, developments summarized under the term 'globalization' have put this entire constellation into question."[52] Under the auspices of globalization, the national models, including those employed in the study of literature and culture, are no longer reliable or even desirable. The "historical constellation" in which the nation-state constituted the dominant force in social, political, economic, and spatial organization of the world system is as much an imaginative projection as other constellations. However, just as the ideological comes to appear natural, the national model has seemed so constitutive of human sociality that it is hard to imagine alternatives. The radical alterity of fantasy or of the fantastic mode broadly conceived enables and promotes a projection of a world that can, if only provisionally, be mapped.

Therefore, it is not surprising that literary and cultural critics such as Walter Benjamin or Theodor Adorno (or their Frankfurt School successor Jürgen Habermas) should find the figure of the constellation so useful for critical theory. In organizing the swirling, vicissitudinous elements of modern culture and society, the critic draws imaginary lines *not* to fix such phenomena in place as a way of determining their true meaning or of constraining their mobile diversity but to arrange them in a cognizable pattern for further use. Amid the disorienting and dynamic phenomena of the postmodern condition, one may wish to "project a world," in other words, to create patterns that, while obviously artificial, provisional, and imaginary, can aid us in conceptualizing and navigating the planetary space we inhabit. As Oedipa Maas knowingly concluded, "Anything might help."

Along these lines, a fantastic, postnational criticism may enable a new way of seeing and mapping this planetary space that now provides the ultimate ground or horizon of thought in the age of globalization. Like those Apollo 8 astronauts who ventured into the universe and beyond the moon, quite literally "beyond the flaming walls of the world," a critical practice such as geocriticism, operating as it does in a fantastic mode, may thereby achieve novel vistas, look back on the worldly world from our radically otherworldly perspective, project new constellations and maps, and maybe just perceive things a bit differently. In navigating the planetary space of a postnational constellation geocritically, we may thus embrace the strangeness of the contemporary world system, imagine radical alternatives, and descry—if only in uncertain, tentative, and momentary glimpses—the features of other worlds.

Notes

1. Sir Walter Scott, "On the Supernatural in Fictitious Composition," in *Sir Walter Scott on Novelists and Fiction*, ed. Ioan Williams (London: Routledge and Kegan Paul, 1968), 348.
2. Ibid.
3. See, e.g., Wai Chee Dimock, *Through Other Continents: American Literature across Deep Time* (Princeton, NJ: Princeton University Press, 2006), 1–6.
4. See Georg Lukács, *The Theory of the Novel*, trans. Anna Bostock (Cambridge, MA: MIT Press, 1971); see also Georg Lukács, *The Historical Novel*, trans. Hannah and Stanley Mitchell (Lincoln: University of Nebraska Press, 1983), especially 19–88.
5. See Jonathan Arac, *The Emergence of American Literary Narrative, 1820–1860* (Cambridge, MA: Harvard University Press, 2005), 6–8.

6. See Martin Heidegger, *Being and Time*, trans. J. Macquarrie and E. Robinson (New York: Harper and Row, 1962), 233.

7. See Fredric Jameson, *Postmodernism, or, the Cultural Logic of Late Capitalism* (Durham, NC: Duke University Press, 1991), 51–54.

8. In addition to the relatively obvious uses of national myths or legends, I include here the "fantasy" that underlies and promotes nationalism, as discussed in Lauren Berlant's significant *Anatomy of a National Fantasy: Hawthorne, Utopia, and Everyday Life* (Chicago: University of Chicago Press, 1991); Wai Chee Dimock's *Empire for Liberty: Melville and the Poetics of Individualism* (Princeton, NJ: Princeton University Press, 1989); and more recently Donald E. Pease's *The New American Exceptionalism* (Minneapolis: University of Minnesota Press, 2009), just to mention works in the context of US culture.

9. See Fredric Jameson, *Archaeologies of the Future: The Desire Called Utopia and Other Science Fictions* (London: Verso, 2005), 254–266.

10. As Jameson has put it, "All thinking today is *also*, whatever else it is, an attempt to think the world system as such"; see Fredric Jameson, *The Geopolitical Aesthetic: Cinema and Space in the World System* (Bloomington and London: Indiana University Press and the British Film Institute, 1992), 4.

11. China Miéville, "Editorial Introduction," Symposium: Marxism and Fantasy, *Historical Materialism* 10, no. 4 (2002): 46.

12. Indeed, as a number of environmentalists and ecocritics have noted, the "Earthrise" photo may have sparked the environmentalist movement and led to Earth Day, partially ended the "Space Age" by recalling attention to planet Earth itself, and transformed humanity's attitude toward the planet, confirming a "Spaceship Earth" vision that reimagines the global space, not as an empty backdrop for human activity but a dynamic and affective geographical domain. See Robert Poole, *Earthrise: How Man First Saw the Planet* (New Haven. CT: Yale University Press, 2008), 141–169.

13. Archibald MacLeish, "Riders on the Earth," *New York Times*, December 25, 1968, 1.

14. Ibid. Similar in spirit to MacLeish's conclusion, Arthur C. Clarke declared that the Apollo 8 mission constituted "a second Copernican revolution" and speculated that the children born that year might one day "Live to become citizens of the United Planets." See Poole, *Earthrise*, 5–6.

15. Norman Cousins, quoted in Poole, *Earthrise*, 3.

16. Although subsequent missions would achieve lunar landing and other milestones of the space program, the Apollo 8 astronauts traveled the furthest from the earth's surface, going beyond the moon, hence gaining the vantage from which to capture the "earthrise."

17. On this, see David Harvey, *The Condition of Postmodernity* (Oxford: Blackwell, 1990), 284–307; Giovanni Arrighi, *The Long Twentieth Century: Money, Power, and the Origins of Our Times* (London: Verso, 1994), 325–356; and my "Meta-Capital: Culture and Financial Derivatives," *Works and Days* 30, no. 1/2 (2012): 231–247.

18. For a rather different analysis focusing on environmental criticism in its assessment of globalization or cosmopolitanism, see Ursula K. Heise, *Sense of Place and Sense of Planet: The Environmental Imagination of the Global* (Oxford: Oxford University Press, 2008).

19. Poole, *Earthrise*, 11.

20. Gayatri Chakravorty Spivak, *Death of a Discipline* (New York: Columbia University Press, 2003), 102.

21. See, e.g., Jameson, *Archaeologies of the Future*, and David Harvey, *Spaces of Hope* (Berkeley: University of California Press, 2000).

22. Significantly, in Thomas More's *Utopia*, the utopian island is discovered on one of Amerigo Vespucci's transatlantic voyages; see More, *Utopia*, trans. Paul Turner (New York: Penguin, 2003).

23. See my *Utopia in the Age of Globalization: Space, Representation, and the World System* (New York: Palgrave Macmillan, 2013).

24. Fredric Jameson, *The Seeds of Time* (New York: Columbia University Press, 1994), xii.

25. Jameson, *Archaeologies of the Future*, 232.

26. See Darko Suvin, *Metamorphoses of Science Fiction: On the Poetics and History of a Literary Genre* (New Haven, CT: Yale University Press, 1979), 4; Jameson, *Archaeologies of the Future*, 56–71.

27. J. R. R. Tolkien, "On Fairy-Stories," in *The Tolkien Reader* (New York: Ballantine Books, 1966), 60–61.

28. Miéville, "Editorial Introduction," 42.

29. Ibid., 42–43; note, however, that Miéville quite rightly does not claim that fantasy is itself a revolutionary mode or "acts as a guide to political action" (46). The value of fantasy lies less in its politics—which could lie anywhere on the political spectrum—than in its imaginative encounter with radical alterity itself.

30. Miéville, "Editorial Introduction," 42.

31. See J. R. R. Tolkien, "Mythopoeia," in *Tree and Leaf* (New York: HarperCollins, 2001), 85.

32. Nathaniel Hawthorne, *The House of the Seven Gables* (Oxford: Oxford University Press, 1991), 1. Hawthorne includes similar statements justifying his use of fanciful or unrealistic matter and methods in the prefatory remarks to his other novels, *The Scarlet Letter*, *The Blithedale Romance*, and *The Marble Faun*.

33. See Kathryn Hume, *Fantasy and Mimesis: Responses to Reality in Western Literature* (New York: Methuen, 1984).

34. Scott, "On the Supernatural in Fictitious Composition," 247.

35. See Lucretius, *On the Nature of the Universe*, trans. Alicia Stallings (New York: Penguin, 2007), 29.

36. Fredric Jameson, *Marxism and Form: Twentieth-Century Dialectical Theories of Literature* (Princeton, NJ: Princeton University Press, 1971), 110–111.

37. Russell Jacoby, *Picture Imperfect: Utopian Thought for an Anti-Utopian Age* (New York: Columbia University Press, 2005), xvii.

38. Jameson, *Archaeologies of the Future*, 416.

39. Fredric Jameson, "A New Reading of *Capital*," *Mediations* 25, no. 1 (Fall 2010), 13.

40. Jameson, *Archaeologies of the Future*, xv.

41. Lukács, *The Theory of the Novel*, 19.

42. See, e.g., my "On Geocriticism," in *Geocritical Explorations: Space, Place, and Mapping in Literary and Cultural Studies*, ed. Robert T. Tally Jr. (New York: Palgrave Macmillan, 2011), 1–9; see also my *Spatiality* (London: Routledge, 2013).

43. Erich Auerbach, "Philology and *Weltliteratur*," trans. M. and E. W. Said, *Centennial Review* 13 (Winter 1969), 17.

44. Ibid.

45. Ibid.; for the translation of the Latin, see Jerome Taylor, *The Didascalion of Hugh of Saint Victor: A Medieval Guide to the Arts*, trans. Jerome Taylor (New York: Columbia University Press, 1991), 101.

46. Edward Said, "Reflections on Exile," in *Reflections on Exile and Other Essays* (Cambridge, MA: Harvard University Press, 2000), 186.

47. See, e.g., my *"Mundus Totus Exilium Est*: Reflections on the Critic in Exile," *Transnational Literature* 3, no. 2 (May 2012): 1–10.

48. For a more nuanced critical reading of the new cosmopolitanism in the age of globalization, see Timothy Brennan, *At Home in the World: Cosmopolitanism Now* (Cambridge, MA: Harvard University Press, 1997).

49. Thomas Pynchon, *The Crying of Lot 49* (New York: Harper and Row, 1966), 82.

50. See Daniel Engber, "Starry Blight: How a Bunch of Mesopotamian Peasants Ruined the Night Sky," *Slate Magazine* (posted July 12, 2012), accessed September 10, 2012, http://www.slate.com/articles/health_and_science/a_fine_whine/2012/07/against_constellations _why_are_we_stuck_with_bronze_age_graffiti_.html.

51. On the postnational approach to American literature in the world today, see Wai Chee Dimock and Lawrence Buell, eds., *Shades of the Planet: American Literature as World Literature* (Princeton, NJ: Princeton University Press, 2007); Paul Giles's fascinating trilogy, *Transatlantic Insurrections: British Culture and the Formation of American Literature, 1730–1860* (Philadelphia, PA: University of Pennsylvania Press, 2001), *Virtual Americas: Transnational Fictions and the Transatlantic Imaginary* (Durham, NC: Duke University Press, 2002), and *Atlantic Republic: The American Tradition in English Literature* (Oxford: Oxford University Press, 2006); and Yunte Huang's *Transpacific Imaginations: History, Literature, Counterpoetics* (Cambridge, MA: Harvard University Press, 2008).

52. Jürgen Habermas, *The Postnational Constellation*, trans. Max Pensky (Cambridge, MA: MIT Press, 2001), 60.

Conclusion: A Map of the Pyrenees

THE CZECH POET Miroslav Holub relates the story, itself a retelling of a tale formerly told by the Nobel Prize winner Albert Szent-Györgyi, of a Hungarian reconnaissance unit hopelessly lost in a snowstorm in the Alps during World War I. At the brink of despair and resigning themselves to death, they find a map that one soldier had kept in his pocket. Using it to locate their bearings, the soldiers manage to make it back safely to camp. There the commanding officer, who had been wracked with anguish and guilt over the loss of his troops, asked to see this miraculous map that had saved their lives. A soldier handed it over, and it was revealed to be a map not of the Alps but of the Pyrenees! The moral of the story appears to differ among its tellers. Szent-Györgyi's point in originally recounting the anecdote was to show that, in science, even errors or false starts can lead to success. Holub's broader intention in retelling the tale, however, may have been to show how, in the words of his poem, "Life is on its way somewhere or another," regardless of one's sense of orientation.[1] The map, even the wrong map, can aid us in getting to where we need to go.

Arguably, the study of literature itself serves a similar purpose, as Peter Barry has suggested in *English in Practice*.[2] Literature provides innumerable examples of fictional "maps," filled with figural representations of real and imaginary places, which can be used by readers to orient themselves in their own lives and lived spaces. The study of literature thus involves a kind of history, theory, and analysis of cartography, figuratively speaking, as scholars may chart the development of literary maps over time, may come to understand the various ways in which these maps function in relation to others and to society and culture, and may interpret the maps, revealing the significance of this or that feature, making connections between different points, and disclosing the potential meanings of the text as a whole. This consideration of texts as maps is not entirely metaphorical, since poems, plays, narratives, and other literary forms have often performed the task of literally depicting real social and geographical spaces while allowing readers to gain their bearings within the represented landscape.

In recent years, especially as a result of what has been called the spatial turn in the humanities, scholars and critics have paid increasing attention to matters of space, place, and mapping in literature. In some cases, this has also included explicitly interdisciplinary research that brings the insights of architecture, art history, geography, urban studies, and other disciplinary fields to bear on literary and cultural studies. In others, the spatial turn has led to distinctive new approaches to literature, including geocriticism, geopoetics, literary geography, and spatially oriented critical theory, all operating more or less within the traditional boundaries of the work done in language and literature departments. However these practices are conducted, the enhanced role of space and place in literary studies in the past few decades is noteworthy. The new literary critical, historical, and theoretical approaches associated with the spatial turn have engendered corresponding changes to the ways in which literature is taught and studied. With a heightened sense of awareness of space and place, modern language and literature scholars have helped to develop new readings of familiar texts, to introduce texts and themes previously ignored, and to open up alternative spaces for inquiry in the classroom and beyond.

The spatial turn in the humanities deserves a word of explanation, particularly since one could argue that, in a manner of speaking, literary studies have always included a large number of spatial concepts or concerns.[3] Geography, for example, has never been too distant from literature, and the very categories by which literary studies have been organized are not infrequently geographical or spatial. National languages and literatures, of course, imply such geographical and political constructions as nation-states, territories, realms, or domains, with attendant borders, transgressions, contact zones, and so forth. Regionalism offers another clearly geographical category for literary studies, as do courses organized around geographical features, such as maritime writing, travel narratives, urban literature, and so on. Additionally, many traditional genres or movements are associated with the places or types of space that characterize their subjects, such as the rolling hills of pastoral poetry, the urban exposé in detective fiction, the distinctive landscapes of the western, the science-fictional societies of utopian literature, or the alternative worlds of fantasy. Even within the forms of the texts themselves, critics have long paid attention to spatial structure in poems, for instance, or to the ways in which epics or novels represent places, or to the spatial arrangement of sets and characters in a play. In many respects, critical attention to spatiality or to matters of space, place, and mapping in literary studies is nothing new, and students of literature have long viewed space and place as crucial elements of their work.

However, the spatial turn in recent years has disclosed a certain new spatiality associated with the present, and spatially oriented critics have convincingly argued that earlier methods of literary analysis, even those that examined spatial or geographical features of the texts under consideration, tended to downplay or overlook the significance of space and place, sometimes subordinating space to time, geography to history, or the setting to the characters and events taking place there. Space was conceived largely as "an empty container," a "mere backdrop for time," in which the events unfold progressively, subject to the teleological sense of progress, as Bertrand Westphal has put it.[4] According to this view, time and history were the dominant categories, where space or geography merely designated those areas in which important events occurred. As Michel Foucault observed, with respect to philosophy and the human sciences,

> The great obsession of the nineteenth century was, as we know, history: with its themes of development and of suspension, of crisis, and cycle, themes of the ever-accumulating past, with its great preponderance of dead men and the menacing glaciation of the world. . . . The present epoch will perhaps be above all the epoch of space. We are in the epoch of simultaneity: we are in the epoch of juxtaposition, the epoch of the near and far, of the side-by-side, of the dispersed. We are at a moment, I believe, when our experience of the world is less that of a long life developing through time than that of a network that connects points and intersects with its own skein.[5]

The shift in focus that Foucault sees as typical of late twentieth-century thought has been observed by others as well, from geographers and historians to visual artists and creative writers. In recent literary and cultural studies, notably with the advent of the discourses of postmodernism, postcolonial theory, and globalization but also with respect to other interdisciplinary approaches to literature, space has reemerged as a principal concern.[6]

The spatial turn was aided by a new aesthetic sensibility that came to be understood as postmodernism in the arts, architecture, literature, and philosophy, combined with a strong theoretical critique provided by poststructuralism. Fredric Jameson has famously identified a "new spatiality implicit in the postmodern," which comports with Foucault's sense that ours is "the epoch of space."[7] Jameson called for a project of "cognitive mapping" as the most suitable response to the bewildering novelty and velocity of postmodern culture. Geographers such as David Harvey, Edward W. Soja, Derek Gregory, and Nigel Thrift have demonstrated how the postmodern condition has occasioned a "reassertion of space" in critical theory, particularly with respect to urban studies.[8] In postcolonial studies, critics such as Edward W. Said have proposed a "geographical inquiry into historical experience" in which careful attention must be paid to spatial experience.[9] The transformational effects of postcolonialism, globalization, and the rise of ever more advanced information technologies helped to push space and spatiality into the foreground, as traditional spatial or geographic limits were erased or redrawn.[10] At the same time, the work of ecocritics or environmentalists have called attention to serious concerns over the development and management of natural and social spaces, particularly emphasizing problems with preservation, sustainability, and ecological disaster.[11] The sense that recent history, if not the present moment, calls for a greater awareness of the importance of space in culture and in society seems to be reaffirmed as the twenty-first century's natural and geopolitical order, what has been celebrated or criticized as a "borderless world" in an era of globalization, brings issues of spatiality to the fore.[12] Although late modernity or postmodernity might be characterized by a heightened awareness of spatiality, it is not accurate to identify this reassertion of space in literary or cultural studies as an exclusively modern or postmodern phenomenon. Scholars working with ancient, medieval, and renaissance texts, among others, have contributed invaluable research into the ways that spatially oriented criticism can enable significant new readings of texts and contexts.[13] Today, spatial literary studies—whether conceived of as *geocriticism*, *literary geography*, or the *spatial humanities* more generally—offers an approach to literary and cultural texts, ranging across periods and genres, that emphasizes the relations between space and writing. All of this work contributes to the formation of new critical perspectives that seem particularly timely today.

As noted above, spatial or geographical considerations have no doubt always been a part of literary and critical practice, but the effects of the recent resurgence of spatiality and the explosion in the number of spatially oriented works of criticism and scholarship cannot be underestimated. The spatial turn has no particular date of inception, but one may perceive more critical attention being paid to matters of space in the 1970s and 1980s. Yet sometimes transformative concepts, approaches, or theories only become noticeable *after* the turn, as it were. For example, a significant collection of essays published in 1990 and designed to register the field-altering changes to literary studies in the aftermath of "theory," Frank Lentricchia and Thomas McLaughlin's *Critical Terms for Literary Study*, contained no entries for space, place, mapping, or geography.[14] Raymond Williams's enormously influential *Keywords*, which first appeared in 1975, also contained no entry for space or place; the second edition, published in 1983, included twenty-one additional entries, but *space* and *place* remained absent.[15] Harvey felt the need to redress this omission in an essay titled "Space as a Key Word," which began by stating that "If Raymond Williams were contemplating the entries for his celebrated text on *Keywords* today, he would have surely have included the word 'space'."[16] In a 2006 essay with the deceptively simple, keyword-like title of "Space," Thrift dates the "spatial turn in the humanities and social sciences" to roughly the span of "the last 20 years or so," and he predicts that the relatively recent critical phenomenon will have lasting results on how we think about ourselves and the world.[17]

Understandably, the spatial turn in the humanities and social sciences has begun to affect the ways in which literature and culture are taught. Recently, a number of courses in spatial literary criticism and theory have appeared in university curricula, and far more courses using geocritical or spatial approaches to existing fields have emerged. Examples include classes on spatiality in medieval literature, postcolonial geographies, representations of the city in literature, feminist spaces, regional writing, travel narrative, and studies on individual authors and their environments. In some cases, technologies such as geographic information systems (GIS) or Google Maps have been used to examine texts in new and exciting ways; for instance, students might map out the trajectory of an itinerant character, look up the physical geography of a characteristic setting, or contrast scenes of a novel through an examination of the different places on a map. Examinations of exemplary types of space, such as urban versus pastoral, have a long history in literary studies, and such classics as Raymond Williams's *The Country and the City* can be viewed as important precursors to current geocritical practices.[18] The enhanced attention to space, place, or geography in literary studies makes possible innovative approaches to traditional literary criticism, while also enabling students to make connections between textual interpretation and scholarly practices in other disciplines. Spatial literary studies, broadly conceived, thus highlight the relations between texts and the world represented in them, offering students new ways of seeing literature, literary history, and criticism.

I expect that spatial literary studies will continue to expand, increase in complexity and nuance, and chart new directions for further inquiry in the future. Whether considered as a singular subfield within literary scholarship more generally or as diverse examples of multiple critical practices, the field of spatial literary studies has exploded in recent years, and the number of books and essays that might be legitimately listed on any comprehensive bibliography of spatial literary studies is almost beyond count.[19] Given the diversity of critical practices, it is probably worth asking what constitutes *spatial literary studies*, even if one must admit up front that such a discussion could never be complete or that such a definition could scarcely be definitive, at least not in a way that all practitioners would readily agree upon. For my own part, especially in my role as an editor, I have tried to err on the side of expansiveness and inclusiveness. That is, I consider spatial literary studies, doing business as geocriticism, literary geography, the spatial humanities, or using some other moniker, as a multiform critical practice that would include almost any approach to the text that focuses attention on space, place, or mapping, whether within the confines of the text, in reference to the outside world, or in some combination of the two, as in Soja's suggestive notion of "real-and-imagined places."[20] The real, imagined, and real-and-imagined spaces of literature, criticism, history, and theory, as well as of our own abstract conceptions and lived experience, all constitute the practical domain for spatial literary studies.

Similarly, in my use of the term *geocriticism*, I have tried to indicate something like a general comportment toward the text, rather than a discrete methodology with its own set of rules and conventions. It is a critical practice associated with the sort of topophrenia that, I maintain, influences the relations among individual and collective subjects and the spaces and places of their world. As I discussed in chapter 2, I first began employing the term in order to give a sense of the reader's work in examining the "maps" created by a writer's *literary cartography*. That is, if a writer, through the act of writing, produces maps of the social spaces represented in the text, the geocritical reader, sensitive to the text's spatiality and its inherently cartographic project, is able to read these maps. Geocriticism, to my mind, represents a critical counterpart to the aesthetic production of literary cartograph. For others, perhaps, the practices associated with what are variously called geocriticism, literary cartography, or literary geography understandably entail something much more specific, such as focusing on a single, recognizable topos, making the connection to a geographic body of knowledge exterior to the text under consideration or bringing new technologies such as GIS to bear on literary scholarship. But I have found that a looser definition serves to unite disparate critical practices under a meaningful, if also contested, changing, and maybe even aleatory, sign. Geocriticism, like the more general spatial literary studies, makes possible any number of interpretive, analytical approaches to textual geographies, themselves conceived broadly enough to include the real and imagined spaces of literature, which in turn reflect, shape, and transform the real and imagined spaces and places of the world.

In my writings on spatiality, literary cartography, and geocriticism, I have frequently discussed critics and theorists one might expect to see in these domains, including contemporary critics, theorists, geographers, philosophers, and others directly engaged in spatiality studies. But I have also drawn most heavily upon earlier examples of spatial theory and criticism from such forerunners as Walter Benjamin (whose unfinished *Passagenwerk*, among other writings, represents a major effort to write a spatial history of the present), Mikhail Bakhtin (whose conception of the chronotope alone merits a place of high distinction in spatial literary studies), or Edward W. Said (whose attention to geography in his inquiry into the historical experience reflected and repressed in cultural texts has proven so influential upon so many other scholars). However, some might have questioned the appearance of Erich Auerbach or Georg Lukács in my survey of writers essential to a theory of literary cartography, yet I have found their analyses of narrative figuration necessary antecedents to Fredric Jameson's concept of cognitive mapping, which has served as my principal model in imagining the project of literary cartography and has played a large role in spatial criticism more generally.[21]

Hence, my working definition of spatial literary studies would have to include not only the sort of work done by critics employing geographical science or focusing on representations of a particular place but also those working with spaces or places in a more metaphorical sense. I do acknowledge that my expansive view of what counts as a spatially oriented approach has sometimes meant that I have elided crucial differences among critical practices, allowing certain distinctions to remain relatively indistinct. After all, scholars using GIS to chart a novel's character or plot trajectories along the physical topography of a given region are engaged in a rather different project than that of critics examining the concepts of deterritorialization and reterritorialization in theorizing matters of poststructuralist geophilosophy. The differences are real and may have important consequences for future research and teaching. Nevertheless, I am far less interested in turf wars among various types of spatially oriented critics than in the prospects for richer, more innovative, and perhaps more useful ways of seeing and reading made possible by this renewed and heightened attention to spatiality, broadly considered.

The wide range of critical approaches currently being taken by a diverse array of scholars working in the spatial humanities reflects the richness and diversity of the field itself. Just as some of the characteristic demarcations among different sorts of spatial literary studies may not ultimately hold, as certain distinctive approaches blend with others or as what had seemed clear boundaries between them suddenly shift or blur, so too the divisions I have employed must be viewed as artificial, provisional, and even, if the reader does not find them especially helpful, disposable. For instance, one may speak of places represented in the text or of texts circulating in spaces, but the distinction quickly becomes untenable, as it is clear that the relations between the text and the place, "between the paper and the stone," as Westphal referred to it, are thoroughly bound up in each other.[22] Similarly, the old rivalry between theory and practice cannot long maintain its opposition, as even the most metatheoretical essays must find their substance in literary critical practices, even as the most traditional close readings cannot function without an operative theoretical framework. And so on. But the complexity or fluidity of categories is no reason to abandon them. If they must be perceived as tentative and heuristic, as labels whose value obtains only while needed, like the scaffolding that may be judiciously put away and forgotten when the edifice is completed or, better, like the ladder one may choose to use or to ignore, depending on one's climbing strategy.

The renewed or enhanced attention to space, place, and mapping in literary and cultural studies following the spatial turn has made possible a wide array of interesting readings. At the same time, the focus on spatial or geographical aspects of literature has served to highlight the dynamic relations between the text and the geospaces represented in it, bridging the divide between the word and the world, enabling new perspectives on textual geographies. Drawing upon multiple literary, critical, and theoretical traditions, geocritical or spatial literary studies today present many different ways of approaching questions of space, place, or geography and literature. By engendering novel perspectives, geocriticism and other spatially oriented approaches have opened up alternative vistas, which in turn may help to create new spaces for critical inquiry in the future. The study of literary spaces inevitably requires the invention and reinvention of ever more imaginative cartographies. Indeed, even if the maps we create or consult turn out to be maps of the Pyrenees when we had thought we were exploring the Alps, we may still find our way home, but we will likely do so only after having had many extraordinary, transformative experiences in the meanwhile. Mapping, along with map reading, is after all part of the adventure.

Notes

1. Miroslav Holub, "Brief Thoughts on Maps," trans. Jarmila and Ian Milner, *Times Literary Supplement* (February 4, 1977): 118.

2. Peter Barry, *English in Practice: In Pursuit of English Studies*, 2nd ed. (London: Bloomsbury, 2014), 3.

3. See, e.g., Barney Warf and Santa Arias, eds., *The Spatial Turn: Interdisciplinary Perspectives* (London: Routledge, 2008).

4. Bertrand Westphal, *Geocriticism: Real and Fictional Spaces*, trans. Robert T. Tally Jr. (New York: Palgrave Macmillan, 2011), 10.

5. Michel Foucault, "Of Other Spaces," trans. Jay Miskowiec, *Diacritics* 16 (Spring 1986), 22.

6. See Edward W. Soja, *Postmodern Geographies: The Reassertion of Space in Critical Social Theory* (London: Verso, 1989); on the ways in which this new spatiality has influenced literature in particular, see Peta Mitchell, *Cartographic Strategies of Postmodernity: The Figure of the Map in Contemporary Theory and Fiction* (London: Routledge, 2007).

7. Fredric Jameson, *Postmodernism, or, the Cultural Logic of Late Capitalism* (Durham, NC: Duke University Press, 1991), 418.

8. See, e.g., David Harvey, *The Condition of Postmodernity* (Oxford: Blackwell, 1990).

9. Edward Said, *Culture and Imperialism* (New York: Knopf, 1993), 7.

10. See, e.g., Jane Stadler, Peta Mitchell, and Stephen Carleton, *Imagined Landscapes: Geovisualizing Australian Spatial Narratives* (Bloomington, IN: Indiana University Press, 2016).

11. See, e.g., Christine M. Battista and Robert T. Tally Jr., eds., *Ecocriticism and Geocriticism: Overlapping Territories in Environmental and Spatial Literary Studies* (New York: Palgrave Macmillan, 2016).

12. See Kenichi Ohmae, *The Borderless World: Power and Strategy in the Interlinked Economy* (New York: HarperCollins, 1990); needless to say, this term has become increasingly problematic in the years since Ohmae first introduced it.

13. Arguably, research in medieval or early modern cultures has proven as influential upon the spatial humanities as that in any field, with a number of influential studies setting the tone. See, e.g., Tom Conley, *The Self-Made Map: Cartographic Writing in Early Modern France* (Minneapolis: University of Minnesota Press, 1996); Ricardo Padrón, *The Spacious Word: Cartography, Literature, and Empire in Early Modern Spain* (Chicago: University of Chicago Press, 2004); and José Rabasa, *Inventing America: Spanish Historiography and the Formation of Eurocentrism* (Norman: Oklahoma University Press, 1993).

14. Frank Lentricchia and Thomas McLaughlin, eds., *Critical Terms for Literary Study* (Chicago: University of Chicago Press, 1990).

15. Raymond Williams, *Keywords: A Vocabulary of Culture and Society* (Oxford: Oxford University Press, 1983). See also the Keywords Project (http://keywords.pitt .edu), a collaborative, revisionary extension of Williams's endeavor to create a lexicon for contemporary cultural studies currently underway at the University of Pittsburgh.

16. David Harvey, "Space as a Keyword," in *Spaces of Global Capitalism: Towards a Theory of Uneven Geographical Development* (London: Verso, 2006), 119.

17. Nigel Thrift, "Space," *Theory, Culture, and Society* 23, no. 2–3 (2006), 139.

18. Raymond Williams, *The Country and the City* (Oxford: Oxford University Press, 1973). 19 Although a truly comprehensive list is probably impossible, the editors of a new journal, *Literary Geographies*, have compiled and regularly augment an impressive bibliography of relevant scholarship. The bibliography is available online at http://literarygeographies .wordpress.com/.

20. See Edward Soja, *Thirdspace: Journeys to Los Angeles and Other Real-and-Imagined Places* (Oxford: Blackwell, 1996).

21. See, e.g., my *Spatiality* (London: Routledge, 2013), especially 44–78.

22. Westphal, *Geocriticism*, 158.

Bibliography

Anderson, Perry. *The Origins of Postmodernity*. London: Verso, 1998.

Anonymous. "Myvatn, Mystery, and Magic: *Game of Thrones*-Themed Tour." Accessed August 16, 2017. https://www.icelandtravel.is/tour/item700728 /myvatn-mystery-magic-game-of-thrones-themed-tour-2/.

Anonymous. "Viator Exclusive: 'Game of Thrones' Tour." Accessed August 16, 2017. https://www.lonelyplanet.com/croatia/southern-dalmatia/activities /viator-exclusive-game-of-thrones-tour/a/pa-act/v-5360GAMETHRONES/1319358.

Arac, Jonathan. *The Emergence of American Literary Narrative, 1820–1860*. Cambridge, MA: Harvard University Press, 2005.

———. *Impure Worlds: The Institution of Literature in the Age of the Novel*. New York: Fordham University Press, 2011.

———. "'A Romantic Book': *Moby-Dick* and Novel Agency." *boundary 2* 17, no. 2 (Summer 1990): 40–59.

———. "What Kind of History Does the Theory of the Novel Require?" *NOVEL: A Forum on Fiction* 42, no. 2 (2009): 190–195.

Aristotle. *The Poetics*. Translated by Samuel Henry Butcher. New York: Hill and Wang, 1961.

Arrighi, Giovanni. *The Long Twentieth Century: Money, Power, and the Origins of Our Times*. London: Verso, 1994.

Auerbach, Erich. *Dante: Poet of the Secular World*. Translated by Ralph Manheim. New York: New York Review Books, 2007.

———. *Mimesis: The Representation of Reality in Western Literature*. Translated by Willard R. Trask. Princeton, NJ: Princeton University Press, 1953.

———. "Philology and *Weltliteratur*." Translated by Mariam and Edward W. Said. *Centennial Review* 13 (Winter 1969): 1–17.

Augé, Marc. *Non-Place: Introduction to an Anthropology of Supermodernity*. Translated by John Howe. London: Verso, 1995.

Bachelard, Gaston. *The Poetics of Space*. Translated by Maria Jolas. Boston, MA: Beacon Press, 1964.

Bakhtin, Mikhail. *The Dialogic Imagination: Four Essays*. Edited and translated by Caryl Emerson and Michael Holquist. Austin: University of Texas Press, 1981.

Bal, Mieke. *Narratology: Introduction to the Theory of Narrative*. Translated by Christine van Boheemen. Toronto: University of Toronto Press, 1985.

Balasopoulos, Antonis. "'*Utopiae Insulae Figura*': Utopian Insularity and the Politics of Form." *Transtext(e)s/Transcultures: Journal of Global Cultural Studies* 3 (2008): 22–38.

Barry, Peter. *English in Practice: In Pursuit of English Studies*. 2nd ed. London: Bloomsbury, 2014.

Barthes, Roland. *Image-Music-Text*. Translated by Stephen Heath. New York: Hill and Wang, 1977.

Baudrillard, Jean. *Simulacra and Simulation*. Translated by Sheila Faria Glaser. Ann Arbor: University of Michigan Press, 1994.

Beecroft, Alexander. *An Ecology of World Literature: From Antiquity to the Present Day.* London: Verso, 2015.

Benjamin, Walter. *The Arcades Project.* Translated by Howard Eiland and Kevin McLaughlin. Cambridge, MA: Harvard University Press, 1999.

Berlant, Lauren. *Anatomy of a National Fantasy: Hawthorne, Utopia, and Everyday Life.* Chicago: University of Chicago Press, 1991.

Bhabha, Homi. *The Location of Culture.* London: Routledge, 1994.

Bodenhamer, David J., John Corrigan, and Trevor M. Harris. *The Spatial Humanities: GIS and the Future of Humanities Scholarship.* Bloomington: Indiana University Press, 2010.

Borges, Jorge Luis. "On Exactitude in Science." *Collected Fictions*, 325. Translated by Andrew Hurley. New York: Penguin, 1999.

Braudel, Fernand. *The Mediterranean and the Mediterranean World in the Age of Phillip II.* Translated by Siân Reynolds. New York: Harper & Row, 1972.

Brennan, Timothy. *At Home in the World: Cosmopolitanism Now.* Cambridge, MA: Harvard University Press, 1997.

Budgen, Frank. *James Joyce and the Making of* Ulysses, *and Other Writings.* Edited by Clive Hart. Oxford: Oxford University Press, 1989.

Bulson, Eric. *Novels, Maps, Modernity: The Spatial Imagination, 1850–2000.* New York: Routledge, 2006.

Calvino, Italo. *Invisible Cities.* Translated by William Weaver. New York: Harcourt, 1974.

Carroll, Lewis. *Sylvie and Bruno Concluded.* London: Macmillan, 1893.

Carroll, Siobhan. "Atopia/Non-Place." In *The Routledge Handbook of Literature and Space*, edited by Robert T. Tally Jr., 159–167. London: Routledge, 2017.

Carter, Paul. *The Road to Botany Bay: An Essay in Spatial History.* London: Faber and Faber, 1987.

Certeau, Michel de. *The Practice of Everyday Life.* Translated by Steven Randall. Berkeley: University of California Press, 1984.

Cervantes, Miguel de. *Don Quixote.* Translated by J. M. Cohen. New York: Penguin, 1950.

Cevasco, Maria. "Imagining a Space That Is Outside: An Interview with Fredric Jameson," *minnesota review* 78 (2012): 83–94.

Chesterton, G. K. *Charles Dickens: A Critical Study.* New York: Dodd Mead and Co., 1906.

Chin-Tanner, Wendy. "No Moon." *Turn.* Alexander, AR: Sibling Rivalry Press, 2014. 38.

———. "On Truth in a Nonmoral Sense," *Vinyl Poetry* 9. http://vinylpoetry.com/volume-9/page-30/.

Conley, Tom. *The Self-Made Map: Cartographic Writing in Early Modern France.* Minneapolis: University of Minnesota Press, 1996.

Conrad, Joseph. "Geography and Some Explorers." In *Last Essays*, 1–31. London: J. M. Dent, 1921.

———. *Heart of Darkness.* New York: Bantam, 1969.

———. "An Outpost of Progress." In *Tales of Unrest*, edited by Allan H. Simmons and J. H. Stape, 75–100. Cambridge: Cambridge University Press, 2012.

Cresswell, Tim. *Place: A Short Introduction.* Oxford: Blackwell, 2004.

Cusset, François. *French Theory: How Foucault, Derrida, Deleuze & Co. Transformed the Intellectual Life of the United States.* Translated by Jeff Fort. Minneapolis: University of Minnesota Press, 2008.

Dante. *The Divine Comedy.* Vol. I, *Inferno.* Translated by Mark Musa. New York: Penguin, 1984.

Davis, Lennard J. *Resisting Novels: Ideology and Fiction*. London: Routledge, 2014.

Dear, Michael, Jim Ketchum, Sarah Luria, and Doug Richardson, eds. *GeoHumanities: Art, History, Text at the Edge of Place*. London: Routledge, 2011.

Deleuze, Gilles. *Desert Islands and Other Texts, 1953–1974*. Edited by David Lapoujade. Translated by Michael Taormina. New York: Semiotext(e), 2004.

———. *Nietzsche and Philosophy*. Translated by Hugh Tomlinson. New York: Columbia University Press, 1982.

Deleuze, Gilles, and Félix Guattari. *A Thousand Plateaus*. Translated by Brian Massumi. Minneapolis: University of Minnesota Press, 1987.

———. *What Is Philosophy?* Translated by Hugh Tomlinson and Graham Burchell. New York: Columbia University Press, 1994.

Dimock, Wai Chee. *Empire for Liberty: Melville and the Poetics of Individualism*. Princeton, NJ: Princeton University Press, 1989.

———. *Through Other Continents: American Literature across Deep Time*. Princeton, NJ: Princeton University Press, 2006.

Dimock, Wai Chee, and Lawrence Buell, eds. *Shades of the Planet: American Literature as World Literature*. Princeton, NJ: Princeton University Press, 2007.

Downey, Dara, Ian Kinane, and Elizabeth Parker, eds. *Landscapes of Liminality: Between Space and Place*. Lanham, MD: Rowman & Littlefield International, 2016.

Eagleton, Terry. *After Theory*. New York: Basic Books, 2003.

———. *Literary Theory: An Introduction*. 2nd ed. Minneapolis: University of Minnesota Press, 1996.

Eco, Umberto. *Six Walks in the Fictional Woods*. Cambridge, MA: Harvard University Press, 1994.

Elden, Stuart. *The Birth of Territory*. Chicago: University of Chicago Press, 2014.

Elias, Amy J., and Christian Moraru, eds. *The Planetary Turn: Relationality and Geoaesthetics in the Twenty-First Century*. Evanston, IL: Northwestern University Press, 2015.

Engber, Daniel. "Starry Blight: How a Bunch of Mesopotamian Peasants Ruined the Night Sky," *Slate Magazine* (July 12, 2012): http://www.slate.com/articles/health_and _science/a_fine_whine/2012/07/against_constellations_why_are_we_stuck_with _bronze_age_graffiti_.html.

Entrikin, J. Nicholas. *The Betweenness of Place: Towards a Geography of Modernity*. Baltimore, MD: Johns Hopkins University Press, 1991.

Felski, Rita. *The Limits of Critique*. Chicago: University of Chicago Press, 2015.

Foucault, Michel. *The Archaeology of Knowledge*. Translated by Alan Marc Sheridan Smith. New York: Pantheon, 1972.

———. *The Birth of the Clinic: An Archaeology of Medical Perception*. Translated by A. M. Sheridan Smith. New York: Vintage, 1973.

———. *Discipline and Punish: The Birth of the Prison*. Translated by Alan Sheridan. New York: Vintage, 1977.

———. *The History of Sexuality, Volume I: An Introduction*. Translated by Robert Hurley. New York: Random House, 1978.

———. "Intellectuals and Power: A Conversation between Michel Foucault and Gilles Deleuze." In *Language, Counter-Memory, Practice*, edited by Donald Bouchard, 205–217. Ithaca, NY: Cornell University Press, 1977.

———. "Of Other Spaces." Translated by Jay Miskowiec. *Diacritics* 16 (Spring 1986): 22–27.

——. *The Order of Things: An Archaeology of the Human Sciences*. Translated by anon. New York: Vintage, 1973.

Frank, Joseph. *The Idea of Spatial Form*. New Brunswick, NJ: Rutgers University Press, 1991.

Freedman, Carl. *Critical Theory and Science Fiction*. Middletown, CT: Wesleyan University Press, 2000.

Freud, Sigmund. *Civilization and Its Discontents*. Translated by James Strachey. New York: W.W. Norton, 2010.

Frye, Northrop. *The Educated Imagination*. Bloomington: Indiana University Press, 1964.

Gaiman, Neil. *Fragile Things: Short Fictions and Wonders*. New York: HarperCollins, 2006.

——. *The Graveyard Book*. New York: HarperCollins, 2008.

Giles, Paul. *Atlantic Republic: The American Tradition in English Literature*. Oxford: Oxford University Press, 2006.

——. *Transatlantic Insurrections: British Culture and the Formation of American Literature, 1730–1860*. Philadelphia: University of Pennsylvania Press, 2001.

——. *Virtual Americas: Transnational Fictions and the Transatlantic Imaginary*. Durham, NC: Duke University Press, 2002.

Goldstein, Leonard. *The Social and Cultural Roots of Linear Perspective*. Minneapolis, MN: MEP Publications, 1988.

Gregory, Derek. *Geographical Imaginations*. Oxford: Blackwell, 1994.

Habermas, Jürgen. *The Philosophical Discourse of Modernity: Twelve Lectures*. Translated by Thomas McCarthy. Cambridge, MA: MIT Press, 1987.

——. *The Postnational Constellation*. Translated by Max Pensky. Cambridge, MA: The MIT Press, 2001.

Harley, John Brian. *The New Nature of Maps: Essays in the History of Cartography*. Edited by Paul Laxton. Baltimore, MD: Johns Hopkins University Press, 2001.

Hartog, François. *The Mirror of Herodotus: The Representation of the Other in the Writing of History*. Translated by Janet Lloyd. Berkeley: University of California Press, 1988.

Harvey, David. *The Condition of Postmodernity*. Oxford: Blackwell, 1990.

——. *Spaces of Global Capitalism: Towards a Theory of Uneven Geographical Development*. London: Verso, 2006.

——. *Spaces of Hope*. Berkeley: University of California Press, 2000.

Hawthorne, Nathaniel. *The House of the Seven Gables*. Oxford: Oxford University Press, 1991.

Hegel, Georg Wilhelm Friedrich. *Hegel's Philosophy of Right*. Translated by T. M. Knox. Oxford: Oxford University Press, 1967.

Heidegger, Martin. *Being and Time*. Translated by John Macquarrie and Edward Robinson. New York: Harper and Row, 1962.

Heise, Ursula K. *Sense of Place and Sense of Planet: The Environmental Imagination of the Global*. Oxford: Oxford University Press, 2008.

Holub, Miroslav. "Brief Thoughts on Maps." Translated by Jarmila and Ian Milner. *Times Literary Supplement* (February 4, 1977): 118.

Homer. *The Odyssey*. Translated by Robert Fagles. New York: Penguin, 1996.

Hones, Sheila. *Literary Geographies: Narrative Space in* Let the Great World Spin. New York: Palgrave Macmillan, 2014.

Horkheimer, Max, and Theodor W. Adorno. *Dialectic of Enlightenment: Philosophical Fragments*. Translated by Edmund Jephcott. Palo Alto, CA: Stanford University Press, 2002.

Huang, Yunte. *Transpacific Imaginations: History, Literature, Counterpoetics*. Cambridge, MA: Harvard University Press, 2008.

Hume, Kathryn. *Fantasy and Mimesis: Responses to Reality in Western Literature*. New York: Methuen, 1984.

Hunter, Ian. "The History of Theory." *Critical Inquiry* 33, no. 1 (Autumn 2006): 78–112.

Jacoby, Russell. *Picture Imperfect: Utopian Thought for an Anti-Utopian Age*. New York: Columbia University Press, 2005.

Jameson, Fredric. *The Antinomies of Realism*. London: Verso, 2013.

———. *Archaeologies of the Future: The Desire Called Utopia and Other Science Fictions*. London: Verso, 2005.

———. *The Geopolitical Aesthetic: Cinema and Space in the World System*. Bloomington and London: Indiana University Press and the British Film Institute, 1992.

———. *The Hegel Variations: On the Phenomenology of Spirit*. London: Verso, 2010.

———. "How Not to Historicize Theory." *Critical Inquiry* 34, no. 3 (Spring 2008): 563–582.

———. *The Ideologies of Theory: Essays, 1971–1986*. Vol. 1, *Situations of Theory*. Minneapolis: University of Minnesota Press, 1988.

———. *The Ideologies of Theory: Essays, 1971–1986*. Vol. 2, *The Syntax of History*. Minneapolis: University of Minnesota Press, 1988.

———. *Jameson on Jameson: Conversations on Cultural Marxism*. Edited by Ian Buchanan. Durham, NC: Duke University Press, 2007.

———. *Marxism and Form: Twentieth-Century Dialectical Theories of Literature*. Princeton, NJ: Princeton University Press, 1971.

———. "Modernism and Imperialism." In *The Modernist Papers*, 152–169. London: Verso, 2007.

———. "A New Reading of *Capital*." *Mediations* 25, no. 1 (Fall 2010): 5–14.

———. "On Politics and Literature." *Salmagundi* 2, no. 3 (Spring–Summer 1968): 17–26.

———. *The Political Unconscious: Narrative as a Socially Symbolic Act*. Ithaca, NY: Cornell University Press, 1981.

———. *Postmodernism, or, the Cultural Logic of Late Capitalism*. Durham, NC: Duke University Press, 1991.

———. *Representing Capital: A Reading of Volume One*. London: Verso, 2011.

———. *The Seeds of Time*. New York: Columbia University Press, 1994.

———. *Signatures of the Visible*. London: Routledge, 1990.

———. *Valences of the Dialectic*. London: Verso, 2009.

Kant, Immanuel. "What Is Enlightenment?" *On History*, edited and translated by Lewis White Beck, 3–10. Indianapolis, IN: Bobbs-Merrill, 1963.

Kehlmann, Daniel. *Measuring the World*. Translated by Carol Brown Janeway. New York: Vintage, 2006.

Kermode, Frank. *The Sense of an Ending: Studies in the Theory of Fiction*. Oxford: Oxford University Press, 1967.

Kracauer, Siegfried. *History: The Last Things before the Last*. Edited by Paul Oskar Kristeller. Oxford: Oxford University Press, 1969.

Le Guin, Ursula K. "95. 'Are They Going to Say This Is Fantasy?'" *Ursula K. Le Guin's Blog* (March 5, 2015), accessed March 27, 2016, http://www.ursulakleguin.com/Blog2015.html.

Lefebvre, Henri *The Production of Space*. Translated by Donald Nicholson-Smith. Oxford: Blackwell, 1991.

Lentricchia, Frank, and Thomas McLaughlin, eds. *Critical Terms for Literary Study*. Chicago: University of Chicago Press, 1990.

Linde, Charlotte, and William Labov. "Spatial Networks as a Site for the Study of Language and Thought." *Language* 51, no. 4 (December 1975): 924–939.

Loukaki, Argyro. *The Geographical Unconscious*. London: Ashgate, 2014.

Lucretius. *On the Nature of the Universe*. Translated by Alicia Stallings. New York: Penguin, 2007.

Lukács, Georg. *The Historical Novel*. Translated by Hannah and Stanley Mitchell. Lincoln: University of Nebraska Press, 1983.

———. *History and Class Consciousness: Studies in Marxist Dialectics*. Translated by Rodney Livingstone. Cambridge, MA: MIT Press, 1971.

———. "Narrate or Describe." In *Writer and Critic and Other Essays*, translated by Arthur D. Kahn, 110–148. New York: Grosset, 1970.

———. *The Theory of the Novel*. Translated by Anna Bostock. Cambridge, MA: MIT Press, 1971.

Lynch, Kevin. *The Image of the City*. Cambridge, MA: MIT Press, 1960.

MacLeish, Archibald. "Riders on the Earth." *New York Times*, December 25, 1968, 1.

Manguel, Alberto, and Gianni Guadalupi. *The Dictionary of Imaginary Places*. Rev. ed. New York: Harcourt, 1999.

Marcus, Sharon. "Space." In *The Encyclopedia of the Novel*, edited by Paul Shellinger, 1259–1262. Chicago: Fitzroy Dearborn Publishers, 1998.

Marcuse, Herbert. *Eros and Civilization: A Philosophical Inquiry into Freud*. Boston, MA: Beacon, 1966.

———. *Five Lectures: Psychoanalysis, Politics, and Utopia*. Translated by Jeremy J. Shapiro and Shierry M. Weber. Boston, MA: Beacon Press, 1970.

Marin, Louis. *Utopics: The Semiological Play of Textual Spaces*. Translated by Robert A. Vollrath. Atlantic Highlands, NJ: Humanities Press International, 1984.

Marx, Karl. *Capital: A Critique of Political Economy*. Vol. 1. Translated by Samuel Moore and Edward Aveling. New York: Random House, 1906.

Melville, Herman. *Moby-Dick, or, The Whale*. New York: Penguin, 1992.

Miéville, China. "Cognition as Ideology: A Dialectic of SF Theory." In *Red Planets: Marxism and Science Fiction*, edited by Mark Bould and China Miéville, 231–248. Middletown, CT: Wesleyan University Press, 2009.

———. "Editorial Introduction." *Symposium: Marxism and Fantasy*, in *Historical Materialism* 10, no. 4 (2002): 39–49.

———. "There and Back Again," *Omnivoracious* blog, guest post (June 15, 2009). Accessed September 14, 2012, http://www.omnivoracious.com/2009/06/there-and-back-again -five-reasons-tolkien-rocks.html.

———. "Tolkien—Middle-earth Meets Middle England," *Socialist Review* 259 (January 2002): http://socialistreview.org.uk/259/tolkien-middle-earth-meets-middle-england.

Miller, J. Hillis. *Topographies*. Stanford, CA: Stanford University Press, 1995.

Mitchell, Peta. *Cartographic Strategies of Postmodernity: The Figure of the Map in Contemporary Theory and Fiction*. London: Routledge, 2007.

Monmonier, Mark. *How to Lie with Maps*. Chicago: University of Chicago Press, 1991.

Moorcock, Michael. *Wizardry and Wild Romance: A Study of Epic Fantasy*. London: Victor Gollancz Ltd., 1987.

Moraru, Christian. *Reading for the Planet: A Geomethodology.* Ann Arbor: University of Michigan Press, 2015.

More, Thomas. *Utopia.* Translated by Paul Turner. New York: Penguin, 2003.

Moretti, Franco. *Graphs, Maps, Trees: Abstract Models for a Literary History.* London: Verso, 2005.

———. "Lukács's Theory of the Novel: Centenary Reflections." *New Left Review* 91 (January–February 2014): 39–42.

———. *The Novel, Volume 1: History, Geography, and Culture.* Princeton, NJ: Princeton University Press, 2007.

———. *The Novel, Volume 2: Forms and Themes.* Princeton, NJ: Princeton University Press, 2007.

Nietzsche, Friedrich. "On Truth and Lie in an Extra-Moral Sense." In *The Portable Nietzsche*, translated by Walter Kaufmann, 42–47. New York: Penguin, 1976.

O'Hara, Daniel T. *The Art of Reading as a Way of Life: On Nietzsche's Truth.* Evanston, IL: Northwestern University Press, 2009.

Ohmae, Kenichi. *The Borderless World: Power and Strategy in the Interlinked Economy.* New York: HarperCollins, 1990.

Olson, Charles. *Call Me Ishmael.* San Francisco: City Lights, 1947.

Padrón, Ricardo. "Mapping Imaginary Worlds." In *Maps: Finding Our Place in the World*, edited by James R. Akerman and Robert W. Karrow Jr., 255–287. Chicago: University of Chicago Press, 2007.

———. *The Spacious Word: Cartography, Literature, and Empire in Early Modern Spain.* Chicago: University of Chicago Press, 2004.

Pease, Donald E. *The New American Exceptionalism.* Minneapolis: University of Minnesota Press, 2009.

Peraldo, Emmanuelle, ed. *Literature and Geography: The Writing of Space throughout History.* Newcastle-upon-Tyne: Cambridge Scholars, 2016.

Perec, Georges. *An Attempt at Exhausting a Place in Paris.* Translated by Marc Lowenthal. Cambridge, MA: Wakefield Press, 2010.

Piatti, Barbara. *Die Geographie der Literatur: Schauplätze, Handlungsräume, Raumphantasien.* Göttingen: Wallstein Verlag, 2008.

Poole, Robert. *Earthrise: How Man First Saw the Planet.* New Haven, CT: Yale University Press, 2008.

Pratchett, Terry. *The Color of Magic.* New York: Harper, 1989.

Prieto, Eric. "Geocriticism, Geopoetics, Geophilosophy, and Beyond." In *Geocritical Explorations: Space, Place, and Mapping in Literary and Cultural Studies*, edited by Robert T. Tally Jr., 13–27. New York: Palgrave Macmillan, 2011.

———. *Literature, Geography, and the Postmodern Poetics of Place.* New York: Palgrave Macmillan, 2012.

Pynchon, Thomas. *The Crying of Lot 49.* New York: Harper and Row, 1966.

Rabasa, José. *Inventing America: Spanish Historiography and the Formation of Eurocentrism.* Norman: Oklahoma University Press, 1993.

Rodaway, Paul. *Sensuous Geographies: Body, Sense, and Place.* London: Routledge, 1994.

Ross, Kristin. *The Emergence of Social Space: Rimbaud and the Paris Commune.* Minneapolis: University of Minnesota Press, 1988.

Ryan, Marie-Laure, Kenneth Foote, and Maoz Azaryahu. *Narrating Space / Spatializing Narrative: Where Narrative Theory and Geography Meet.* Columbus: Ohio State University Press, 2016.

Said, Edward W. *Beginnings: Intention and Method.* New York: Columbia University
    Press, 1985.
———. *Culture and Imperialism.* New York: Knopf, 1993.
———. "Introduction to *Moby-Dick.*" In *Reflections on Exile,* 356–371. Cambridge, MA:
    Harvard University Press, 2000.
———. *Orientalism.* New York: Vintage, 1978.
———. "Reflections on Exile." In *Reflections on Exile and Other Essays,* 173–186. Cambridge,
    MA: Harvard University Press, 2000.
Sartre, Jean-Paul. *Nausea.* Translated by Lloyd Alexander. New York: New Directions, 1964.
Scott, Walter. "On the Supernatural in Fictitious Composition." In *Sir Walter Scott on
    Novelists and Fiction,* edited by Ioan Williams, 312–353. London: Routledge and Kegan
    Paul, 1968.
Shippey, Tom. *J. R. R. Tolkien: Author of the Century.* Boston, MA: Houghton Mifflin, 2000.
———. *The Road to Middle-earth: How J. R. R. Tolkien Created a New Mythology.* Boston,
    MA: Houghton Mifflin, 2003.
Soja, Edward W. *Postmodern Geographies: The Reassertion of Space in Critical Social Theory.*
    London: Verso, 1989.
———. *Thirdspace: Journeys to Los Angeles and Other Real-and-Imagined Places.* Oxford:
    Blackwell, 1996.
Spivak, Gayatri Chakravorty. *Death of a Discipline.* New York: Columbia University
    Press, 2003.
———. *In Other Worlds.* London: Routledge, 1987.
Stadler, Jane, Peta Mitchell, and Stephen Carleton. *Imagined Landscapes: Geovisualizing
    Australian Spatial Narratives.* Bloomington: Indiana University Press, 2016.
Suvin, Darko. *Metamorphoses of Science Fiction: On the Poetics and History of a Literary
    Genre.* New Haven, CT: Yale University Press, 1979.
Tally, Robert T., Jr. *Fredric Jameson: The Project of Dialectical Criticism.* London: Pluto
    Press, 2014.
———. "In the File Drawer Labeled 'Science Fiction': Genre after the Age of the Novel,"
    Journal of English Language and Literature 63, no. 2 (2017), 201–217.
———. "Introduction: The World, the Text, and the Geocritic." In *The Geocritical
    Legacies of Edward W. Said,* edited by Robert T. Tally Jr., 1–16. New York:
    Palgrave Macmillan, 2015.
———. "Jameson's Project of Cognitive Mapping: A Critical Engagement." In *Social
    Cartography: Mapping Ways of Seeing Social and Educational Change,* edited by
    Rolland G. Paulston, 399–416. New York: Garland, 1996.
———. *Melville, Mapping, and Globalization: Literary Cartography in the American Baroque
    Writer.* London: Continuum, 2009.
———. "Meta-Capital: Culture and Financial Derivatives." *Works and Days* 30, no. 1/2
    (2012): 231–247.
———. "*Mundus Totus Exilium Est*: Reflections on the Critic in Exile," *Transnational
    Literature* 3, no. 2 (May 2012): 1–10.
———. "On Geocriticism." In *Geocritical Explorations: Space, Place, and Mapping in
    Literary and Cultural Studies,* edited by Robert T. Tally Jr., 1–9. New York: Palgrave
    Macmillan, 2011.
———. *Spatiality.* London: Routledge, 2013.

———. *Utopia in the Age of Globalization: Space, Representation, and the World System.* New York: Palgrave Macmillan, 2013.

Tally, Robert T., Jr., and Christine M. Battista, eds. *Ecocriticism and Geocriticism: Overlapping Territories in Environmental and Spatial Literary Studies.* New York: Palgrave Macmillan, 2016.

Taylor, Jerome. *The Didascalion of Hugh of Saint Victor: A Medieval Guide to the Arts.* Translated by Jerome Taylor. New York: Columbia University Press, 1991.

Thacker, Andrew. *Moving through Modernity: Space and Geography in Modernism.* Manchester: Manchester University Press, 2003.

Thrift, Nigel. "Space." *Theory, Culture, and Society* 23, no. 2–3 (2006): 139–146.

———. *Spatial Formations.* London: SAGE Publications, 1996.

Tolkien, J. R. R. *The Hobbit.* New York: Del Rey, 1982.

———. *The Letters of J. R. R. Tolkien.* Edited by Humphrey Carpenter. Boston, MA: Houghton Mifflin, 2000.

———. *The Monsters and the Critics and Other Essays.* Edited by Christopher Tolkien. New York: HarperCollins, 2006.

———. "Mythopoeia." In *Tree and Leaf,* 83–90. New York: HarperCollins, 2001.

———. "On Fairy-Stories." In *The Tolkien Reader,* 33–99. New York: Ballantine Books, 1966.

———. *The Return of the King.* New York: Del Rey, 1986.

———. *The Silmarillion.* New York: Del Rey, 2002.

Toscano, Alberto, and Jeff Kinkle, *Cartographies of the Absolute.* Winchester, UK: Zero Books, 2015.

Trauvitch, Rhona. "Charting the Extraordinary: Sentient and Transontological Spaces." In *Literary Cartographies: Spatiality, Representation, and Narrative,* edited by Robert T. Tally Jr., 199–213. New York: Palgrave Macmillan, 2014.

Trigg, Dylan. "Place and Non-Place: A Phenomenological Perspective." In *Place, Space, and Hermeneutics,* edited by Bruce B. Janz, 127–139. New York: Springer, 2017.

———. *Topophobia: A Phenomenology of Anxiety.* London: Bloomsbury, 2016.

Tuan, Yi-Fu. *Landscapes of Fear.* New York: Pantheon, 1979.

———. *Space and Place: The Perspective of Experience.* Minneapolis: University of Minnesota Press, 1977.

———. *Topophilia: A Study of Environmental Perception, Attitudes, and Values.* New York: Columbia University Press, 1990.

Turchi, Peter. *Maps of the Imagination: The Writer as Cartographer.* San Antonio, TX: Trinity University Press, 2004.

Vattimo, Gianni. "Dialectics, Difference, Weak Thought." In *Weak Thought,* edited by Gianni Vattimo and Pier Aldo Rovatti, translated by Peter Carravetta, 39–52. Albany, NY: SUNY Press, 2012.

Vonnegut, Kurt. *Breakfast of Champions.* New York: Delacorte Press, 1973.

Wallerstein, Immanuel. *The Modern World-System.* 3 vols. New York: Academic Press, 1974.

Warf, Barney, and Santa Arias, eds. *The Spatial Turn: Interdisciplinary Perspectives.* London: Routledge, 2008.

Wegner, Phillip E. *Imaginary Communities: Utopia, the Nation, and the Spatial Histories of Modernity.* Berkeley: University of California Press, 2002.

———. *Life between Two Deaths, 1989–2001: U.S. Culture in the Long Nineties.* Durham, NC: Duke University Press, 2009.

Wells, Amy. "Bending the Bars of the Meridian Cage." *American Book Review* 37, no. 6 (September/October 2016): 7–8.

Westphal, Bertrand. *La Cage des méridiens: La littérature et l'art contemporain face à la globalization*. Paris: Minuit, 2016.

———. *Geocriticism: Real and Fictional Spaces*. Translated by Robert T. Tally Jr. New York: Palgrave Macmillan, 2011.

———. *La Géocritique: Réel, fiction, espace*. Paris: Minuit, 2007.

———. "Îles dalmates: L'odysée des îles." In *L'Œil de la Méditerranée: Une Odyssee Litteraire*, edited by Bertrand Westphal, 177–198. La Tour d'Aigues: Éditions de l'Aube, 2005.

———. *The Plausible World: A Geocritical Approach to Space, Place, and Maps*. Translated by Amy D. Wells. New York: Palgrave Macmillan, 2013.

———. "Pour une approche géocritique des textes: esquisse." In *La Géocritique mode d'emploi*. Edited by Bertrand Westwhal, 9–39. Limoges: Pulim, 2000.

———. *Le Rivage des mythes: Une géocritique méditerranéene*. Limoges: Pulim, 2001.

Williams, Raymond. *The Country and the City*. Oxford: Oxford University Press, 1973.

———. *Keywords: A Vocabulary of Culture and Society*. Rev. ed. Oxford: Oxford University Press, 1983.

Woolf, Virginia. "Literary Geography." *Books and Portraits: Some Further Selections from the Literary and Biographical Writings of Virginia Woolf*, edited by Mary Lyon, 158–61. New York: Harcourt, Brace, Jovanovitch, 1977.

Yeung, Heather H. *Spatial Engagement with Poetry*. New York: Palgrave Macmillan, 2015.

Index

ROBERT T. TALLY Jr. is Professor of English at Texas State University. His books include *Fredric Jameson: The Project of Dialectical Criticism*; *Utopia in the Age of Globalization: Space, Representation, and the World System*; and *Spatiality*.

Printed and bound by CPI Group (UK) Ltd, Croydon, CR0 4YY

09/06/2025

14685940-0001